EBURY

ALL COLOUR COLLECTION

365
VEGETARIAN
DISHES

ALL COLOUR COLLECTION

365

VEGETARIAN DISHES

EBURY PRESS LONDON

First published 1993

1 3 5 7 9 10 8 6 4 2

First published in the United Kingdom in 1993 by
Ebury Press
Random House, 20 Vauxhall Bridge Road, London SW1V 2SA

Random House Australia (Pty) Limited
20 Alfred Street, Milsons Point, Sydney, New South Wales 2061, Australia

Random House New Zealand Limited
18 Poland Road, Glenfield, Auckland 10, New Zealand

Random House South Africa (Pty) Limited
PO Box 337, Bergvlei, South Africa

Random House UK Limited Reg. No. 954009

A CIP catalogue record for this book is available from the British Library

ISBN 0 09 177891 3

Photography by Jan Baldwin, Martin Brigdale, Laurie Evans, Melvin Grey,
Tim Hill, James Jackson, David Johnson, Paul Kemp, James Murphy,
Alan Newnham, Charlie Stebbings, Grant Symon, Rosemary Weller,
Andrew Whittuck, Paul Williams

Typeset by Clive Dorman & Co.
Printed and bound in Italy by New Interlitho S.p.a., Milan

COOK'S NOTES

- Both metric and imperial measures are given in the recipes in this book. Follow one set of measures only as they are not interchangeable.
- All spoon measures are level unless otherwise stated.
- All ovens should be preheated to the specified temperature.
- Microwave cooking instructions are given for some of the recipes in this book. When using these, please note that HIGH refers to 100% full power output of a 600-700 watt cooker; MEDIUM refers to 60% of full power; LOW refers to 35% of full power.

  If your microwave power output is lower than 600 watts, it may be necessary to allow longer than recommended. In any event you should always check food before the end of the cooking time, to ensure that it does not overcook.

CONTENTS

SOUPS

From hearty meal-in-one soups to delicate chilled soups you will find a host of tempting recipes in this collection. Remember that a good vegetable stock is essential for a flavourful soup. Warm crusty bread is the ideal accompaniment.

CREAM OF ONION SOUP

SERVES 4

25 g (1 oz) butter or margarine	salt and pepper
450 g (1 lb) onions, thinly sliced	20 ml (4 tsp) cornflour
	45 ml (3 tbsp) single cream
600 ml (1 pint) milk	parsley sprigs, to garnish

1 Melt the butter in a saucepan, add the onions, cover and cook gently for about 5 minutes or until softened, shaking the pan occasionally to prevent browning.
2 Add the milk and 300 ml (½ pint) water, season to taste and bring to the boil, stirring. Reduce the heat, cover and simmer for about 25 minutes or until the onion is tender.
3 Blend the cornflour to a smooth paste with 45 ml (3 tbsp) water, stir into the soup and bring to the boil. Cook gently for a few minutes or until slightly thickened, stirring. Add the cream, adjust the seasoning and reheat without boiling. Garnish with parsley sprigs.

CREAM OF CELERY SOUP

SERVES 4

25 g (1 oz) butter or margarine	300 ml (½ pint) vegetable stock
1 head of celery, finely chopped	300 ml (½ pint) milk
2 onions, chopped	salt and pepper
	75 ml (3 fl oz) single cream
125 g (4 oz) cottage cheese, sieved	celery leaves, to garnish

1 Melt the butter in a saucepan, add the celery and onions and cook gently for 5 minutes.
2 Stir in the cottage cheese, stock, milk and salt and pepper. Bring to the boil and simmer for 30 minutes; then sieve or purée in a blender or food processor. Reheat and add half the cream.
3 Pour into a soup tureen or individual dishes and float the remaining cream on the top of each serving, with a few celery leaves. Serve immediately.

CAULIFLOWER SOUP

SERVES 6

900 g (2 lb) cauliflower	300 ml (½ pint) buttermilk
1 large onion	pinch of freshly grated nutmeg
60 ml (4 tbsp) oil	salt and pepper
1 garlic clove, crushed	25 g (1 oz) flaked almonds
15 ml (1 tbsp) plain flour	15 ml (1 tbsp) chopped parsley
900 ml (1½ pints) milk	
2 eggs, beaten	

1 Cut away any green stalks from the cauliflower, and cut it into small florets. Roughly chop the onion.
2 Heat 30 ml (1 tbsp) of the oil in a saucepan. Add the onion and garlic and fry for 3-4 minutes until golden.
3 Stir in the flour. Cook, stirring, for 1 minute, then add the milk and cauliflower.
4 Bring to the boil, cover and simmer for 25-30 minutes or until the cauliflower is very soft.
5 Work the soup to a very smooth purée in a blender or food processor, or rub through a sieve.
6 Return to the rinsed-out pan. Beat in the eggs, buttermilk, nutmeg and salt and pepper to taste. Reheat very gently, without boiling.
7 Heat the remaining oil in a small frying pan. Add the almonds and parsley and fry until the nuts are golden. Scatter over the soup before serving.

CREAM OF MUSHROOM SOUP

SERVES 4

25 g (1 oz) butter or margarine	15 ml (1 tbsp) chopped parsley
25 g (1 oz) plain flour	125 g (4 oz) mushrooms, finely chopped
300 ml (½ pint) vegetable stock	salt and pepper
300 ml (½ pint) milk	15 ml (1 tbsp) lemon juice
	30 ml (2 tbsp) cream

1 Melt the butter in a saucepan, stir in the flour and cook, stirring, for 1 minute. Gradually stir in the stock and milk. Bring to the boil, whisking continuously. Stir in the parsley, mushrooms and seasoning. Cover and simmer for 10 minutes.
2 Remove from the heat and add the lemon juice and cream, stirring well.
3 Pour into a tureen or individual dishes, and serve immediately with Melba toast.

CHEESE AND COURGETTE SOUP

SERVES 4

450 g (1 lb) courgettes, sliced	175 g (6 oz) garlic and herb cheese
1 large onion, chopped	150 ml (¼ pint) single cream
1 litre (1¾ pints) vegetable stock	chopped herbs, to garnish
salt and pepper	

1 Put the courgettes and onion in a large saucepan with the stock. Bring to the boil, then lower the heat, cover the pan and simmer for 20 minutes or until the courgettes are really soft.
2 Sieve or purée the soup in a blender or food processor. Put the cheese in the rinsed-out pan and gradually work in the puréed soup with a wooden spoon.
3 Reheat the soup gently, stirring constantly, then add the cream and heat through without boiling.
Taste and adjust the seasoning, then pour into warmed individual soup bowls. Sprinkle with chopped herbs and serve immediately.

STILTON SOUP

SERVES 4-6

50 g (2 oz) butter or margarine	300 ml (½ pint) milk
1 onion, finely chopped	125 g (4 oz) Blue Stilton cheese, crumbled
2 celery sticks, sliced	50 g (2 oz) Cheddar cheese, grated
40 g (1½ oz) plain flour	salt and pepper
45 ml (3 tbsp) dry white wine	60 ml (4 tbsp) double cream
900 ml (1½ pints) vegetable stock	croûtons, to garnish

1 Melt the butter in a saucepan, add the vegetables, and fry gently for 5 minutes. Stir in the flour and cook for 1 minute. Remove from the heat, stir in the wine and stock, then return to the heat. Bring to the boil, lower the heat, cover and simmer for 30 minutes.
2 Add the milk and cheeses, stirring constantly; season. Stir in the cream.
3 Rub through a sieve or purée in a blender or food processor and reheat without boiling. Serve garnished with croûtons.

BRUSSELS SPROUT SOUP

SERVES 4-6

225 g (8 oz) Brussels sprouts	salt and pepper
225 g (8 oz) potatoes, peeled	150 ml (¼ pint) milk
25 g (1 oz) butter or margarine	30 ml (2 tbsp) natural yogurt
900 ml (1½ pints) vegetable stock	chopped walnuts, to garnish

1 Remove and discard the outer leaves of the sprouts. Chop the sprouts roughly. Slice the potatoes. Melt the butter in a saucepan, add the sprouts and cook gently for 2 minutes, stirring.

2 Add the potatoes, stock and salt and pepper to taste. Bring to the boil, cover and simmer for 25 minutes or until the potatoes are tender.

3 Sieve or purée the soup in a blender or food processor. Return to the rinsed-out pan, stir in the milk and heat thoroughly.

4 Add the yogurt and heat through, without boiling. Taste and adjust seasoning. Serve hot, garnished with chopped walnuts.

WINTER VEGETABLE SOUP

SERVES 4

10 ml (2 tsp) lemon juice	75 g (3 oz) butter or margarine
225 g (8 oz) Jerusalem artichokes	125 g (4 oz) dried haricot beans, soaked in cold water overnight and drained
½ small cabbage	bouquet garni
450 g (1 lb) carrots	vegetable stock or water
225 g (8 oz) turnips	salt and pepper
2 onions, or 2 leeks	chopped parsley and grated cheese, to serve
2-3 celery sticks	

1 Fill a bowl with cold water and pour the lemon juice into it to acidulate it. Peel the artichokes, slice, then cut into strips. Drop them into the acidulated water as you work, to prevent them from discolouring.

2 Shred the cabbage coarsely, discarding all thick or woody stalks. Cut the remaining vegetables into fairly small pieces.

3 Melt the butter in a large saucepan, add all the vegetables (except the cabbage and beans) and fry for about 10 minutes, stirring, until soft but not coloured. Add the beans, bouquet garni and enough stock or water to cover. Add plenty of pepper and bring to the boil, then lower the heat, cover and simmer for 45 minutes to 1 hour.

4 Add the cabbage and salt to taste. Cook for a further 20-30 minutes, adding more liquid as required. When all the ingredients are soft, discard the bouquet garni and adjust the seasoning.

5 Serve the soup hot, sprinkled with chopped parsley and hand grated cheese separately.

SERVING SUGGESTION

This is a really substantial soup, best served as a meal in itself, with crusty French bread or crisp bread rolls.

CURRIED POTATO AND APPLE SOUP

SERVES 4

50 g (2 oz) butter or margarine	1.2 litres (2 pints) vegetable stock or water
4 medium old potatoes, peeled and diced	salt and pepper
2 eating apples, peeled, cored and diced	150 ml (¼ pint) natural yogurt, at room temperature
10 ml (2 tsp) curry powder	

1 Melt the butter in a large saucepan. Add the potatoes and apples and fry gently for about 10 minutes until lightly coloured, shaking the pan and stirring frequently.
2 Add the curry powder and fry gently for 1-2 minutes, stirring. Pour in the stock or water and bring to the boil. Add salt and pepper to taste. Lower the heat, cover the pan and simmer for 20-25 minutes.
3 Sieve the soup or purée in a blender or food processor, then return to the rinsed-out pan.
4 Stir the yogurt until smooth, then pour half into the soup. Heat through, stirring constantly.
5 Pour the hot soup into warmed individual bowls and swirl in the remaining yogurt.

CURRIED PARSNIP AND ORANGE SOUP

SERVES 4

50 g (2 oz) butter or margarine	15 ml (1 tbsp) flour
2 parsnips, diced	1.1 litres (2 pints) vegetable stock
1 onion, chopped	finely grated rind and juice of 2 large oranges
1 garlic clove, crushed	salt and pepper
5 ml (1 tsp) curry powder	150 ml (¼ pint) single cream, to serve
5 ml (1 tsp) ground cumin	

1 Melt the butter in a large heavy-based saucepan. Add the parsnips and onion, cover the pan and fry gently for about 10 minutes until softened, shaking the pan frequently.
2 Add the garlic and spices and fry uncovered, for 2 minutes, stirring constantly to prevent burning. Stir in the flour and cook for a further 2 minutes, then pour in the stock and the orange juice. Bring to the boil, stirring, then add seasoning to taste. Lower the heat, cover and simmer for about 20 minutes until the parsnips are tender.
3 Work the soup in a blender or food processor until smooth, then turn into a bowl, cover and leave overnight in a cool place or the refrigerator until cold, to allow the flavours to develop.
4 To serve, reheat the soup until bubbling, then lower the heat, stir in half the cream and heat through without boiling. Taste and adjust the seasoning.
5 Pour the hot soup into a warmed tureen or individual bowls, swirl with the remaining cream and sprinkle with the grated orange rind. Serve immediately.

MIXED BEAN AND VEGETABLE SOUP

SERVES 6

CREAM OF JERUSALEM ARTICHOKE SOUP

SERVES 4

15 ml (1 tbsp) olive oil	2 bay leaves
1 onion, roughly chopped	about 1.1 litres (2 pints) vegetable stock
450 g (1 lb) mixed root vegetables, including carrots, potatoes and parsnips, roughly chopped	425 g (15 oz) can red kidney beans, drained and rinsed
450 g (1 lb) mixed vegetables, such as peppers, celery and fennel, roughly chopped	425 g (15 oz) can black-eyed beans, drained and rinsed
	2 courgettes, sliced
1 garlic clove, crushed	45 ml (3 tbsp) chopped parsley or coriander
10 ml (2 tsp) mild curry powder	salt and pepper

1 Heat the oil in a large heavy-based saucepan. Add all the vegetables, except the beans and courgettes, and cook over a high heat for 4-5 minutes, stirring all the time. Add the garlic, curry powder and bay leaves and continue cooking for 2-3 minutes.
2 Pour in the stock. (There should be enough to cover the vegetables; if not, add a little more.) Bring to the boil, then reduce the heat, cover and simmer for 20 minutes.
3 Add the beans and cook for a further 10 minutes. Remove the bay leaves. Purée about half the soup in a blender.
4 Return the puréed soup to the saucepan and bring to the boil, then add the courgettes and herbs. Season to taste with salt and pepper and simmer gently for 3-4 minutes or until the courgettes are just tender. Add a little extra stock, if necessary, to thin the soup. Serve as a main course.

COOK'S TIP

Use this basic recipe to make soup from any mixture of vegetables and beans available. Freshly cooked beans could be used, but we've used cans to make the soup quick to cook. Cut the vegetables into generous chunks to give the soup a good, hearty texture.

900 g (2 lb) Jerusalem artichokes	25 ml (1½ tbsp) lemon juice
2 lemon slices	30 ml (2 tbsp) chopped parsley
25 g (1 oz) butter or margarine	150 ml (¼ pint) single cream
1 onion, chopped	salt and pepper
450 ml (¾ pint) milk	croûtons, to garnish

1 Wash the artichokes well and put them in a large saucepan with the lemon slices. Cover with 900 ml (1½ pints) cold water. Bring to the boil and cook until tender, about 20 minutes.
2 Drain off the water, reserving 600 ml (1 pint). Leave the artichokes to cool.
3 Peel the artichokes with your fingers, then mash them roughly.
4 Melt the butter in a clean saucepan, add the onion and cook gently for 10 minutes until soft but not coloured. Stir in the reserved artichoke water, artichokes and milk. Bring the soup to the boil, stirring, then simmer for 2-3 minutes.
5 Sieve or purée the soup in a blender or food processor. Return to the rinsed-out pan and stir in the lemon juice, parsley, cream and salt and pepper to taste. Reheat gently, without boiling. Serve hot, garnished with croûtons.

HARVEST VEGETABLE SOUP

SERVES 4

25 g (1 oz) butter or margarine	50 g (2 oz) lentils
450 g (1 lb) carrots, diced	salt and pepper
1 onion, sliced	½ bay leaf
2 medium potatoes, peeled and diced	40 g (1½ oz) plain flour
1 small green pepper, seeded and chopped	450 ml (¾ pint) milk
	125 g (4 oz) Cheddar cheese, grated
	croûtons, to garnish

1 Melt the butter in a large saucepan and fry the carrots, onion, potatoes and green pepper until soft.
2 Add 450 ml (¾ pint) water, the lentils, salt and pepper to taste and the bay leaf and simmer for 30 minutes.
3 Mix the flour with a little of the milk and gradually blend in the rest. Stir well into the soup until it thickens. Simmer for 5 minutes, then stir in 75 g (3 oz) cheese.
4 Pour into a serving dish, sprinkle with the remaining cheese and garnish with croûtons. Serve immediately.

VARIATION

Vegetable and Oatmeal Broth
Substitute 25 g (1 oz) medium oatmeal and 225 g (8 oz) swede for the lentils and potatoes.

VEGETABLE AND OATMEAL BROTH

SERVES 4-6

1 onion	25 g (1 oz) medium oatmeal
175 g (6 oz) swede	1.1 litres (2 pints) vegetable stock
2 carrots	salt and pepper
1 leek	150 ml (¼ pint) milk
40 g (1½ oz) butter or margarine	chopped parsley, to garnish (optional)

1 Dice the onion, swede and carrots finely. Slice the leek into 1 cm (½ inch) rings, then wash well under cold running water to remove any grit.
2 Melt the butter in a large saucepan, add the vegetables and cook gently without browning for 5 minutes. Add the oatmeal, stir well and cook for a few minutes.
3 Stir in the stock and salt and pepper to taste and bring to the boil. Lower the heat, cover and simmer for about 45 minutes or until tender.
4 Add the milk and reheat to serving temperature. Taste and adjust the seasoning before serving, sprinkled with chopped parsley, if liked.

WATERCRESS SOUP

SERVES 4

2 bunches watercress	750 ml (1¼ pints) vegetable stock
50 g (2 oz) butter or margarine	300 ml (½ pint) milk
1 onion, chopped	salt and pepper
50 g (2 oz) plain flour	

1 Wash and trim the watercress, leaving some of the stem, then chop roughly.
2 Melt the butter in a saucepan, add the watercress and onion and cook gently for 10 minutes until soft but not coloured.
3 Add the flour and cook gently, stirring, for 1-2 minutes. Remove from the heat and gradually blend in the stock and milk. Bring to the boil, stirring constantly, then simmer for 3 minutes. Add salt and pepper to taste.
4 Sieve or purée the soup in a blender or food processor. Return to the rinsed-out pan and reheat gently, without boiling. Taste and adjust seasoning, if necessary. Serve hot.

SERVING SUGGESTION

Try serving this delicately flavoured soup with a swirl of Greek yogurt over the top of each bowl.

CREAM OF PARSLEY SOUP

SERVES 8

225 g (8 oz) parsley	2 litres (3½ pints) vegetable stock
2 onions	salt and pepper
125 g (4 oz) celery	150 ml (¼ pint) single cream
50 g (2 oz) butter or margarine	parsley sprigs, to garnish
45 ml (3 tbsp) plain flour	

1 Wash the parsley, drain and chop roughly. Slice the onions and celery.
2 Melt the butter in a large saucepan and add the parsley, onions and celery. Cover the pan and cook gently for about 10 minutes until the vegetables are soft. Shake the pan occasionally.
3 Stir in the flour until smooth, then mix in the stock. Add salt and pepper to taste and bring to the boil.
4 Cover the pan and simmer for 25-30 minutes. Cool a little, then purée in a blender or food processor. Leave to cool completely, then chill for 2-3 hours or overnight to allow the flavours to develop.
5 Reheat the soup until bubbling, taste and adjust seasoning and swirl in the cream. Serve immediately, garnished with the parsley.

SPICED DAL SOUP

SERVES 4-6

125 g (4 oz) channa dal	225 g (8 oz) tomatoes, skinned and roughly chopped
5 ml (1 tsp) cumin seeds	
10 ml (2 tsp) coriander seeds	2.5 ml ($\frac{1}{2}$ tsp) turmeric
5 ml (1 tsp) fenugreek seeds	5 ml (1 tsp) treacle
3 dried red chillies	5 ml (1 tsp) salt
15 ml (1 tbsp) shredded coconut	lemon slices and coriander sprigs, to garnish
30 ml (2 tbsp) ghee or vegetable oil	

1   Pick over the dal and remove any grit or discoloured pulses. Put into a sieve and wash thoroughly under cold running water. Drain well.
2   Place the dal in a large saucepan, cover with 600 ml (1 pint) water and bring to the boil. Cover and simmer for at least 1 hour, or until tender.
3   Finely grind the cumin, coriander, fenugreek, chillies and coconut in a small electric mill or with a pestle and mortar. Heat the ghee or oil in a heavy-based frying pan, add the spice mixture and fry, stirring, for 30 seconds. Set the spices aside.
4   Mash or purée the dal in a blender or food processor, then transfer to a large saucepan. Stir in the tomatoes, spices, treacle, salt and a further 300 ml ($\frac{1}{2}$ pint) water.
5   Bring to the boil, then lower the heat, cover and simmer for about 20 minutes. Taste and adjust seasoning and turn into a warmed serving dish. Garnish with lemon slices and coriander sprigs and serve immediately.

COOK'S TIP

The shredded coconut in this recipe can be fresh if you want to go to the trouble of preparing a fresh coconut, but for such a small quantity it is more practical to buy ready shredded coconut. It has larger flakes than desiccated coconut, and a fuller flavour.

PARSNIP AND APPLE SOUP

SERVES 6-8

25 g (1 oz) butter or margarine	4 fresh sage leaves or 2.5 ml ($\frac{1}{2}$ tsp) dried sage
700 g (1$\frac{1}{2}$ lb) parsnips, roughly chopped	2 cloves
1 Bramley cooking apple, cored, peeled and roughly chopped	150 ml ($\frac{1}{4}$ pint) single cream
	salt and pepper
1.1 litres (2 pints) vegetable stock	sage leaves or parsley and croûtons, to garnish

1   Melt the butter in a large saucepan, add the parsnips and apple, cover and cook gently for 10 minutes, stirring occasionally.
2   Pour in the stock, add the sage and cloves. Bring to the boil, cover then simmer for 30 minutes, until the parsnips are softened.
3   Remove the sage leaves and cloves, leave to cool slightly, then purée in a blender or food processor.
4   Return to the saucepan and reheat gently with the cream. Season to taste. Serve hot, garnished with the sage or parsley and croûtons.

COOK'S TIP

The velvety texture of a creamy soup is always welcoming, and the unmistakable flavour of parsnips, blended with a hint of tart cooking apple, is very warming. Root crops of all types thrive in fertile East Anglian soil, but parsnips don't reach their peak until after one or two hard frosts.

GOLDEN
VEGETABLE SOUP

SERVES 4

CARROT
AND ORANGE SOUP

SERVES 4-6

25 g (1 oz) butter or margarine	225 g (8 oz) cauliflower, broken into florets
1 large carrot, cut into 4 cm (1½ inch) matchsticks	1 medium onion, sliced
2 celery sticks, cut into 4 cm (1½ inch) matchsticks	2.5 ml (½ tsp) turmeric
125 g (4 oz) swede, cut into 4 cm (1½ inch) matchsticks	1 litre (1¾ pints) vegetable stock
	salt and pepper
	snipped chives, to garnish

1 Melt the butter in a saucepan, add all the vegetables and cook for 2 minutes, stirring occasionally.
2 Add the turmeric and cook for 1 minute. Pour over the stock and adjust seasoning. Bring to the boil and simmer for 20 minutes. Garnish with snipped chives and serve with crusty brown bread.

VARIATIONS

Served in larger quantities this hearty soup can make a meal in itself. You can use any other orange or light coloured vegetables – such as potatoes, sweetcorn, yellow courgettes, pumpkins, turnips – that have a firm enough texture not to disintegrate during cooking. Be sparing with the turmeric; it is for colour only and too much will spoil the taste.

30 ml (2 tbsp) oil	1 litre (1¾ pints) vegetable stock
700 g (1½ lb) carrots, sliced	salt and pepper
2 medium onions, sliced	1 orange

1 Heat the oil in a saucepan, add the vegetables and cook gently for 10 minutes until softened.
2 Add the stock, season with salt and pepper to taste and bring to the boil. Lower the heat, cover and simmer for about 40 minutes, or until the vegetables are tender.
3 Sieve the vegetables or purée with half of the stock in a blender or food processor. Add this mixture to the stock remaining in the pan.
4 Meanwhile pare half of the orange rind thinly, using a potato peeler, then cut it into shreds. Cook the shreds in gently boiling water until tender.
5 Finely grate the remaining orange rind into the soup. Stir well to combine with the ingredients.
6 Squeeze the juice of the orange into the pan, then reheat the soup gently. Drain the shreds of orange rind and use to garnish the soup before serving.

CARROT AND CARDAMOM SOUP

SERVES 4

60 ml (4 tbsp) oil	50 g (2 oz) lentils
200 g (7 oz) carrots, grated	1.1 litres (2 pints) vegetable stock
1 onion, finely sliced	salt and pepper
10 whole green cardamoms	parsley sprigs, to garnish

1 Heat the oil in a heavy-based saucepan, add the carrots and onion and cook gently for 4-5 minutes without browning.

2 Meanwhile split each cardamom and remove the black seeds. Crush the seeds with a pestle in a mortar, or use the end of a rolling pin on a wooden board.

3 Add the crushed cardamom seeds to the vegetables with the lentils. Cook, stirring, for a further 1-2 minutes.

4 Add the stock and bring to the boil. Lower the heat, cover the pan with a lid and simmer gently for about 20 minutes, or until the lentils are just tender. Season to taste with salt and pepper. Serve hot, garnished with parsley.

CELERIAC AND STILTON SOUP

SERVES 8

50 g (2 oz) butter or margarine	10 ml (2 tsp) chopped fresh sage or 5 ml (1 tsp) dried
2 leeks, roughly chopped	salt and pepper
juice of 1 lemon	225 g (8 oz) Blue Stilton cheese, rinded and roughly chopped
2 heads of celeriac, total weight about 900 g (2 lb)	300 ml (½ pint) single cream
1.7 litres (3 pints) vegetable stock	shredded sage leaves, to garnish

1 Melt the butter in a large saucepan, add the leeks and fry very gently for 10 minutes until softened.

2 Meanwhile, fill a bowl with cold water and add the lemon juice. Peel the celeriac thickly with a sharp knife. Cut into chunks, dropping them into the bowl of acidulated water.

3 Drain the celeriac, then add to the pan of leeks. Fry gently, for a further 10 minutes.

4 Add the stock and bring to the boil, stirring, then add the sage and salt and pepper to taste. Lower the heat, cover and simmer for about 20 minutes or until the celeriac is very soft.

5 Crumble the Stilton cheese into a blender or food processor. Add the soup and work to a smooth purée, in batches if necessary.

6 Return the soup to the rinsed-out pan and stir in the cream. Reheat, stirring, then adjust seasoning. Pour into warmed bowls and garnish with sage to serve.

SPINACH SOUP

SERVES 4

MINESTRONE

SERVES 6-8

450 g (1 lb) fresh spinach	salt and pepper
900 ml (1½ pints) vegetable stock	450 ml (¾ pint) buttermilk
15 ml (1 tbsp) lemon juice	few drops of Tabasco sauce

1 Strip the spinach leaves from their stems and wash in several changes of water. Place the spinach, stock, lemon juice and seasoning in a pan. Bring to the boil, then lower the heat, cover and simmer for 10 minutes.

2 Work the spinach through a sieve, or strain off most of the liquid and reserve, then purée the spinach in a blender or processor.

3 Reheat the spinach purée gently with the cooking liquid, 300 ml (½ pint) of the buttermilk and the Tabasco sauce. Swirl in the remaining buttermilk. Serve with warm wholemeal rolls.

175 g (6 oz) dried cannellini beans, soaked overnight in cold water	125 g (4 oz) shelled fresh or frozen peas
60 ml (4 tbsp) olive oil	175 g (6 oz) French beans, sliced
2 onions, chopped	225 g (8 oz) dark green cabbage, tough stalks removed and roughly chopped
3 garlic cloves, crushed	
2 carrots, diced	
2 celery sticks, diced	75 ml (5 tbsp) parsley, chopped
400 g (14 oz) can chopped tomatoes	60 ml (4 tbsp) Pesto (see page 172)
2.3 litres (4 pints) vegetable stock	salt and pepper
350 g (12 oz) floury potatoes (such as King Edward or Maris Piper), peeled and diced	TO SERVE
	Pesto (see page 172)
125 g (4 oz) small pasta shapes	freshly grated Parmesan cheese

1 Drain the beans, put them in a very large saucepan and cover with fresh water. Bring to the boil and boil rapidly for 10 minutes, then cover and simmer for 1 hour; drain.

2 Heat the oil in a large saucepan, add the onions and garlic and fry for 5-10 minutes or until golden brown. Add the carrots and celery and cook for 2 minutes.

3 Stir in the beans, tomatoes, stock, potatoes, pasta and fresh peas, if using. Bring to the boil, then reduce the heat, half-cover and simmer for 1 hour.

4 Add the frozen peas, if using, French beans, cabbage, parsley and Pesto. Season with salt and pepper and simmer for 30 minutes or until the vegetables are all tender. Serve immediately in a warmed soup tureen, as a main course. Hand the Pesto and cheese in separate bowls for guests to stir into their soup.

ASPARAGUS SOUP

SERVES 2

1 medium potato, peeled and diced	150 ml (¼ pint) milk
450 ml (¾ pint) vegetable stock	salt and pepper
275 g (10 oz) can asparagus, drained	30 ml (2 tbsp) soured cream
	25 g (1 oz) Gruyère cheese, grated

1 Put the diced potato and stock into a medium saucepan and bring to the boil. Simmer gently for 10-15 minutes until the potato is cooked.

2 Pour this mixture into a blender or food processor, add the drained asparagus and purée until smooth. Return to the saucepan, stir in the milk and reheat the soup thoroughly. Taste and season with salt and pepper.

3 Just before serving, stir in the soured cream and grated Gruyére cheese. Serve hot.

COOK'S TIP

For a special occasion, why not top this soup with a special garnish? Sprinkle grated Gruyére cheese on to buttered toast, then pop under the grill until melted and bubbling. Cut into small squares, removing the crusts, then float on top of the soup just before serving.

CREAM OF LEMON SOUP

SERVES 6

25 g (1 oz) butter or margarine	1.1 litres (2 pints) vegetable stock
2 onions, thinly sliced	2 bay leaves
75 g (3 oz) carrot, thinly sliced	salt and pepper
75 g (3 oz) celery, thinly sliced	150 ml (¼ pint) single cream or Greek-style yogurt
2 lemons	spring onion tops or chives and lemon slices, to garnish

1 Melt the butter in a large saucepan and add the vegetables. Cover and cook gently for 10-15 minutes until the vegetables begin to soften.

2 Meanwhile, thinly pare the lemons using a potato peeler. Blanch the rinds in boiling water for 1 minute, then drain. Squeeze the juice from the lemons to give 75-90 ml (5-6 tbsp).

3 Add the lemon rind and juice, stock and bay leaves to the pan; season. Bring to the boil, cover and simmer for 40 minutes or until the carrots and celery are both very soft.

4 Cool the soup a little, remove the bay leaves, then purée the pan contents in a blender or food processor until quite smooth.

5 Return the soup to the clean pan, reheat gently, stirring in the cream or yogurt. Do not boil. Adjust seasoning to taste. Serve hot or chilled, garnished with chopped spring onions or chives and lemon slices. Serve with pitta bread.

TOMATO SOUP WITH BASIL

SERVES 6

50 g (2 oz) butter or margarine	900 ml (1½ pints) vegetable stock
2 onions, thinly sliced	30 ml (2 tbsp) tomato purée
900 g (2 lb) tomatoes	7.5 ml (1½ tsp) chopped fresh basil or 2.5 ml (½ tsp) dried
45 ml (3 tbsp) plain flour	basil leaves and single cream, to garnish

1 Melt the butter in a saucepan, add the onions and fry gently until golden brown.
2 Meanwhile, halve the tomatoes and scoop out the seeds into a sieve placed over a bowl. Press to extract all the tomato pulp and juice; discard the seeds.
3 Remove the pan from the heat. Stir in the flour and cook gently for 1 minute, stirring. Remove from the heat and gradually stir in the stock. Bring to the boil slowly and continue to cook, stirring, until thickened.
4 Stir in the tomato purée, herbs and the tomatoes with reserved juice and seasoning. Cover the pan and simmer gently for about 30 minutes.
5 Leave the soup to cool slightly, then sieve or purée in a blender or food processor. Strain into a clean pan and reheat gently. Garnish with basil and cream.

LETTUCE SOUP

SERVES 4

350 g (12 oz) lettuce leaves	600 ml (1 pint) vegetable stock
125 g (4 oz) spring onions, trimmed	150 ml (¼ pint) milk
50 g (2 oz) butter or margarine	salt and pepper
15 ml (1 tbsp) plain flour	shredded lettuce or 60 ml (4 tbsp) soured cream, to finish (optional)

1 Chop the lettuce leaves and spring onions roughly. Melt the butter in a deep saucepan, add the lettuce and spring onions and cook gently for about 10 minutes until both the lettuce and onions are very soft.
2 Stir in the flour and cook, stirring, for 1 minute, then add the stock. Bring to the boil, cover and simmer for 45 minutes to 1 hour.
3 Work the soup to a purée in a blender or food processor, or rub through a sieve. Return to the rinsed-out pan and add the milk with salt and pepper to taste. Reheat to serving temperature. Finish with a garnish of shredded lettuce or a swirl of soured cream, if liked.

SERVING SUGGESTION

This soup has a pretty colour and delicate flavour. It makes a lovely summer starter served with Melba toast.

CHILLED MEDITERRANEAN SOUP

SERVES 4

2 very large Marmande or Beefsteak tomatoes	4 garlic cloves
1 medium Spanish onion	60 ml (4 tbsp) wine vinegar
1 green pepper, cored and seeded	30 ml (2 tbsp) olive oil
	2.5 ml (½ tsp) paprika
450 g (1 lb) can potatoes, drained	salt and pepper
	few ice cubes and mint sprigs, to serve

1 Chop all the vegetables and the garlic roughly and then put half of them in a blender or food processor with the vinegar and about 150 ml (¼ pint) water. Work to a smooth purée.
2 Sieve the purée to remove the tomato skins, working it into a large soup tureen or bowl.
3 Repeat the puréeing and sieving with the remaining vegetables and another 150 ml (¼ pint) water. Add to the purée in the tureen or bowl.
4 Add 750 ml (1¼ pints) water to the soup with the oil, paprika and seasoning to taste. Stir well to mix, cover and chill in the refrigerator for at least 1 hour before serving.
5 To serve, taste and adjust the seasoning, then stir in the ice cubes. Float mint sprigs on top.

SERVING SUGGESTION

Serve as a starter for a summer luncheon or barbecue party, with bowls of garnish such as tiny bread croûtons (fried or toasted), diced red and green pepper, diced cucumber and finely chopped hard-boiled eggs.

CHILLED MELON SOUP

SERVES 4

1 ripe honeydew or cantaloupe melon, weighing about 700 g (1½ lb)	salt and white pepper
	1 egg yolk
25 g (1 oz) butter or margarine	60 ml (4 tbsp) double cream
5 ml (1 tsp) ground ginger	thin slices of preserved (stem) ginger or cream, to garnish
900 ml (1½ pints) vegetable stock	

1 Cut the melon in half and scoop out the seeds with a sharp-edged teaspoon.
2 Remove the flesh from the melon and cut into small chunks.
3 Melt the butter in a large saucepan, add the cubes of melon and cook very gently for 5 minutes until softened.
4 Sprinkle in the ginger and cook for a further 1-2 minutes, stirring constantly. Pour in the stock, add salt and pepper to taste and bring to the boil. Lower the heat, cover the pan and simmer for 30 minutes.
5 Sieve or purée the soup in a blender or food processor. Mix the egg yolk and cream together in a bowl, then stir in a little of the soup.
6 Return the soup to the rinsed-out pan and stir in the egg yolk liaison. Heat through gently without boiling, stirring constantly until thickened. Leave to cool, then chill in the refrigerator for at least 4 hours. Taste and adjust seasoning before serving garnished with ginger slices, or cream feathered into a pattern.

COOK'S TIP

Both honeydew and cantaloupe melons are widely available in the summer months. Honeydew melons have green flesh and a delicate flavour, whereas cantaloupes have yellow flesh and are sweeter, with a scented flesh. Both types of melon are suitable for making soup, as long as they are ripe and juicy. To test for ripeness, press gently with your thumbs at both ends the melon should give slightly if it is ripe.

ICED COURGETTE SOUP

SERVES 4

50 g (2 oz) butter or margarine	5 ml (1 tsp) chopped basil or 2.5 ml (½ tsp) dried
450 g (1 lb) courgettes, chopped	salt and pepper
1 medium potato, peeled and diced	125 g (4 oz) ripe Blue Brie cheese
750 ml (1¼ pints) vegetable stock or water	sliced courgette, to garnish (optional)

1 Melt the butter in a large heavy-based saucepan. Add the courgettes and potato, cover the pan and fry gently for about 10 minutes until softened, shaking frequently.
2 Add the stock or water with the basil and seasoning to taste. Bring to the boil, stirring, then lower the heat and simmer for 20 minutes until the vegetables are tender.
3 Remove the rind from the Brie and chop the cheese into small dice. Put into a blender or food processor, then pour in the soup. Blend until smooth, then turn into a bowl, cover and leave until cold. Chill in the refrigerator overnight.
4 To serve, whisk the soup vigorously to ensure an even consistency, then taste and adjust seasoning. Pour into a chilled soup tureen or individual bowls and float the courgette slices on the top if liked.

CHILLED WATERCRESS AND PEA SOUP

SERVES 6

1 large bunch of watercress	1.1 litres (2 pints) milk
50 g (2 oz) butter or margarine	900 g (2 lb) peas, shelled
1 onion, thinly sliced	salt and pepper
	150 ml (¼ pint) single cream

1 Remove any tough stalks and roughly chop the watercress, reserving a few sprigs for garnish.
2 Melt the butter in a saucepan, add the watercress and onion, cover and cook gently for about 15 minutes, without browning.
3 Remove from the heat and stir in the milk, peas and seasoning. Bring to the boil, stirring.
4 Cover and simmer gently for about 30 minutes, until the peas are really soft. Cool slightly, then rub through a sieve or purée in a blender or food processor.
5 Pour into a large bowl. Adjust seasoning, then allow to cool. Stir in the cream and chill well before serving. Garnish with watercress sprigs.

CHILLED MUSHROOM AND LEMON SOUP

SERVES 6-8

450 g (1 lb) open mushrooms	15 ml (1 tbsp) chopped thyme
grated rind and juice of 1 lemon	900 ml (1½ pints) vegetable stock
1 garlic clove, crushed	150 ml (¼ pint) single cream
salt and pepper	parsley sprigs, to garnish

1 Reserve one or two mushrooms for garnish and roughly slice the rest. Put the sliced mushrooms in a shallow dish and add the lemon rind and juice, garlic, seasoning and herbs. Leave to marinate for several hours, turning occasionally.
2 Purée the mushrooms and the marinade with the stock in a blender or food processor. Stir in the cream and adjust seasoning.
3 Chill well before serving. Garnish with the remaining mushrooms, very finely sliced, and parsley sprigs.

CHILLED APPLE AND AVOCADO SOUP

SERVES 2

2 Golden Delicious apples	10 ml (2 tsp) lemon juice
15 g (½ oz) butter or margarine	1 ripe avocado
5 ml (1 tsp) garam masala	150 ml (¼ pint) single cream
300 ml (½ pint) chilled vegetable stock	salt and pepper

1 Quarter, core and peel the apples, then slice thickly. Place in a heavy-based saucepan with the butter and garam masala. Cook, stirring, for about 5 minutes, until the apples are tender.
2 Transfer the contents of the pan to a blender or food processor. Add the stock and lemon juice and work to a smooth purée.
3 Peel and stone the avocado. Dice the flesh roughly, then add to the apple mixture. Work again until smooth.
4 Pour the soup into a chilled bowl and stir in half of the cream. Add salt and pepper to taste. Cover the bowl tightly with cling film, then chill in the refrigerator for 1 hour.
5 To serve, pour the soup into individual bowls and swirl in the remaining cream. Serve immediately, or the avocado may discolour.

SERVING SUGGESTION

This chilled soup is cool and delicate. Serve with Melba toast for a refreshing starter in hot summer weather.

ICED SWEET PEPPER SOUP

SERVES 4

60 ml (4 tbsp) chopped coriander	225 g (8 oz) ripe tomatoes, sliced
225 g (8 oz) red peppers, seeded and sliced	900 ml (1½ pints) vegetable stock
1 onion, sliced	150 ml (¼ pint) milk
	salt and pepper

1 To make the coriander ice cubes, put the chopped coriander into an ice-cube tray, top up with water and freeze.
2 Place the peppers in a large saucepan with the onion, tomatoes and stock. Bring to the boil, then lower the heat, cover and simmer for about 15 minutes or until the vegetables are tender. Drain, reserving the liquid.
3 Sieve the vegetables, or purée them in a blender or food processor, then sieve the purée to remove the tomato seeds.
4 Combine the reserved liquid, vegetable purée and milk in a bowl with seasoning to taste. Cool for 30 minutes, then chill in the refrigerator for at least 2 hours before serving, with coriander ice cubes.

COOK'S TIP

Do not confuse the herb coriander with the spice of the same name. In this recipe, the fresh herb is used. Looking rather like frondy parsley, it is available at many supermarkets and also at continental and oriental specialist shops. Its flavour is highly aromatic, much stronger than parsley. The spice coriander is used extensively in Indian cookery; it is available as whole seeds and in ground form. The herb and the spice are not interchangeable in recipes.

ANDALUSIAN SUMMER SOUP

SERVES 4-6

60 ml (4 tbsp) olive oil	450 g (1 lb) ripe tomatoes, roughly chopped
1 large onion, roughly chopped	30 ml (2 tbsp) wine vinegar
2 garlic cloves, roughly chopped	1 dried red chilli, finely chopped
2 large red peppers, seeded and roughly chopped	salt and pepper
	60 ml (4 tbsp) mayonnaise

1 Heat the oil in a large saucepan, add the onion and garlic and fry gently for 5 minutes until soft but not coloured.
2 Add the red peppers and fry, stirring, for a further 5 minutes, then add the tomatoes and stir to break them up. Add 900 ml (1½ pints) water, the wine vinegar, chilli and salt and pepper to taste.
3 Bring to the boil, then lower the heat, cover the pan with a lid and simmer for 45 minutes, stirring occasionally.
4 Sieve the soup or purée in a blender or food processor. If blending or processing, sieve to remove the tomato skins.
5 Put the mayonnaise in a large bowl and gradually whisk in the soup. Chill in the refrigerator for at least 4 hours before serving. Accompany the chilled soup with bowls of finely chopped cucumber, onion and red or green pepper, if liked.

VICHYSOISSE

SERVES 4

50 g (2 oz) butter or margarine	2 potatoes, peeled and thinly sliced
4 leeks	salt and pepper
1 onion, sliced	200 ml (7 fl oz) single cream
1 litre (1¾ pints) vegetable stock	snipped chives, to garnish

1 Melt the butter in a heavy-based saucepan, add the leeks and onion and cook gently for about 10 minutes, until soft but not coloured. Add the stock and potatoes and bring to the boil.
2 Lower the heat, add salt and pepper to taste and cover the pan with a lid. Simmer for about 30 minutes until the vegetables are completely soft.
3 Sieve or purée the soup in a blender or food processor. Pour into a large serving bowl and stir in the cream. Taste and adjust seasoning. Chill for at least 4 hours. Sprinkle with chives to serve.

CHILLED CUCUMBER SOUP

SERVES 4

2 medium cucumbers, peeled	1 garlic clove, crushed
125 g (4 oz) walnuts, chopped	30 ml (2 tbsp) chopped dill
30 ml (2 tbsp) olive oil, or a mixture of walnut and olive oil	salt and pepper
	300 ml (½ pint) natural yogurt or soured cream
300 ml (½ pint) vegetable stock, skimmed	dill sprigs, to garnish

1 Cut the cucumbers into small dice and place in a bowl. Add the walnuts, oil, stock, garlic and chopped dill and season to taste with salt and pepper.
2 Stir the soup well, cover the bowl with cling film and chill in the refrigerator for at least 8 hours, or overnight.
3 To serve, uncover and whisk in the yogurt or soured cream. Ladle into individual soup bowls surrounded by crushed ice and garnish with the sprigs of dill.

SERVING SUGGESTION

Cool, creamy and refreshing, this cucumber soup is best served with crisp Melba toast and chilled dry white wine.

ICED PEA
AND MINT SOUP

SERVES 4

225 g (8 oz) green split peas	2 bay leaves
2 litres (3½ pints) unsalted vegetable stock or water	salt and pepper
1 cooking apple	90 ml (3 fl oz) natural yogurt, to serve
25 g (1 oz) mint leaves	mint sprigs, to garnish
juice of 1 lemon	

1 Rinse the split peas well under cold running water. Put the peas in a large saucepan and add the stock or water.
2 Bring the liquid slowly to the boil, then skim off any scum with a slotted spoon.
3 Peel and core the cooking apple, then chop roughly. Add to the pan with half of the mint, the lemon juice and the bay leaves.
4 Half cover the pan with a lid and simmer gently for about 1 hour or until the peas are very tender.
5 Discard the bay leaves. Work the soup to a purée in a blender or food processor, then work through a sieve into a bowl, pressing with the back of a metal spoon. Add the remaining mint, with salt and pepper to taste. Leave until cold, then chill in the refrigerator for at least 4 hours, preferably overnight.
6 To serve, taste and adjust seasoning, then pour into individual bowls and swirl with yogurt. Garnish with mint sprigs. Serve chilled.

COOK'S TIP

Split peas are most often associated with warming winter soups. This recipe for iced split pea soup is cool and delicate, quite the opposite. You can buy two types of split pea, green and yellow; either can be used for this soup, but the green ones give a prettier colour. Both kinds have been split through the middle, as the name suggests, then skinned. This makes them easy to cook – and ideal for puréed soups.

AVOCADO
SOUP

SERVES 4

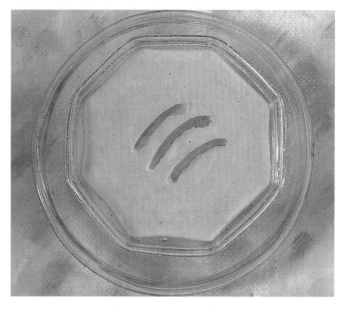

1 avocado	5 ml (1 tsp) golden syrup
450 ml (¾ pint) vegetable stock	pinch of cayenne pepper
30 ml (2 tbsp) lemon juice	salt and pepper
200 ml (7 fl oz) milk	2 ripe tomatoes, to garnish

1 Halve the avocado, discard the stone and peel and roughly chop the flesh.
2 Put the avocado into a blender or food processor with the stock, lemon juice, milk, golden syrup and cayenne and blend until smooth. Season to taste with salt and pepper. Pour into a bowl, cover and chill in the refrigerator for no longer than 2 hours. (The soup will begin to discolour if you leave it for longer.)
3 Meanwhile, plunge the tomatoes into boiling water for 10 seconds, remove from the water and peel off the skin. Halve the tomatoes, remove the seeds, then cut each half into thin slivers.
4 Taste and adjust the seasoning of the soup. Garnish with the tomato slivers just before serving.

ICED TOMATO
AND HERB SOUP

SERVES 4

450 g (1 lb) ripe tomatoes	salt and pepper
1 small onion, sliced	25 g (1 oz) fresh white breadcrumbs
20 ml (4 tsp) tomato purée	
450 ml (¾ pint) vegetable stock	150 ml (¼ pint) soured cream
30 ml (2 tbsp) chopped herbs (eg basil, coriander, parsley)	basil leaves, to garnish (optional)

1 Roughly chop the tomatoes and process them in a blender or food processor with the onion, tomato purée, stock and herbs until smooth.
2 Rub the tomato mixture through a nylon sieve into a saucepan. Heat gently to remove the frothy texture, then add plenty of salt and pepper.
3 Pour the soup into a large serving bowl and stir in the breadcrumbs. Chill in the refrigerator for at least 2 hours.
4 Stir the soured cream until smooth, then stir in. Float basil leaves on top to serve if liked.

CHILLED
ASPARAGUS SOUP

SERVES 6

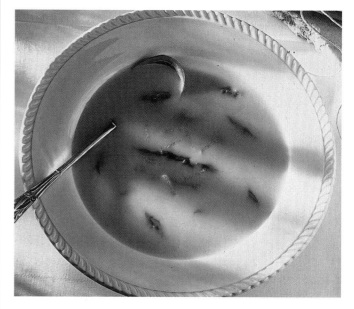

700 g (1½ lb) asparagus	1.4 litres (2½ pints) vegetable stock
salt and pepper	
25 g (1 oz) butter or margarine	150 ml (¼ pint) single cream
2 onions, chopped	grated lemon rind, to garnish

1 Cut the tips off the asparagus and simmer them very gently in salted water for 3-5 minutes, until just tender. Drain well and refresh with cold water.
2 Scrape the asparagus stalks with a potato peeler or knife and cut off the woody ends. Thinly slice the stalks.
3 Melt the butter in a large saucepan. Add the asparagus stalks and onions, cover and cook for 5-10 minutes, until beginning to soften.
4 Add the stock and season to taste. Bring to the boil, cover and simmer for 30-40 minutes, until the asparagus and onions are tender.
5 Allow to cool slightly, then purée in a blender or food processor until smooth. Sieve to remove any stringy particles, then stir in the cream.
6 Chill in the refrigerator for 2-3 hours. Serve, garnished with the reserved asparagus tips and lemon rind.

STARTERS

This mouth-watering selection of starters includes tasty dips and crudités; pâtés, terrines and mousses; delicious grilled and baked vegetable dishes; tempura, samosas and bhajias; plus refreshing chilled starters for summer meals.

GARLIC DIP

SERVES 6

1 onion, finely chopped	150 ml (¼ pint) soured cream
1 small garlic clove, crushed	crudités, to serve (see page 29)

1 Combine the onion with the crushed garlic and soured cream in a bowl.
2 Serve with crudités, cocktail biscuits, crisps, etc.

BLUE CHEESE DIP

SERVES 6-8

150 ml (¼ pint) soured cream	juice of 1 lemon
1 garlic clove, crushed	salt and pepper
175 g (6 oz) Blue Stilton cheese, crumbled	snipped chives, to garnish

1 Combine all the ingredients in a bowl and beat together well. Do not add too much salt as Stilton is salty.
2 Put into a small dish and chill well. Garnish with snipped chives. Serve with savoury cocktail biscuits, pretzels, stuffed olives, etc.

VARIATION

Corn Dip
Omit the Stilton and garlic, adding instead 125 g (4 oz) cottage cheese and a 227 g (8 oz) drained can of corn niblets.

WATERCRESS DIP

SERVES 6

225 g (8 oz) cottage cheese	½ bunch of watercress, chopped
60 ml (4 tbsp) milk	salt and pepper
½ small onion, chopped	crudités, to serve (see right)
1 small garlic clove, crushed	

1 Beat the cheese in a bowl with a wooden spoon and gradually add the milk until the mixture is smooth.
2 Stir the onion, garlic and watercress into the cheese.
3 Leave for at least 2 hours in a cool place to allow the flavours to develop. Season with salt and pepper to taste and serve with crudités.

SPICY CHEESE AND TOMATO DIP

SERVES 6

125 g (4 oz) Cheshire cheese, grated	30 ml (2 tbsp) single cream
50 g (2 oz) butter, softened	few drops of Worcestershire sauce
1 small onion	cayenne pepper
5 ml (1 tsp) mustard powder	parsley sprig, to garnish
15 ml (1 tbsp) tomato ketchup	crudités, to serve (see right)

1 In a bowl, beat together the cheese and softened butter with a wooden spoon.
2 Grate in the onion, add the mustard powder, tomato ketchup, cream and Worcestershire sauce. Season with a little cayenne pepper and mix well.
3 Put into a serving dish and chill. Garnish with a parsley sprig. Serve with crudités.

CRUDITES WITH AIOLI

SERVES 4-6

4 garlic cloves, skinned	1 large red pepper, seeded and cut into strips
1 egg yolk	1 large green pepper, seeded and cut into strips
300 ml (½ pint) olive oil	175 g (6 oz) button mushrooms
lemon juice, to taste	
salt and pepper	1 small cauliflower, cut into florets
CRUDITES	
6 celery sticks	1 bunch radishes
4 carrots, peeled	6 spring onions
½ cucumber	

1 First make the aïoli. Pound the garlic in a mortar and pestle. Stir in the egg yolk. Add the oil a drop at a time, beating until the mixture begins to thicken. This may happen quite suddenly.
2 Continue adding the oil in a thin, steady stream to make a smooth, thick mayonnaise. Stir in lemon juice and salt and pepper to taste. Turn into a bowl, cover and keep in a cool place.
3 Meanwhile, prepare the vegetables. Cut the celery in half crossways, then cut into sticks lengthways. Cut the carrot and cucumber into thin sticks. Slice the mushrooms.
4 To serve, arrange all the vegetables on one large or two small serving dishes. Serve with the dip.

COOK'S TIP

If you want to make this starter ahead of time, the aïoli will keep in a covered container for several days in the refrigerator. The vegetables can be prepared 1-2 hours ahead of time and kept in a bowl of iced water in the refrigerator.

AVOCADO AND GARLIC DIP WITH CRUDITES

SERVES 4-6

2 ripe avocados	CRUDITES
juice of 1 lemon	4 carrots
225 g (8 oz) low-fat soft cheese	4 celery sticks
	1 head chicory
2 large garlic cloves, crushed	125 g (4 oz) button mushrooms
dash of Tabasco sauce, to taste	
salt and pepper	8 cherry tomatoes or large radishes
celery leaves, to garnish	

1 Cut the avocados in half, then twist the halves in opposite directions to separate them. Remove the stones.
2 With a teaspoon, scoop the avocado flesh from the shells into a bowl.
3 Mash the avocado flesh with a fork, adding half of the lemon juice to prevent discolouration.
4 Whisk in the cheese and garlic until evenly mixed, then add Tabasco and seasoning to taste.
5 Transfer the dip to a serving bowl. Cover tightly then chill in the refrigerator until serving time (but no longer than 2 hours).
6 Before serving, prepare the crudités. Scrape the carrots and cut them into thin sticks. Trim the celery and cut into thin sticks. Separate the chicory into leaves. Toss the mushrooms in the remaining lemon juice.
7 To serve, uncover the dip, place the bowl in the centre of a large serving platter and garnish with celery leaves. Surround with the prepared crudités. Serve immediately, or the avocado in the dip may discolour.

AUBERGINE DIP

SERVES 4

2 large aubergines	juice of about 3 lemons
3 garlic cloves, skinned	coriander leaves, black olives and lemon wedges, to garnish
salt	
about 150 ml (¼ pint) tahini paste	

1 Place the aubergines under the grill and cook for about 20 minutes, turning constantly until the skin blisters and the flesh feels soft. Remove from the heat and leave until cool enough to handle. Then peel off the skins and discard them.
2 Put the aubergine flesh in a blender or food processor and blend to form a smooth purée, or push through a sieve.
3 Crush the garlic with salt, then add to the aubergine flesh. Add half the tahini paste and the juice of 1½ lemons and work again until evenly incorporated.
4 Taste the dip and add a little more tahini paste and lemon juice. Continue adding tahini and lemon gradually until the flavour is to your liking. Add more salt if liked.
5 Turn the dip into a shallow serving bowl and smooth the surface. Garnish with coriander, olives and lemon wedges. Refrigerate for 2-3 hours until serving time. Serve with hot pitta bread.

HUMMUS

SERVES 8

225 g (8 oz) dried chick peas, soaked in cold water overnight, or two 400 g (14 oz) cans chick peas	60 ml (4 tbsp) olive oil
	1-2 garlic cloves, crushed
juice of 2 large lemons	salt and pepper
150 ml (¼ pint) tahini paste	black olives and chopped parsley, to garnish

1 If using dried chick peas, drain, place in a saucepan and cover with cold water. Bring to the boil and simmer gently for 2 hours or until tender.
2 Drain the cooked or canned chick peas, reserving a little of the liquid. Put them in a blender or food processor, reserving a few for garnish, and gradually add the reserved liquid and the lemon juice, blending well after each addition in order to form a smooth purée.
3 Add the tahini paste, all but 10 ml (2 tsp) oil and the garlic. Season with salt and pepper to taste. Blend again until smooth.
4 Spoon into a serving dish and sprinkle with the reserved oil, chick peas, and the olives and chopped parsley. Serve with warm pitta bread.

SERVING SUGGESTION

Hummus – or as it is more correctly called – hummus bi tahina – is a traditional dip from the Middle East, where it is served as part of the mezze.
The mezze course is similar to the French hors d'oeuvre, a collection of savoury titbits designed to titilate the appetite before the main meal is served. In this country you can serve hummus on its own as a starter.

GUACAMOLE
DIP WITH CRUDITES

SERVES 8

1 small onion	10 ml (2 tsp) ground coriander
2-3 garlic cloves	
2.5 cm (1 inch) piece fresh root ginger, peeled	10 ml (2 tsp) ground cumin
	5 ml (1 tsp) chilli powder
4 large ripe avocados	2 ripe tomatoes, seeded and roughly chopped
finely grated rind and juice of 2 small limes	
	salt and pepper
60 ml (4 tbsp) chopped fresh coriander	coriander sprigs, to garnish

1 Using a food processor or blender and with the machine running, drop the onion, garlic and ginger through the funnel. Process until finely chopped.

2 Peel and stone the avocados, then put in the food processor or blender with all the remaining ingredients, except the tomato. Process until almost smooth. Stir in the tomato, taste and adjust seasoning as necessary.

3 Transfer to a serving bowl and chill for 30 minutes to let the flavours develop. Garnish with coriander and serve with crudités.

COOK'S TIP

If you don't own a food processor, finely chop the onion, garlic, ginger and tomato then mash the avocado before mixing with the remaining ingredients.

CRUDITÉS

Serve an assortment of crudités chosen and prepared to appeal to the eye as well as the taste buds. Baby vegetables such as carrots, baby corn, cherry tomatoes and button mushrooms can be served whole. Traditionally, crudités are cut into neat strips, all about the same size and arranged in tidy rows of colour. You may prefer to simply clean and trim vegetables to a manageable size retaining their original shape. Sliced fresh fruit such as apples, pears, nectarines, grapes, mangoes, star fruit and fresh dates also make good crudités.

POTTED
CHEESE WITH MINT

SERVES 6

75 g (3 oz) butter or margarine, at room temperature	60 ml (4 tbsp) soured cream
	pepper
225 g (8 oz) Red Leicester or Cheddar cheese	mint leaves, to garnish
15 ml (1 tbsp) chopped mint	

1 Put the butter in a bowl and beat until really soft. Grate in the cheese, then beat it gradually into the butter.

2 Stir in the chopped mint and soured cream, adding pepper to taste. (Salt should not be required as the cheese contains sufficient.)

3 Spoon into individual serving dishes and garnish with mint leaves. Cover and chill for at least 2 hours. To serve, spread on slices of wholemeal bread or crispbreads.

NUTTY CAMEMBERT PATE

SERVES 4-6

175 g (6 oz) soft ripe Camembert cheese	salt and pepper
225 g (8 oz) full-fat soft cheese	75 g (3 oz) finely chopped blanched almonds
2.5 ml (½ tsp) paprika	paprika, to garnish

1 Cut the rind off the Camembert, then work the cheese through a sieve into a bowl, or mix in a food processor until smooth.
2 Add the soft cheese, paprika and seasoning to taste. Beat vigorously with a wooden spoon to combine the ingredients well together.
3 Spoon the pâté into a greased and base-lined 300 ml (½ pint) dish or mould. Press down well and smooth the surface with the back of the spoon. Cover the dish and freeze for 1 hour.
4 Loosen the pâté from the dish by running a palette knife between the two. Turn the pâté out upside down on to a serving plate and peel off the lining paper. Chill before serving.
5 Sprinkle the nuts over the pâté, then press evenly over the top and around the sides with the palette knife. Sprinkle with paprika. Serve chilled with wholemeal toast, crispbreads or crackers.

BUTTER BEAN PATE

SERVES 6-8

225 g (8 oz) dried butter beans, soaked in cold water overnight	30 ml (2 tbsp) chopped coriander
60 ml (4 tbsp) olive oil	salt and pepper
juice of 2 lemons	coriander sprigs and lemon wedges, to garnish
2 garlic cloves, crushed	

1 Drain the butter beans in a sieve and rinse thoroughly under cold running water. Put in a saucepan, cover with cold water and bring to the boil.
2 With a slotted spoon, skim off any scum that rises to the surface. Half cover the pan with a lid and simmer for 1½-2 hours until the beans are very tender.
3 Drain the beans and rinse under cold running water. Put half of the beans in a blender or food processor with half of the oil, lemon juice, garlic and coriander. Blend to a smooth purée, then transfer to a bowl. Repeat with the remaining beans, oil, lemon juice, garlic and coriander.
4 Beat the 2 batches of purée together until well mixed, then add seasoning to taste.
5 Turn the pâté into a serving bowl and rough up the surface with the prongs of a fork. Chill in the refrigerator until required.
6 Garnish this creamy dip with coriander and lemon wedges. Serve with fingers of hot wholemeal pitta bread or granary toast.

VARIATION

If you want to make this dip really quickly, use two 400 g (14 oz) cans butter beans and start the recipe from the beginning of step 3.

DEEP-FRIED CAMEMBERT

SERVES 4

8 individual portions of ripe Camembert cheese	25 g (1 oz) blanched almonds, very finely chopped
15 ml (1 tbsp) plain flour	oil, for deep-frying
salt and pepper	cranberry or redcurrant jelly, to serve
1 egg, size 2	
50 g (2 oz) dried breadcrumbs	

1 Coat the portions of Camembert in the flour seasoned with salt and pepper.
2 Beat the egg in a shallow dish, add the Camembert and turn to coat in the egg.
3 Mix the breadcrumbs and almonds together and use to coat the Camembert. Repeat with more egg, breadcrumbs and almonds to make a second coating. Freeze or chill for 30 minutes.
4 Heat the oil in a deep-fat fryer to 190°C (375°F). Deep-fry the Camembert for about 4 minutes, turning to ensure even browning. Remove with a slotted spoon and drain on absorbent kitchen paper. Serve hot, with the cranberry or redcurrant jelly handed separately, for dipping.

COOK'S TIP

The appeal of this delicious starter is the way in which the ripe Camembert cheese oozes out of its crisp coating when cut. Make sure the cheese is just ripe before coating, then keep it well chilled right up to the moment of deep-frying. If the cheese is allowed to stand at room temperature, it will become over-ripe and ooze out of the coating during frying.

CRUNCHY BAKED POTATO SKINS

SERVES 4

4 medium baking potatoes	300 ml (½ pint) natural yogurt
60 ml (4 tbsp) oil	30 ml (2 tbsp) snipped chives
salt and pepper	salad leaves, to garnish

1 Pierce the potatoes all over with a skewer, then place directly on the oven shelf. Bake in the oven at 200°C (400°F) mark 6 for 1¼ hours until tender.
2 Cut each potato in half lengthways and scoop out most of the flesh with a sharp-edged teaspoon, taking care not to split the skins.
3 Stand the potato skins on a lightly oiled baking sheet. Brush them inside and out with the oil and sprinkle with plenty of salt and pepper.
4 Increase the oven temperature to 220°C (425°F) mark 7 and bake for 10 minutes until crisp.
5 Meanwhile, whisk the yogurt and chives together with seasoning to taste. Spoon into a serving bowl.
6 Serve the potato skins piping hot, with the yogurt dressing. Garnish with salad leaves.

SERVING SUGGESTION

Crunchy baked potato skins are an American idea. Put a spoonful or two of dressing in each potato skin and either eat with the fingers as the Americans do, or with a knife and fork if you prefer. They are equally good served as a starter or as a quick and easy snack.

BRIE TOASTS

MAKES ABOUT 60

350 g (12 oz) Blue Brie cheese, rind removed	10 thick slices of crustless bread
45 ml (3 tbsp) mayonnaise	butter, for spreading
salt and pepper	

1 Beat together the cheese, mayonnaise and seasoning.
2 Spread one side of each slice of bread with butter, the other with the cheese and mayonnaise mixture, and cut into triangles.
3 Place buttered side down, on baking sheets and bake in the oven at 200°C (400°F) mark 6 for 12 minutes or until crisp and brown underneath. Serve hot.

COOK'S TIP

The toasts can be prepared ahead, covered and refrigerated until you're ready to bake them.

BRUSCHETTA

SERVES 4

700 g (1½ lb) very ripe, juicy tomatoes, roughly chopped	15 ml (1 tbsp) virgin olive oil
pinch of sugar	8-10 thick slices of white bread cut from a day-old loaf
salt and pepper	few basil leaves
2-3 large garlic cloves, skinned	few black olives (optional)

1 Put the tomatoes in a bowl, add the sugar and season generously with salt and pepper. Crush one of the garlic cloves and add it to the tomatoes with the olive oil. Cover and leave to stand for 30 minutes-1 hour.
2 Lightly toast the bread on both sides until golden brown. Cut the remaining garlic cloves in half and rub all over both sides of the toast. (The more you rub, the stronger the garlic flavour will be.)
3 Arrange the toast on four individual serving plates. Spoon the tomatoes on top with a little of their juice. Tear the basil leaves into small pieces and sprinkle over the bruschetta. Scatter the olives, if using, on top and serve.

COOK'S TIP

Bruschetta is Tuscan garlic bread made with dense Italian bread, rich green virgin olive oil and garlic. The success of this dish depends entirely on the ingredients; soggy pre-sliced white bread and bland vegetable oil just will not do!

STUFFED VINE LEAVES

SERVES 4-6

175 g (6 oz) bulgar wheat	2.5 ml (½ tsp) ground allspice
4 tomatoes, skinned and finely chopped	salt and pepper
2 garlic cloves, crushed	225 g (8 oz) packet vine leaves preserved in brine, soaked and drained
125 g (4 oz) pine nuts or almonds, finely chopped	150 ml (¼ pint) olive oil
30 ml (2 tbsp) chopped mint	juice of 1 lemon
5 ml (1 tsp) ground cinnamon	lemon slices, to garnish

1 Put the bulgar wheat in a bowl, pour in boiling water to cover, stir and leave to soak for 10 minutes until all the water is absorbed.

2 Transfer the bulgar wheat to a clean tea towel, wrap tightly and ring out as much moisture as possible.

3 Put the bulgar wheat in a bowl with the remaining ingredients, except the vine leaves, olive oil and lemon juice. Add salt sparingly, but plenty of pepper. Mix well.

4 Place 1 vine leaf, vein side upwards, flat on a board or work surface. Put a little filling on the edge of it. Fold the opposite sides of the leaf into the centre, then roll the leaf up around the filling like a cigar.

5 Squeeze the vine leaves gently in the palm of your hand to seal the parcel. Repeat with the remaining filling and vine leaves, putting any ragged or torn vine leaves in the base of a large heavy-based saucepan.

6 Put the stuffed vine leaves in the pan, packing them in layers as close together as possible to prevent them from opening.

7 Mix the olive oil and lemon juice with 150 ml (¼ pint) water and pour slowly into the pan. Put a plate immediately on top of the vine leaves, then cover the pan with a lid. Simmer very gently for 2 hours, then leave the vine leaves to cool in the liquid. Serve chilled, garnished with lemon slices.

SPANAKOPITTES

MAKES 60

30 ml (2 tbsp) olive oil	75 g (3 oz) Feta cheese, crumbled
1 small onion, chopped	1 egg, beaten
227 g (8 oz) packet frozen chopped spinach, thawed and squeezed dry	pepper
	175 g (6 oz) filo pastry sheets
	125 g (4 oz) butter, melted

1 Heat the oil in a saucepan, add the onion and fry gently for 5 minutes until soft. Remove the pan from the heat and stir in the spinach, cheese, egg and pepper to taste.

2 Cut the filo pastry sheets widthways into 5 cm (2 inch) strips. Place the strips on non-stick baking parchment and cover with a slightly damp tea towel.

3 Brush one strip of the pastry with melted butter and place 5 ml (1 tsp) of the spinach mixture at the end of the strip.

4 Fold one corner of the strip diagonally over the filling, so the short edge lies on top of the long edge and forms a right angle.

5 Continue folding the pastry at right angles until you reach the end of the strip, forming a neat triangular package. Repeat with remaining strips and filling to make 60 triangles.

6 Place the packages seam side down in a large roasting tin, and brush with melted butter. Bake in the oven at 220°C (425°F) mark 7 for 15 minutes until golden brown. Serve hot.

VARIATION

Replace the filo pastry with two 386 g (13 oz) packets bought puff pastry. Divide each packet into 6 equal pieces and roll out each piece to a 25 cm (10 inch) square. Cut each square into ten 5 cm (2 inch) strips, and continue from step 2.

AUBERGINE SAMOSAS

SERVES 4

1 small aubergine, about 225 g (8 oz)	2 tomatoes, skinned and chopped
salt and pepper	30 ml (2 tbsp) chopped coriander
15 ml (1 tbsp) oil	Wholemeal Pastry made with 175 g (6 oz) flour (see page 80)
1 garlic clove, crushed	
1.25 ml (¼ tsp) ground allspice	oil, for deep-frying

1 Chop the aubergine finely. Place in a colander, sprinkling each layer with salt. Cover with a plate, place heavy weights on top and leave for 30 minutes, then rinse well under cold running water and dry with absorbent kitchen paper.

2 Heat the oil in a heavy-based saucepan, add the aubergine, garlic and allspice and fry gently for 5-7 minutes or until softened. Stir in the tomatoes and coriander. Season with pepper only, then remove from the heat and leave to cool for 15-20 minutes.

3 Roll out the pastry thinly on a well-floured surface. Stamp out eight 10 cm (4 inch) rounds. Spoon a little filling on each, brush the pastry edges with water and fold over to form semi-circular shapes. Press the edges well together to seal. Place on a plate, cover loosely and chill for 30 minutes.

4 Heat the oil in a deep-fat fryer to 180°C (350°F). Deep-fry the samosas in batches for 4-5 minutes until golden. Drain well and serve immediately.

ONION BHAJIAS

SERVES 4

150 g (5 oz) gram or besan flour	5 ml (1 tsp) chilli powder
5 ml (1 tsp) bicarbonate of soda	4 green cardamoms
10 ml (2 tsp) salt	30 ml (2 tbsp) chopped mint or coriander (optional)
10 ml (2 tsp) coriander seeds, crushed	2 large onions, chopped
2.5 ml (½ tsp) garam masala	salt and pepper
5 ml (1 tsp) turmeric	oil, for deep-frying
	lemon or lime wedges, to garnish

1 Sift the flour, bicarbonate of soda and salt into a bowl. Add the crushed coriander seeds, garam masala, turmeric and chilli powder and mix well.

2 Open the cardamom pods and take out the seeds. Discard the husks and crush the seeds lightly. Add these to the flour mixture together with the mint or coriander, if using, onions, salt and pepper to taste and 30 ml (2 tbsp) water. Mix together thoroughly to a fairly stiff paste.

3 Heat the oil in a deep-fat fryer to 180°C (350°F). Using 2 wet dessertspoons, drop 6 spoonfuls of the mixture into the hot oil and deep-fry the fritters for 3-4 minutes or until darkish brown in colour.

4 Remove from the oil with a slotted spoon and transfer to absorbent kitchen paper to drain. Repeat with the remaining mixture.

5 Serve piping hot, with lemon or lime wedges.

TEMPURA

SERVES 4

25 g (1 oz) fresh root ginger	salt and pepper
60 ml (4 tbsp) sake or dry sherry	125 g (4 oz) cauliflower florets
45 ml (3 tbsp) soy sauce	2 large carrots
125 g (4 oz) plain flour, plus 30 ml (2 tbsp)	16 button mushrooms
30 ml (2 tbsp) maize flour	2 medium courgettes
30 ml (2 tbsp) arrowroot	2 red peppers
	oil, for deep-frying

1 First make the dipping sauce. Peel the fresh root ginger, then grate the flesh into a bowl. Add the sake or sherry and the soy sauce, and 200 ml (7 fl oz) boiling water. Stir well to mix, then set aside while preparing the vegetables and batter.
2 Sift the 125 g (4 oz) plain flour, the maize flour and arrowroot into a large bowl with a pinch each of salt and pepper. Gradually whisk in 300 ml (½ pint) ice cold water to form a smooth, thin batter. Chill in the refrigerator while preparing the vegetables.
3 Divide the cauliflower into tiny sprigs, discarding any thick, woody stalks. Peel the carrots and cut into thin sticks. Wipe the mushrooms and trim the stalks, if necessary. Trim the courgettes, then cut into thin slices.
4 Cut the red peppers in half, remove the core and seeds and slice the flesh into thin strips. Toss the vegetables in the 30 ml (2 tbsp) plain flour.
5 Heat the oil in a wok or deep-fat fryer to 190°C (375°F). Dip the vegetables in the batter in batches, then remove with a slotted spoon taking up a lot of the batter with the vegetables. Deep-fry for 4-5 minutes until crisp, then remove with a slotted spoon. Drain on absorbent kitchen paper. Serve immediately, with the dipping sauce handed separately in individual bowls.

BROCCOLI FRITTERS

SERVES 4

100 g (3½ oz) plain wholemeal flour	salt and pepper
pinch of salt	2 egg whites, beaten
20 ml (4 tsp) oil	oil, for deep-frying
900 g (2 lb) broccoli	300 ml (½ pint) Tomato Sauce (see page 171), to serve
plain wholemeal flour, for dusting	

1 Sift the flour and salt into a bowl and make a well in the centre. Add 90 ml (6 tbsp) water and the oil and beat to form a smooth batter.
2 Trim off and discard the thick ends of the broccoli, then cut into large florets. Cook in boiling salted water for about 5 minutes until nearly tender. Drain the broccoli well. Dust with flour seasoned with salt and pepper.
3 Fold the egg whites into the batter. Lightly turn the broccoli in the batter, using a spoon and fork to coat evenly. Heat the oil in a deep-fat fryer to 180°C (350°F). Deep-fry broccoli in batches for 1-2 minutes until golden.
4 With a slotted spoon, transfer the fritters to a wire rack. Keep warm in a cool oven, uncovered, while cooking the remainder. Serve immediately with hot tomato sauce.

VARIATIONS

Aubergine Fritters
Cut 2 aubergines into 1 cm (½ inch) slices. Blanch for 1 minute in boiling salted water, drain well and proceed as from step 2.
Carrot Fritters
Cut 900 g (2 lb) carrots into finger-sized sticks. Do not blanch, but proceed as from step 2.
Mushroom Fritters
Wipe 450 g (1 lb) button mushrooms and proceed from step 2.
Courgette Fritters
Cut 900 g (2 lb) courgettes into 1 cm (½ inch) slices. Blanch for 1 minute in boiling salted water, drain well and proceed as from step 2.

FRIED COURGETTES WITH ROSEMARY AIOLI

SERVES 4

15 ml (1 tbsp) very finely chopped rosemary	300 ml (½ pint) olive oil
2-4 garlic chives, crushed	pepper
1.25 ml (¼ tsp) salt	900 g (2 lb) thin courgettes
2 egg yolks	plain flour, for coating
30 ml (2 tbsp) lemon juice	oil, for deep-frying
	rosemary sprigs, to garnish

1   To make the aïoli, put the rosemary, garlic and a little of the salt in a bowl and mash with a fork until a paste is formed. Add the egg yolks, the remaining salt and 5 ml (1 tsp) of the lemon juice, and beat well.

2   Gradually add the olive oil, drop by drop, whisking all the time, until the mixture is thick and smooth. When all of the oil has been added, whisk in the remaining lemon juice. Season with pepper, cover and leave to stand for at least 1 hour to allow the flavours to develop.

3   Just before serving, thinly slice the courgettes. Put some plain flour in a bowl and season with salt and pepper. Add the courgettes and toss until coated.

4   Heat the oil in a deep frying pan or deep-fat fryer to 190°C (375°F). Put enough courgette slices into the frying basket to quarter fill it, shaking off excess flour, and lower the basket into the oil. Cook for 3-4 minutes or until golden brown. Drain on crumpled absorbent kitchen paper and keep warm while cooking the remainder.

5   Pile the fried courgettes on to warmed individual serving plates and add a spoonful of rosemary aïoli. Garnish with sprigs of rosemary and serve immediately.

COUNTRY MUSHROOMS

SERVES 4

25 g (1 oz) butter or margarine	10 ml (2 tsp) chopped fresh tarragon or 2.5 ml (½ tsp) dried
450 g (1 lb) button mushrooms	45 ml (3 tbsp) soured cream
15 ml (1 tbsp) plain flour	radicchio and lettuce, to serve
150 ml (¼ pint) milk	tarragon leaves, to garnish
10 ml (2 tsp) wholegrain mustard	

1   Melt the butter in a medium saucepan, add the mushrooms and fry for 2 minutes.

2   Stir in the flour, then gradually stir in the milk. Heat, stirring continuously, until the sauce thickens, boils and is smooth. Simmer for 1-2 minutes.

3   Stir in the mustard, tarragon and soured cream.

4   Serve hot on a nest of radicchio and lettuce leaves, garnished with tarragon.

COOK'S TIP

Choose button mushrooms for their delicate flavour. There's no need to wash or peel them - a wipe with a damp cloth is all that's needed. Tarragon has a very distinctive flavour which marries well with mushrooms. Soured cream gives a hint of piquancy.

BAKED STUFFED MUSHROOMS

MAKES 12

12 large cup mushrooms, about 350 g (12 oz) total weight	60 ml (4 tbsp) chopped parsley
4 sticks celery	30 ml (2 tbsp) lemon juice
1 small onion	salt and pepper
50 g (2 oz) walnuts	1 egg, beaten
75 g (3 oz) butter	50 g (2 oz) Cheddar cheese, grated
75 g (3 oz) fresh breadcrumbs	90 ml (6 tbsp) vegetable stock

1 Wipe the mushrooms and pull out the stalks. Chop the stalks finely with the celery, onion and walnuts.
2 Heat the butter in a medium-sized frying pan and lightly brown the rounded sides of the mushrooms, a few at a time.
3 Remove from the pan, add the chopped mushroom stalks with the celery, onion and walnuts. Fry quickly for 2-3 minutes, stirring occasionally.
4 Remove from the heat and stir in the breadcrumbs, parsley, lemon juice and seasoning, binding with the beaten egg.
5 Spoon into the mushroom caps and place side by side in a shallow ovenproof dish to just fit. Sprinkle a little cheese over each mushroom and pour the stock around the edges of the dish. Bake in the oven at 180°C (350°F) mark 4 for 20-25 minutes. Serve hot.

GRILLED CHICORY WITH PEARS AND HAZELNUTS

SERVES 8

4 large or 8 small heads of chicory, halved and cored	15 ml (1 tbsp) chopped fresh thyme or 5 ml (1 tsp) dried
olive oil, for basting	freshly ground pepper
2 ripe pears, halved, cored and sliced	50 g (2 oz) hazelnuts, toasted and chopped
45 ml (3 tbsp) hazelnut oil	thyme sprigs, to garnish

1 Brush the chicory all over with olive oil. Place in a grill pan cut side up, and cook under a really hot grill, as near to the heat as possible, for about 3-4 minutes; 2-3 minutes for smaller heads; or until just beginning to char and soften. Turn, baste with more oil and cook for a further 2-3 minutes; 1-2 minutes for smaller heads.
2 Carefully turn the chicory again and top with slices of pear. Brush with hazelnut oil, sprinkle on the thyme, season with pepper and grill for 5-6 minutes, 4-5 minutes for smaller heads. The chicory will be very soft, so carefully transfer it to warmed plates.
3 Scatter with the hazelnuts, garnish with extra sprigs of thyme and drizzle with remaining hazelnut oil. Serve with crusty Italian bread.

COOK'S TIP

Grilling the chicory transforms it by caramelising the juices. Pears brushed with hazelnut oil cut any bitterness associated with the vegetable.

ARTICHOKES WITH HOLLANDAISE SAUCE

SERVES 4

4 globe artichokes	300 ml (½ pint) Hollandaise Sauce (see page 172)
½ lemon	

1 Break off the toughest outer leaves from each artichoke. With a sharp knife, cut off the stem quite close to the base leaves.

2 Trim the spiky leaf tops, according to variety, with a sharp knife or scissors. Rub the cut surfaces with the lemon half to prevent discolouration.

3 Place the artichokes in a large saucepan of boiling salted water. Simmer gently for 35-40 minutes, according to size. To test whether the artichoke is cooked, try pulling out a leaf. If it comes out easily, the artichoke is cooked. Turn the heads upside down in a colander to drain for a few minutes.

4 The 'choke' must never be eaten as the little barbs can irritate the throat. You can easily recognise the choke: it is a mass of yellowish silky hairs arising out of the firm-textured heart. To remove the chokes, carefully peel back the leaves until it is exposed then scoop them out with a spoon. Serve the artichokes while still hot, with the warm hollandaise sauce.

ASPARAGUS MALTAISE

SERVES 6

450 g (1 lb) asparagus, trimmed	125 g (4 oz) unsalted butter, softened
3 egg yolks	15 ml (1 tbsp) lemon juice
grated rind and juice of 1 orange	30-45 ml (2-3 tbsp) double cream
salt and white pepper	orange twists, to garnish

1 Tie the asparagus in bundles of six to eight stalks. Standing them upright in a saucepan of boiling water, cook for 10-15 minutes until tender.

2 Meanwhile, make the sauce. Beat together the egg yolks, orange rind and salt and pepper to taste in a bowl with a knob of the softened butter.

3 Place the bowl over a pan of hot water and whisk in the orange and lemon juice. Cook over a gentle heat and beat in the remaining butter a little at a time.

4 Once the sauce begins to thicken, remove from the heat and continue beating for 1 minute. Adjust seasoning to taste. Stir in the cream.

5 Remove the asparagus from the pan and drain well. Remove the string. Serve immediately, garnished with orange twists, with the orange sauce handed separately.

AVOCADO AND KIWI FRUIT VINAIGRETTE

SERVES 8

1 egg	salt and pepper
150 ml (¼ pint) olive oil	4 kiwi fruit
60 ml (4 tbsp) white wine vinegar	3 small ripe avocados
45 ml (3 tbsp) chopped parsley	watercress sprigs, to garnish

1 Boil the egg for 6 minutes only. Meanwhile, whisk together the oil, vinegar, parsley and salt and pepper to taste in a medium bowl.

2 Run cold water over the boiled egg to cool. Shell and halve the egg. Scoop out the yolk into the dressing. Chop the egg white finely and add to the dressing, whisking well to ensure it is evenly mixed.

3 Peel the kiwi fruit and slice it into rings, discarding the ends. Stir into the dressing, cover and refrigerate for at least 2 hours.

4 Halve, peel and slice the avocados and arrange on individual serving plates together with the drained kiwi fruit slices.

5 Spoon the dressing over the avocados and kiwi fruit and garnish with watercress sprigs. Serve with wholemeal French-style bread.

ROASTED PEPPERS WITH PISTACHIO NUTS

SERVES 8

8 large sweet peppers	few salad leaves
60 ml (4 tbsp) virgin olive oil	300 ml (½ pint) Greek-style yogurt
salt and pepper	125 g (4 oz) shelled pistachio nuts, roughly chopped
60 ml (4 tbsp) chopped marjoram or oregano	herb sprigs, to garnish

1 Place the peppers in a grill pan and cook under a hot grill until the skin is blackened. Turn the peppers over and cook until the other side is blackened. This will take at least 10-15 minutes.

2 Cover with a damp cloth and leave until cool enough to handle. Carefully peel off the skins. Cut the peppers into chunky strips and place in a shallow dish. Pour over the olive oil and season generously with salt and pepper. Sprinkle with the marjoram. Leave to marinate until ready to serve.

3 To serve, arrange the peppers on individual serving plates with a few salad leaves. Place a large spoonful of yogurt on each plate and sprinkle with the pistachio nuts. Generously grind black pepper over the top and garnish with herb sprigs.

COOK'S TIP

If making the pepper and yogurt starter a long time in advance keep it covered in the refrigerator. Remove from the refrigerator at least 1 hour before serving. It should be served at room temperature, not chilled.

ARTICHOKE HEARTS
A LA GRECQUE

SERVES 6

75 ml (5 tbsp) olive oil	salt and pepper
15 ml (1 tbsp) white wine vinegar	175 g (6 oz) button onions, skinned
10 ml (2 tsp) tomato purée	5 ml (1 tsp) caster sugar
1 large garlic clove, crushed	225 g (8 oz) small button mushrooms
7.5 ml (1½ tsp) chopped thyme or basil	two 400 g (14 oz) cans artichoke hearts

1 To make the dressing, place 45 ml (3 tbsp) oil, the vinegar, tomato purée, garlic, thyme and seasoning in a bowl and whisk together.
2 Blanch the onions in boiling water for 5 minutes; drain well. Heat the remaining oil in a heavy-based pan, add the onions and the sugar and cook for 2 minutes.
3 Add the mushrooms and toss over a high heat for a few seconds. Tip the contents of the pan into dressing. Drain the artichoke hearts, rinse and drain thoroughly. Add them to the dressing and toss together. Cover and chill for at least 30 minutes before serving.

MARINATED
MUSHROOMS

SERVES 4

450 g (1 lb) small button mushrooms	pinch of mustard powder
30 ml (2 tbsp) wine vinegar	pinch of muscovado sugar
90 ml (6 tbsp) sunflower oil	salt and pepper
	chopped parsley, to garnish

1 Leave small mushrooms whole and cut larger ones in quarters.
2 Put the vinegar, oil, mustard and sugar in a bowl with seasoning to taste. Whisk together with a fork until well blended.
3 Add the mushrooms and stir to coat in the marinade. Cover and leave to marinate in the refrigerator for 6-8 hours, stirring occasionally.
4 Taste and adjust the seasoning, then divide the mushrooms equally between 4 individual shallow serving dishes. Sprinkle with chopped parsley and serve immediately.

SERVING SUGGESTION

Marinated mushrooms make a refreshingly light start to a substantial main course. Serve with a little crusty wholemeal bread to mop up the juices.

MUSHROOMS IN SOURED CREAM

SERVES 4

450 g (1 lb) button mushrooms	juice of 1 lemon
1 bunch of spring onions	150 ml (¼ pint) soured cream
4 cardamom pods	30 ml (2 tbsp) chopped coriander
25 g (1 oz) butter or margarine	salt and pepper
30 ml (2 tbsp) olive oil	coriander and paprika, to garnish
2 garlic cloves, crushed	

1 Wipe the mushrooms. Slice them thickly and evenly into 'T' shapes. Trim the spring onions and slice finely.
2 Split open the cardamom pods with your fingernails to release the seeds. Crush the seeds with a mortar and pestle or the end of a rolling pin.
3 Melt the butter with the oil in a large frying pan. Add the spring onions and garlic and fry gently for 5 minutes until the onions soften slightly.
4 Add the crushed cardamom seeds to the pan and fry for 1-2 minutes, then increase the heat and add the mushrooms. Cook the mushrooms for a few minutes only until tender, stirring frequently and shaking the pan to ensure even cooking.
5 Transfer the mushrooms and cooking juices to a bowl. Leave to cool then stir in the lemon juice, soured cream and coriander with salt and pepper to taste. Chill in the refrigerator until serving time. Stir well and garnish with coriander and paprika just before serving, with fresh wholemeal or poppyseed rolls.

CAPONATA

SERVES 4-6

450 g (1 lb) aubergines	45 ml (3 tbsp) wine vinegar
salt and pepper	oil, for deep-frying
30 ml (2 tbsp) olive oil	4 large celery sticks
1 large onion, sliced	50 g (2 oz) large green olives
2 garlic cloves, crushed	15 ml (1 tbsp) capers
450 g (1 lb) tomatoes, skinned and roughly chopped	25 g (1 oz) pine nuts

1 Dice the aubergines, then place in a colander, sprinkling each layer with salt. Cover with a plate, put heavy weights on top and leave to dégorge for 30 minutes.
2 Meanwhile, heat the 30 ml (2 tbsp) olive oil in a heavy-based saucepan or flameproof casserole. Add the onion and garlic and fry gently for about 10 minutes until soft and lightly coloured.
3 Add the tomatoes, wine vinegar and salt and pepper to taste. Simmer for about 20 minutes, breaking up the tomatoes occasionally with a wooden spoon.
4 Heat the oil to 180°C (350°F) in a deep-fat fryer. Rinse the aubergines under cold running water, then pat dry with absorbent kitchen paper.
5 Deep-fry the aubergines in batches until crisp and golden brown, then drain again on absorbent kitchen paper and add to the tomato sauce.
6 Cut the celery sticks diagonally into chunky pieces, then deep-fry and drain as with the aubergines. Add to the tomatoes and aubergines. Continue cooking for a further 10 minutes.
7 Stone the olives, then add to the caponata with the capers and pine nuts. Remove from the heat and leave to cool, then chill in the refrigerator overnight. Taste and adjust seasoning before serving. Serve chilled with chunky slices of French bread, or Italian rolls.

MOZZARELLA STUFFED TOMATOES

SERVES 4

4 large, firm tomatoes	20 ml (4 tsp) chopped basil or 10 ml (2 tsp) dried
salt and pepper	135 ml (9 tbsp) olive oil
50 g (2 oz) black olives	45 ml (3 tbsp) lemon juice
225 g (8 oz) Mozzarella cheese, grated	basil sprigs, to garnish
1-2 garlic cloves, crushed	

1 Skin each tomato by piercing the stalk end with a fork and holding over a gas flame or under the grill. Turn the tomato until the skin bursts. Leave until cool enough to handle, then peel off the skin.

2 Cut a slice off the rounded end of each tomato and reserve. Scoop out the insides of the tomatoes with a teaspoon. Sprinkle the insides with salt and stand cut side down on absorbent kitchen paper.

3 Reserve 4 black olives, then stone and chop the remainder. Put the Mozzarella in a bowl with the chopped olives, garlic and half the basil. Mix well, then add salt and pepper to taste. (Add salt sparingly as olives tend to be salty.)

4 Place the tomatoes in a serving dish and spoon in the Mozzarella mixture. Replace the reserved tomato slices at an angle so that the Mozzarella filling is visible.

5 Whisk together the oil and lemon juice with the remaining basil and salt and pepper to taste. Pour over the tomatoes, then chill for at least 2 hours, spooning the dressing over from time to time. Serve chilled, garnished with the reserved olives and basil sprigs.

CHILLED RATATOUILLE

SERVES 6

1 large aubergine, weighing about 350 g (12 oz)	60 ml (4 tbsp) oil
salt and pepper	125 g (4 oz) button mushrooms
450 g (1 lb) courgettes	150 ml (¼ pint) vegetable stock
225 g (8 oz) trimmed leeks	30 ml (2 tbsp) tomato purée
450 g (1 lb) tomatoes	15 ml (1 tbsp) chopped rosemary or parsley
1 green pepper	

1 Cut the aubergine into 2 cm (¾ inch) pieces.

2 Put the aubergine pieces in a colander, sprinkling each layer lightly with salt. Cover with a plate, weight down, then leave to drain for 30 minutes. Rinse under cold running water and pat dry with absorbent kitchen paper.

3 Slice the courgettes diagonally into 5 mm (¼ inch) pieces. Cut the leeks across into similar sized pieces, discarding the root ends and any tough dark leaves. Wash, pushing the slices apart, and drain well.

4 Skin and quarter the tomatoes; push out the pips into a nylon sieve placed over a bowl; reserve the tomato juice. Halve each tomato quarter lengthwise. Slice the pepper into narrow strips, discarding core and seeds.

5 Heat the oil in a large sauté or frying pan. Add the aubergine and courgettes and fry over high heat for 2-3 minutes, turning frequently. Stir in the remaining vegetables, with the stock, tomato purée, reserved tomato juice, rosemary and salt and pepper to taste.

6 Bring the contents of the pan to the boil, cover and simmer for 8-10 minutes. The vegetables should be just tender with a hint of crispness, not mushy. Adjust the seasoning and pour out into a bowl to cool for 30 minutes. Chill well in the refrigerator for at least 4 hours.

7 To serve, turn into a large serving bowl or individual dishes. Serve with French bread, preferably wholemeal.

PICKLED VEGETABLES

SERVES 4

TOMATO ICE WITH VEGETABLE JULIENNE

SERVES 4-6

400 g (14 oz) can artichoke hearts, drained	30 ml (2 tbsp) white wine vinegar
125 g (4 oz) black olives	grated rind of 1 orange and 45 ml (3 tbsp) juice
2 courgettes, sliced	30 ml (2 tbsp) chopped parsley
150 ml (¼ pint) oil	
10 ml (2 tsp) dry mustard powder	salt and pepper

1 Quarter the artichoke hearts and place in a bowl with the olives and courgettes. Whisk together the remaining ingredients and pour over the vegetable and olives. Stir to coat evenly.
2 Cover and leave to marinate in the refrigerator for at least 12 hours. Spear with wooden cocktail sticks to serve.

COOK'S TIP

The marinade can also be used for other lightly cooked vegetables, smoked oysters, and wild mushrooms.

8 very ripe tomatoes	30 ml (2 tbsp) chopped basil
10 ml (2 tsp) gelatine	2 small leeks
30 ml (2 tbsp) tomato purée	2 medium carrots
30 ml (2 tbsp) lemon juice	2 medium courgettes
few drops of Tabasco	120 ml (4 fl oz) Vinaigrette (see page 173)
salt and pepper	basil leaves, to garnish

1 Put the tomatoes in a blender or food processor and work until smooth. Press the tomato pulp through a sieve into a bowl to remove the seeds and skin.
2 Dissolve the gelatine in 45 ml (3 tbsp) water.
3 Add the tomato purée to the tomato pulp with the lemon juice, Tabasco, salt and pepper to taste. Mix well.
4 Stir in the gelatine and chopped basil leaves. Pour into a chilled shallow freezer container and freeze for about 2 hours until mushy.
5 Remove from the freezer and beat the mixture with a fork to break down any ice crystals. Return to the freezer and freeze for a further 4 hours.
6 Meanwhile, wash the leeks thoroughly and cut into fine julienne strips of equal length. Cut the carrots and courgettes into julienne strips of the same size.
7 Bring a large pan of water to the boil and blanch the leeks for 1 minute, then remove with a slotted spoon and drain on absorbent kitchen paper. Blanch the carrots in the same water for about 4 minutes; drain well. Similarly, blanch the courgettes for 2 minutes and drain well.
8 Put the julienne of vegetables in a bowl, add the vinaigrette and salt and pepper to taste and toss gently to mix. Cover and chill in the refrigerator until required.
9 To serve, allow the tomato ice to soften in the refrigerator for 30 minutes. Arrange small scoops of tomato ice on chilled individual side plates with a 'nest' of julienne vegetables. Garnish with basil sprigs.

CELERIAC REMOULADE

SERVES 6

1 large head of celeriac	30 ml (2 tbsp) French mustard
30 ml (2 tbsp) lemon juice	salt and pepper
300 ml (½ pint) mayonnaise	1 lettuce or curly endive
30 ml (2 tbsp) snipped chives	chopped parsley, to garnish

1 Peel and coarsely grate the celeriac. Toss immediately in the lemon juice to prevent discolouration.
2 Add the mayonnaise, chives and mustard with seasoning to taste and mix well together.
3 Line individual dishes or plates with lettuce, then pile the celeriac mixture in the centre. Sprinkle with chopped parsley and serve immediately.

COOK'S TIP

Celeriac tastes much like celery, but is a knobbly vegetable that looks like a rough turnip and can vary from about the size of a large apple to as big as a coconut.

CARROT AND CELERIAC VINAIGRETTE

SERVES 2

45 ml (3 tbsp) olive or sunflower oil, or 15 ml (1 tbsp) walnut oil and 30 ml (2 tbsp) sunflower oil, mixed	salt and pepper
	125 g (4oz) celeriac
	2 carrots
15 ml (1 tbsp) wine or cider vinegar, or lemon juice	25 g (1 oz) walnut halves, chopped
5 ml (1 tsp) wholegrain mustard	watercress sprigs or lettuce leaves, to garnish
pinch of caster sugar	

1 Put the oil, vinegar, mustard and sugar in a small bowl. Whisk together until thick, then add salt and pepper to taste.
2 Grate the celeriac and add to the bowl of dressing. Grate the carrot and add to the celeriac. Add the chopped walnuts and mix together thoroughly. Cover the bowl tightly with cling film. Chill in the refrigerator for at least 1 hour.
3 To serve, uncover and mix once more. Pile on to individual serving plates and garnish with sprigs of watercress or lettuce leaves, if liked.

SERVING SUGGESTION

Serve this colourful starter in winter, when both carrots and celeriac are plentiful. Granary or wholemeal bread and butter would be the ideal accompaniment.

GORGONZOLA STUFFED PEARS

SERVES 4

125 g (4 oz) Gorgonzola cheese, at room temperature	150 ml (¼ pint) thick homemade mayonnaise (see page 173)
25 g (1 oz) unsalted butter, softened	about 15 ml (1 tbsp) tarragon vinegar
50 g (2 oz) walnuts, finely chopped	2 ripe firm pears (eg Packham)
salt and pepper	juice of ½ lemon
	lettuce leaves, to serve

1 To make the stuffing mixture, work half the cheese and the butter together with a fork. Add half of the walnuts and pepper to taste and mix together until well combined. (Do not add salt as the cheese is quite salty enough.)
2 Soften the remaining cheese and work it into the mayonnaise. Stir the tarragon vinegar into the mayonnaise mixture to thin it down to a light coating consistency. If too thick, add a little more vinegar. Taste and adjust seasoning.
3 Peel the pears and, using a sharp knife, cut each one in half lengthways.
4 Scoop out the cores and a little of the surrounding flesh with a sharp-edged teaspoon. Immediately brush lemon juice over the exposed flesh to prevent discolouration.
5 Fill the scooped-out centres of the pears with the Gorgonzola stuffing mixture.
6 To serve, place 1-2 lettuce leaves on each individual serving plate. Place one pear half, cut side down, on the lettuce. Coat the pears with the mayonnaise, then sprinkle with the remaining chopped walnuts. Serve immediately.

STILTON PEARS

SERVES 4

2 large dessert pears, ripe but firm	15 ml (1 tbsp) mayonnaise
30 ml (2 tbsp) lemon juice	pinch of mustard powder
50 g (2 oz) curd cheese	pinch of sugar
75 g (3 oz) Stilton cheese, crumbled	5 ml (1 tsp) poppy seeds
30 ml (2 tbsp) oil	salt and pepper

1 Using an apple corer, remove the cores from the pears. Sprinkle the cavities with 15 ml (1 tbsp) of the lemon juice.
2 Cream together the two cheeses. Press as much cheese mixture as possible into the pear cavities, then cover and chill until ready to serve.
3 Just before serving, whisk the oil, mayonnaise, remaining lemon juice, mustard, sugar, poppy seeds, salt and pepper together. Spoon on to 4 individual plates. Cut each pear in half lengthways then slice, fan out and arrange, cut side down, in the dressing. Serve at once.

COOK'S TIP

Cheese and pears are a delightful combination, and dessert pears make a refreshing change from avocados in this starter. Comice are a good choice, as they are mouth wateringly juicy when fully ripe. Make sure they are still firm though because, as with all pears, they have to be eaten at just the right moment.

SPINACH TIMBALES

SERVES 6

15 g (½ oz) butter	50 g (2 oz) Cheddar cheese, grated
1 small onion, finely chopped	25 g (1 oz) fresh wholemeal breadcrumbs
450 g (1 lb) fresh spinach, finely chopped, or 225 g (8 oz) frozen chopped spinach, thawed	pinch of freshly grated nutmeg
150 ml (¼ pint) single cream	salt and pepper
2 eggs, beaten	lemon slices, to garnish

1 Melt the butter in a large saucepan, stir in the onion and cook gently for about 5 minutes, until soft.
2 Stir in the spinach and cook for a further 5 minutes if using fresh spinach, 2-3 minutes if using frozen, stirring occasionally, until soft. Stir in the cream.
3 Beat the eggs in a bowl and stir in the spinach mixture, cheese, breadcrumbs and nutmeg. Season to taste. Spoon the mixture into 6 ramekin dishes, level the surfaces, cover each one with foil and place in a roasting tin, half filled with hot water.
4 Bake in the oven at 180°C (350°F) mark 4 for 1 hour, until firm to the touch and a knife inserted in the centre comes out clean. Remove the dishes and leave for 5 minutes. Turn out on to individual plates and garnish with lemon slices.

COOK'S TIP

These light spinach, cheese and egg starters take their name from the round moulds with straight or slightly sloping sides in which they were originally baked, called timbales. This version is cooked in more familiar ramekin dishes.

HOT MUSHROOM TERRINE

SERVES 6

50 g (2 oz) butter or margarine	4 eggs, separated
1 small onion, chopped	salt and pepper
450 g (1 lb) mushrooms, finely chopped	150 g (5 oz) unsalted butter
10 ml (2 tsp) ground coriander	2 egg yolks
225 g (8 oz) curd cheese	15 ml (1 tbsp) lemon juice
	pinch of cayenne and coriander leaves, to garnish

1 Melt the butter in a large saucepan, add the onion and fry gently for 5 minutes until soft. Add the mushrooms and coriander and cook, stirring, for about 20 minutes until all excess liquid has evaporated. Leave for 15 minutes.
2 Turn the mushrooms into a bowl. Add the cheese, egg yolks and seasoning to taste. Mix well, then blend or process in batches.
3 Whisk the egg whites until stiff, then fold into the mushroom mixture. Pour into a well-buttered and base-lined 1 kg (2 lb) loaf tin and cover with well-buttered foil.
4 Place in a roasting tin half filled with hot water. Bake in the oven at 180°C (350°F) mark 4 for 1½ hours or until firm. Remove from the roasting tin.
5 Meanwhile, make a hollandaise sauce. Melt the butter gently in a heavy-based saucepan, then pour into a jug. Put the egg yolks in the warmed goblet of a blender or food processor and turn to low speed.
6 Pour in 25 ml (1½ tbsp) boiling water, then add the warm melted butter very slowly in a thin steady stream. Add the lemon juice and cayenne with salt to taste and continue blending until smooth and creamy.
7 Turn the mushroom terrine out onto a serving dish and peel off the lining paper. Cut into slices and coat with the hollandaise sauce. Garnish with cayenne and coriander leaves to serve.

INDIVIDUAL MUSHROOM SOUFFLES

SERVES 6

75 g (3 oz) butter	40 g (1½ oz) plain flour
125 g (4 oz) flat mushrooms, roughly chopped	275 ml (9 fl oz) milk
20 ml (4 tsp) anchovy essence	salt and pepper
squeeze of lemon juice	4 eggs, size 2, separated
	freshly grated Parmesan

1 Brush the insides of six 150 ml (¼ pint) individual soufflé dishes liberally with 15 g (½ oz) butter and set aside.

2 Melt 25 g (1 oz) butter in a saucepan, add the mushrooms, anchovy essence and lemon juice and stir-fry over high heat for 2-3 minutes. Transfer the mushrooms with a slotted spoon to a large bowl.

3 Melt the remaining butter in the pan, add the flour and cook gently, stirring, for 1-2 minutes. Remove from the heat and gradually blend in the milk. Bring to the boil, stirring constantly, then simmer for 3 minutes until thick and smooth.

4 Remove the pan from the heat and add the sauce to the mushrooms. Stir well to mix, adding salt and pepper to taste. Beat in the egg yolks, one at a time.

5 Whisk the egg whites until stiff, then fold into the soufflé mixture until evenly incorporated. Divide equally between the prepared soufflé dishes and sprinkle with Parmesan. Bake immediately in the oven at 200°C (400°F) mark 6 for 15 minutes or until well risen. Serve immediately, with hot garlic or herb bread.

ASPARAGUS MOUSSES

SERVES 6

700 g (1½ lb) asparagus	150 ml (¼ pint) double cream
50 g (2 oz) butter or margarine	3 egg yolks
1 onion, finely chopped	salt and pepper
30 ml (2 tbsp) lemon juice	1 egg white

1 Cut the tips off the asparagus to a length of about 4 cm (1½ inches) and reserve. Slice the stalks into 1 cm (½ inch) lengths, discarding any tough root ends.

2 Melt the butter in a saucepan. Add the asparagus stalks, onion and lemon juice, then pour in 200 ml (7 fl oz) water. Cover tightly and cook gently for about 30 minutes or until the asparagus is tender.

3 Drain well, then put in a blender or food processor with the cream. Work until almost smooth.

4 Rub the purée through a nylon sieve into a bowl to remove any stringy particles. Beat in the egg yolks with salt and pepper to taste. Whisk the egg white until stiff and fold into the asparagus mixture.

5 Spoon the asparagus mixture into six 150 ml (¼ pint) individual soufflé dishes, then stand the dishes in a roasting tin. Pour in enough hot water to come half way up the sides of the ramekins.

6 Bake the mousses at 170°C (325°F) mark 3 for 40-45 minutes or until just firm when pressed lightly in the centres. Ten minutes before the end of the cooking time, cook the asparagus tips in a steamer for 5-10 minutes until tender.

7 Serve the asparagus mousses immediately, topped with the asparagus tips. Accompany with thin slices of wholemeal toast, if liked.

AUBERGINE
AND CHEESE SOUFFLE

SERVES 4

450 g (1 lb) aubergines	150 ml (¼ pint) milk
salt and pepper	125 g (4 oz) Red Leicester or Cheddar cheese, grated
75 g (3 oz) butter or margarine	4 eggs, separated
30 ml (2 tbsp) plain wholemeal flour	40 g (1½ oz) freshly grated Parmesan cheese

1 Chop the aubergines roughly and place in a colander or sieve. Sprinkle liberally with salt and set aside to drain for 30 minutes. Rinse under cold running water, then pat dry with absorbent kitchen paper.

2 Melt 50 g (2 oz) of the butter in a saucepan and add the aubergines. Cover and cook gently until golden brown and completely soft. Purée in a blender or food processor until nearly smooth.

3 Melt the remaining butter in a clean saucepan, add the flour and cook over a low heat, stirring with a wooden spoon, for 2 minutes. Remove the pan from the heat and gradually blend in the milk, stirring after each addition to prevent lumps forming. Bring to the boil slowly, then simmer for 2-3 minutes, stirring.

4 Remove from the heat and stir in the aubergine purée, the Leicester or Cheddar cheese, the egg yolks and salt and pepper to taste. Turn into a bowl, cover and chill until required.

5 Lightly grease a 1.4 litre (2½ pint) soufflé dish and dust with all but 25 g (1 oz) of the Parmesan cheese.

6 Whisk the egg whites until stiff but not dry. Fold into the aubergine mixture until evenly combined. Spoon into the prepared dish and sprinkle with the remaining Parmesan. Bake in the oven at 200°C (400°F) mark 6 for 25-30 minutes. Serve immediately.

FETA
CHEESE SOUFFLE

SERVES 4

freshly grated Parmesan cheese, for sprinkling	salt and pepper
25 g (1 oz) butter or margarine	225 g (8 oz) Feta cheese, grated
30 ml (2 tbsp) plain flour	50 g (2 oz) stuffed olives, chopped
200 ml (7 fl oz) milk	4 eggs, separated

1 Lightly butter a 1.7 litre (3 pint) soufflé dish and dust out with grated Parmesan.

2 Melt the butter in a saucepan, add the flour and cook for 1 minute, stirring. Off the heat, gradually stir in the milk and black pepper. Bring to the boil; cook for 2-3 minutes, stirring. Allow to cool slightly, then beat in the Feta, olives and egg yolks. Season.

3 Whisk the egg whites until stiff and beat a large spoonful into the sauce. Lightly fold in the rest and pour the mixture into the prepared dish.

4 Bake in the oven at 180°C (350°F) mark 4 for about 40 minutes until the soufflé is golden. Serve immediately.

SPINACH GNOCCHI

SERVES 4

900 g (2 lb) fresh spinach, or 450 g (1 lb) frozen spinach	1.25 ml (¼ tsp) freshly grated nutmeg
225 g (8 oz) Ricotta or curd cheese	125 g (4 oz) freshly grated Parmesan cheese
2 eggs, beaten	salt and pepper
225 g (8 oz) plain flour	125 g (4 oz) butter

1 Place the spinach in a saucepan with just the water clinging to the leaves and cook gently for 5-10 minutes, or until thawed if using frozen spinach. Drain very well and chop the spinach finely.
2 Mix together the Ricotta or curd cheese, eggs, flour, spinach, nutmeg, half the Parmesan, and salt and pepper to taste.
3 With floured hands, form the mixture into cork-sized croquettes, or balls the size of large marbles. Chill in the refrigerator for at least 1 hour.
4 Bring a large pan of salted water to the boil and reduce to barely simmering. Drop in 10-12 gnocchi at a time and cook for 8-10 minutes or until they float to the surface.
5 With a slotted spoon, remove the gnocchi from the pan, then place them in a buttered serving dish. Cover and keep warm while cooking the remaining gnocchi.
6 Melt the butter and pour it over the gnocchi. Sprinkle with the remaining cheese. Serve immediately.

POTATO GNOCCHI

SERVES 4

900 g (2 lb) old potatoes	1 quantity Pesto (see page 172) or Tomato Sauce (see page 171), to serve
salt	
50 g (2 oz) butter	freshly grated Parmesan cheese, to finish
1 egg, beaten	
225-275 g (8-10 oz) plain flour	

1 Cook the potatoes in their skins in boiling salted water for about 20 minutes until tender. Drain well.
2 Sieve the potatoes while still warm into a large bowl. Add 5 ml (1 tsp) salt, the butter, egg and half the flour. Mix well to bind the potatoes together.
3 Turn out on to a floured surface, gradually adding more flour and kneading until the dough is soft, smooth and slightly sticky.
4 With floured hands, roll the dough into 2.5 cm (1 inch) thick ropes. Cut the ropes into 2 cm (¾ inch) pieces.
5 Press a finger into each piece to flatten; draw your finger towards you to curl sides.
6 Alternatively, you can make a decorative shape by using the same rolling technique, but roll the dumpling over the end of the prongs of a fork. Spread out on a floured tea towel.
7 Bring a large pan of salted water to the boil and reduce to barely simmering. Drop in about 10-12 gnocchi at a time and cook gently for 2-3 minutes or until they float to the surface.
8 With a slotted spoon, remove the gnocchi from the pan, then place them in a buttered serving dish. Cover and keep warm while cooking the remaining gnocchi.
9 Toss the gnocchi in the chosen sauce. Serve immediately, sprinkled with Parmesan.

CHOUX BUNS WITH STILTON SAUCE

SERVES 4-6

FOR THE CHOUX PASTRY	FOR THE FILLING
65 g (2½ oz) flour	75 g (3 oz) full-fat soft cheese
pinch of salt	50 g (2 oz) Blue Stilton cheese, crumbled
50 g (2 oz) butter	30 ml (2 tbsp) milk
2 eggs, beaten	25 g (1 oz) walnuts, finely chopped

1 To make the choux pastry, sift together the flour and salt. Put 150 ml (¼ pint) water and the butter into a saucepan. Heat slowly until the butter melts, then bring to a brisk boil. Add the flour all at once, stirring quickly until the mixture forms a soft ball and leaves the sides of the pan clean. Cool slightly.
2 Gradually add the eggs, beating them in until the mixture is smooth, shiny and firm enough to stand in soft peaks.
3 Spoon the choux pastry into 20 equal mounds on a dampened and lightly floured baking sheet. Bake in the oven at 200°C (400°F) mark 6 for 20 minutes; cool.
4 To make the filling, beat together the full-fat soft cheese, Stilton and milk; stir in the nuts.
5 Split the choux puffs and fill with the cheese mixture. Replace the tops and serve immediately.

SPINACH AND MUSHROOM PANCAKES

SERVES 4

450 g (1 lb) fresh spinach, trimmed, or 300 g (10.6 oz) packet frozen spinach	45 ml (3 tbsp) single cream
125 g (4 oz) butter or margarine	3 anchovy fillets, finely chopped (optional)
1 onion, finely chopped	freshly grated nutmeg
225 g (8 oz) mushrooms, thinly sliced	salt and pepper
25 g (1 oz) plain flour	8 pancakes
200 ml (⅓ pint) milk	60 ml (4 tbsp) fresh white breadcrumbs
	30 ml (2 tbsp) chopped parsley

1 Place the spinach in a saucepan with only the water that clings to the leaves. Cook gently, covered, for 5 minutes until wilted, 7-10 minutes if using frozen spinach until thawed. Drain well and chop very finely.
2 Melt 50 g (2 oz) of the butter in a saucepan, add the onion and cook gently for 10 minutes until soft but not coloured. Stir in the mushrooms and cook for a further 2 minutes.
3 Sprinkle the flour over the onion and mushroom mixture and stir well. Cook gently, stirring, for 1-2 minutes. Gradually blend in the milk. Bring to the boil, stirring constantly, then simmer for 3 minutes until very thick. Stir in the spinach, cream, anchovies if using, nutmeg and salt and pepper to taste.
4 Divide the mixture between the pancakes and roll or fold them up. Arrange the pancakes in a buttered shallow ovenproof dish. Melt the remaining butter and pour it over the pancakes.
5 Mix the breadcrumbs and parsley together and sprinkle over the pancakes. Bake in the oven at 190°C (375°F) mark 5 for 10-15 minutes to heat the pancakes through. Serve immediately.

LUNCHES, SUPPERS & SNACKS

Feast your eyes on these tempting recipes for omelettes, crêpes, quick pasta dishes, pizzas and quiches, jacket potatoes and veggie burgers – to name but a few – and you should never run short of inspiration for satisfying light meals.

PIPERADE

SERVES 4

3 large ripe tomatoes	salt and pepper
30 ml (2 tbsp) olive or vegetable oil	50 g (2 oz) butter or margarine, softened
1 red pepper, seeded and chopped	4 slices of crusty bread
1 small onion, chopped	3 eggs, beaten
2 garlic cloves, crushed	chopped parsley, to garnish

1 To skin the tomatoes, plunge into boiling water for 10 seconds, then slip off the skins. Remove the pips and chop the tomato flesh roughly.
2 Heat 15 ml (1 tbsp) of the olive oil in a frying pan, add the tomatoes, red pepper, onion, half of the garlic and salt and pepper to taste and fry gently for about 15 minutes, until the vegetables are soft and pulpy.
3 Meanwhile, cream together the butter and the remaining garlic, spread on both sides of the bread and grill or fry until golden brown. Keep warm.
4 Add the remaining oil and the eggs to the vegetables in the pan and stir gently until the eggs begin to scramble. Serve at once with the hot toast, garnished with plenty of chopped parsley.

SPANISH OMELETTE

SERVES 4

45 ml (3 tbsp) olive oil	2 large onions, coarsely chopped
2 large potatoes, peeled and cut into 1 cm (½ inch) cubes	salt and pepper
	6 eggs, lightly beaten

1 In a medium frying pan, gently heat the olive oil. Add the potatoes and onions and season with salt and pepper. Fry, stirring occasionally, for 10-15 minutes until golden brown.
2 Drain off excess oil and quickly stir in the eggs. Cook for 5 minutes, shaking the pan occasionally to prevent sticking. If you wish, place under a hot grill to brown the top. Serve hot, cut into wedges.

VARIATION

This is a basic Spanish Omelette, but other vegetables may be added, such as chopped red pepper, tomatoes, peas, mushrooms, and spinach. Either add them raw at the beginning, or stir cooked vegetables into the eggs (peas and spinach should be added already cooked).

PEPPER AND TOMATO OMELETTE

SERVES 2

30 ml (2 tbsp) olive oil	4 tomatoes, skinned and sliced
1 onion, sliced	5 eggs
2 garlic cloves, crushed	pinch of dried mixed herbs, or to taste
1 green pepper, seeded and sliced	salt and pepper
1 red pepper, seeded and sliced	50 g (2 oz) hard mature cheese, eg Parmesan or Farmhouse Cheddar, grated

1 Heat the olive oil in a non-stick frying pan. Add the onion and garlic and fry gently for 5 minutes until soft.
2 Add the pepper slices and the tomatoes and fry for a further 2-3 minutes, stirring frequently.
3 In a jug, beat the eggs lightly with the herbs and seasoning to taste. Pour into the pan, allowing the egg to run to the sides.
4 Draw in the vegetable mixture with a palette knife so that the mixture runs on to the base of the pan. Cook over moderate heat for 5 minutes until the underside of the omelette is set.
5 Sprinkle the top of the omelette with the grated cheese, then put under a preheated hot grill for 2-3 minutes until set and browned. Slide onto a serving plate and cut into wedges to serve.

COOK'S TIP

This type of omelette is different from the classic French kind, which is cooked for a very short time and served folded over. It is more like the Spanish tortilla, a flat omelette which is cooked for a longer time, then browned under a hot grill so that both sides become firm.

PERSIAN OMELETTE

SERVES 4

450 g (1 lb) fresh spinach, or 226 g (8 oz) packet frozen spinach	1 onion, chopped
225 g (8 oz) potatoes, peeled	4 eggs, beaten
45 ml (3 tbsp) oil	salt and pepper
	grated rind of ½ lemon
	juice of 1 lemon

1 If using fresh spinach, place in a saucepan with just the water clinging to the leaves after washing. Cover and cook gently for 5 minutes until tender. Drain well and chop finely.
2 If using frozen spinach, place in a saucepan and cook for 7-10 minutes to drive off as much liquid as possible.
3 Cut the potatoes into small dice. Heat 30 ml (2 tbsp) of the oil in a 20 cm (8 inch) non-stick frying pan, add the potatoes and fry gently for 5 minutes until just turning brown. Add the onion and cook for about 10 minutes until golden; the potato should be almost tender. Remove from the heat and set aside.
4 In a large bowl, mix the spinach with the eggs, seasoning, lemon rind and juice. Add the potato and onion and mix well.
5 Heat the remaining oil in the same frying pan, pour in the egg mixture, spreading it evenly over the bottom of the pan. Cover with a lid or foil and cook gently for 15 minutes until just set.
6 Remove the lid or foil and brown under a hot grill before serving.

COOK'S TIP

All this substantial omelette needs as an accompaniment is crusty wholemeal bread and a green salad.

OEUFS GRUYERE

SERVES 4

40 g (1½ oz) butter or margarine	175 g (6 oz) Gruyère cheese, grated
125 g (4 oz) button mushrooms, thinly sliced	1.25 ml (¼ tsp) ground mace
40 g (1½ oz) plain flour	salt and pepper
150 ml (¼ pint) milk	4 eggs, size 1 or 2
150 ml (¼ pint) dry white wine	30 ml (2 tbsp) grated Parmesan cheese
150 ml (¼ pint) double cream	2.5 ml (½ tsp) paprika
	about 60 ml (4 tbsp) dried breadcrumbs

1   Melt the butter in a saucepan, add the mushrooms and fry gently for 5 minutes. Remove with a slotted spoon and set aside.
2   Add the flour to the fat remaining in the pan and cook gently, stirring, for 1-2 minutes. Remove from the heat and gradually blend in the milk and wine. Bring to the boil, stirring constantly, then simmer for 3 minutes until thick and smooth.
3   Lower the heat, stir in the cream and 125 g (4 oz) of the Gruyère, and cook gently until the cheese melts. Add the mace, salt and pepper, and remove from the heat. Stir in the mushrooms.
4   Pour half the sauce into individual gratin dishes. Break an egg into the centre of each dish. Cover with the remaining sauce.
5   Mix the remaining Gruyère with the Parmesan and paprika and sprinkle over the sauce. Cover with the breadcrumbs. Bake in the oven at 190°C (375°F) mark 5 for 10-15 minutes. Serve immediately.

SERVING SUGGESTION

Oeufs Gruyère are deliciously creamy. Serve for a quick lunch or supper, with a tossed mixed salad.

BRUSSELS SPROUT SOUFFLE

SERVES 4

700 g (1½ lb) Brussels sprouts, trimmed weight	40 g (1½ oz) plain wholemeal flour
salt and pepper	300 ml (½ pint) milk
50 g (2 oz) butter or margarine	pinch of freshly grated nutmeg
	3 eggs, separated

1   Grease a 1.3 litre (2¼ pint) soufflé dish. Preheat the oven to 200°C (400°F) mark 6.
2   Cook the Brussels sprouts in boiling salted water for 10-15 minutes until tender. Drain well.
3   Melt the butter in a saucepan, add the flour and cook gently, stirring, for 1-2 minutes. Remove from the heat and gradually blend in the milk. Bring to the boil, stirring constantly, then simmer for 3 minutes until thick and smooth. Add the nutmeg and remove from the heat.
4   Chop half of the sprouts. Work the remaining sprouts in a blender or food processor to a purée with the egg yolks and a little of the sauce. Fold into the rest of the sauce with the chopped sprouts. Season with salt and pepper to taste.
5   Whisk the egg whites until stiff. Gently fold into the sprout mixture. Turn into the soufflé dish. Bake in the oven for 30-35 minutes until risen. Serve immediately.

COOK'S TIP

A hot soufflé is the true soufflé. The tiny bubbles of air trapped within the egg whites expand as they are heated, puffing up the base mixture to which they were added, by as much as two thirds of its original size. When making hot soufflés, it is important to follow the recipe precisely; do not try to cut corners.

CURRIED EGGS

SERVES 4

30 ml (2 tbsp) oil	15 ml (1 tbsp) tomato purée
1 onion, chopped	2.5 ml (½ tsp) chilli powder
1 medium cooking apple, peeled, cored and chopped	salt and pepper
10 ml (2 tsp) garam masala	300 ml (½ pint) natural yogurt
300 ml (½ pint) vegetable stock or water	4 eggs, hard-boiled
225 g (8 oz) can tomatoes	coriander sprigs, to garnish

1 Heat the oil in a deep heavy-based pan. Add the onion, apple and garam masala and fry gently until soft, stirring frequently.

2 Pour in the stock and tomatoes and bring to the boil, stirring to break up the tomatoes as much as possible. Stir in the tomato purée with the chilli powder and seasoning to taste. Lower the heat and simmer, uncovered, for 20 minutes to allow the flavours to develop.

3 Cool the sauce slightly, then pour into a blender or food processor. Add half of the yogurt and work to a purée. Return to the rinsed-out pan.

4 Shell the eggs and cut them in half lengthways. Add them to the sauce, cut side up, then simmer very gently for 10 minutes. Taste the sauce and adjust the seasoning if necessary. Serve hot, with the remaining yogurt drizzled over the top and garnish with coriander.

SERVING SUGGESTION

Serve in a ring of boiled rice, accompanied by mango chutney and a cucumber salad dressed with natural yogurt and flavoured with fresh mint.

COCOTTE EGGS

SERVES 4

25 g (1 oz) butter	10 ml (2 tsp) chopped tarragon
1 small onion, finely chopped	salt and pepper
4 rashers lean back bacon, rinded and finely chopped	4 eggs, size 2
125 g (4 oz) button mushrooms, finely chopped	120 ml (8 tbsp) double cream
10 ml (2 tsp) tomato purée	chopped tarragon, to garnish

1 Melt the butter in a small saucepan, add the onion and fry gently until soft. Add the bacon and fry until beginning to change colour, then add the mushrooms and tomato purée. Continue frying for 2-3 minutes until the juices run, stirring constantly.

2 Remove from the heat and stir in the tarragon and seasoning to taste. Divide the mixture equally between 4 cocottes, ramekins or individual soufflé dishes. Make a slight indentation in the centre of each one.

3 Break an egg into each dish, on top of the mushroom and bacon mixture, then slowly pour 30 ml (2 tbsp) cream over each one. Sprinkle with salt and pepper to taste.

4 Place the cocottes on a baking tray and bake in the oven at 180°C (350°F) mark 4 for 10-12 minutes until the eggs are set. Serve immediately, garnished with tarragon.

VARIATION

Replace the mushrooms with 4 medium tomatoes, skinned and chopped, and substitute the tarragon with basil.

BAKED EGG
WITH MUSHROOMS

SERVES 1

40 g (1½ oz) butter	5 ml (1 tsp) chopped fresh tarragon or 2.5 ml (½ tsp) dried
75 g (3 oz) button mushrooms, finely chopped	salt and pepper
½ small onion, finely chopped	1 egg
	tarragon sprigs, to garnish

1 Melt half of the butter in a small frying pan, add the mushrooms and onion and fry until golden and all the excess moisture has evaporated. Add the herbs and salt and pepper to taste.
2 Spoon the mushroom mixture into a ramekin or cocotte dish and make a well in the centre.
3 Carefully break an egg into the hollow, then dot with the remaining butter.
4 Stand the ramekin in a roasting tin. Pour hot water into the tin to come halfway up the side of the ramekin.
5 Cover the roasting tin with foil and bake in the oven at 180°C (350°F) mark 4 for 12-15 minutes, or until the egg is just set. Serve at once, garnished with tarragon sprigs, and accompanied by toast.

COOK'S TIP

To serve two: double the quantity of ingredients, but use 50 g (2 oz) butter. Follow the recipe above, dividing the mixture between 2 ramekins.

LETTUCE AND
MUSHROOM COCOTTE

SERVES 1

15 g (½ oz) butter or margarine	salt and pepper
50 g (2 oz) mushrooms, sliced	1 egg
¼ small lettuce, finely shredded	15 ml (1 tbsp) single cream (optional)
2.5 ml (½ tsp) freshly grated nutmeg	15 ml (1 tbsp) fresh breadcrumbs

1 Melt the butter in a saucepan, add the mushrooms and cook gently for 2-3 minutes or until the mushrooms are soft. Stir in the lettuce and cook for 1 minute until the lettuce is wilted. Add the nutmeg and plenty of salt and freshly ground pepper.
2 Spoon the lettuce and mushroom mixture into a small, shallow flameproof dish and make a well in the centre.
3 Crack the egg into the hollow and spoon over the cream, if liked. Sprinkle over the breadcrumbs.
4 Cook under a preheated moderate grill for about 5 minutes or until the egg is just set. Serve immediately, with toast or French bread.

SERVING SUGGESTION

Serve with a mixed salad for a light lunch or supper.

WELSH RAREBIT

SERVES 1

50 g (2 oz) Cheddar cheese, grated	1.25 ml (¼ tsp) mustard powder
25 g (1 oz) butter or margarine	salt and pepper
15 ml (1 tbsp) brown ale	1 slice bread, crusts removed

1 Place all the ingredients except the bread in a heavy-based saucepan. Heat very gently, stirring continuously, until a creamy mixture is obtained.
2 Lightly toast the bread on one side only. Pour the sauce over the uncooked side and cook under a preheated hot grill until it is golden and bubbling. Serve immediately with a crisp salad.

COOK'S TIP

To serve two: use the same amount of butter, but double the other ingredients. Follow the recipe above.

VARIATION

To make Buck Rarebit top with a poached egg.

COX'S CHEESE AND NUT TOASTIES

SERVES 4

3 Cox's apples	few drops of Worcestershire sauce
juice of ½ lemon	4 slices of bread
225 g (8 oz) Cheddar cheese, grated	50 g (2 oz) butter
	25 g (1 oz) walnuts, chopped

1 Core the apples and cut one apple into eight thin rings, then dip in lemon juice. Peel and grate the other two apples into a bowl.
2 Mix the grated apple with the cheese and Worcestershire sauce.
3 Toast the bread, then butter one side. Spread the cheese mixture on the toast and sprinkle with chopped nuts. Grill for 3-4 minutes until golden brown. Top each piece of toast with two apple rings.

SPINACH ROULADE

SERVES 3-4

900 g (2 lb) fresh spinach, or 450 g (1 lb) frozen spinach, thawed	1 onion, finely chopped
	125 g (4 oz) curd cheese
4 eggs, size 2, separated	50 g (2 oz) Gruyère cheese, grated
pinch of freshly grated nutmeg	30 ml (2 tbsp) soured cream
salt and pepper	Tomato Sauce, to serve (see page 171)
25 g (1 oz) butter or margarine	

1 Grease a 35 x 25 cm (14 x 10 inch) Swiss roll tin and line with non-stick baking parchment. Set aside. Place the fresh spinach in a saucepan with just the water clinging to the leaves. Cook gently, covered, for about 5 minutes until wilted.

2 Drain the fresh or frozen spinach well and chop finely. Turn into a bowl and allow to cool slightly for about 5 minutes. Beat in the egg yolks, nutmeg and salt and pepper to taste.

3 Whisk the egg whites until stiff, then fold into the spinach mixture with a large metal spoon until evenly incorporated. Spread the mixture in the prepared tin. Bake in the oven at 200°C (400°F) mark 6 for 15-20 minutes until firm.

4 Meanwhile, melt the butter in a saucepan. Add the onion and fry for about 5 minutes until soft. Remove from the heat and stir in the cheeses, soured cream, and salt and pepper to taste.

5 Turn the roulade out on to greaseproof paper and spread immediately and quickly with the cheese mixture. Roll the roulade up by gently lifting the greaseproof paper. Serve hot, cut into thick slices, accompanied by the tomato sauce.

BROCCOLI GOUGERES

SERVES 4

700 g (1½ lb) broccoli	FOR THE CHOUX PASTRY
25 g (1 oz) butter or margarine	65 g (2½ oz) flour
25 g (1 oz) plain flour	pinch of salt
300 ml (½ pint) milk	50 g (2 oz) butter
30 ml (2 tbsp) chopped parsley	2 eggs, beaten
salt and pepper	

1 Cut the broccoli into small florets. Cook in boiling salted water for about 10 minutes until nearly tender. Drain well.

2 Melt the butter in a saucepan, add the flour and cook gently, stirring, for 1-2 minutes. Remove from the heat and gradually blend in the milk. Bring to the boil, stirring constantly, then simmer for 3 minutes. Stir in the parsley, with salt and pepper to taste and remove from the heat. Fold in the broccoli florets.

3 Divide the mixture equally between 4 scallop shells or shallow ovenproof dishes, mounding it up slightly in the centre.

4 To make the choux pastry, sift together the flour and salt. Put 150 ml (¼ pint) water and the butter into a saucepan. Heat slowly until the butter melts, then bring to a brisk boil. Add the flour all at once, stirring quickly until the mixture forms a soft ball and leaves the sides of the pan clean. Cool slightly.

5 Gradually add the eggs, beating them in until the mixture is smooth, shiny and firm enough to stand in soft peaks.

6 Pipe or spoon the choux mixture around the edge of the shells or dishes. Bake in the oven at 200°C (400°F) mark 6 for 35-40 minutes or until well risen and brown. Serve immediately.

GARLIC
AND PEPPER CHEESE

MAKES 450 G (1 LB))

600 ml (1 pint) milk	15 ml (1 tbsp) chopped mixed herbs (parsley, chervil, chives, thyme)
600 ml (1 pint) single cream	
30 ml (2 tbsp) buttermilk	30 ml (2 tbsp) black peppercorns, coarsely crushed
1 garlic clove, skinned	
5 ml (1 tsp) salt	cucumber slices, to garnish

1 Put the milk and cream in a saucepan and heat gently to lukewarm or 32-38°C (90-100°F); stir in the buttermilk. Pour the mixture into a bowl.
2 Cover the bowl tightly and leave in a warm place for 24-48 hours until the cream mixture turns to soft curds.
3 Line a colander with muslin and place in the sink. Pour the curds into the colander and drain for 10 minutes.
4 Place the colander on a rack in a saucepan, cover with cling film and chill for 18-24 hours.
5 On a board, crush the garlic to a smooth purée with the flat of a round-bladed knife and the salt. Spoon the curds from the colander into a bowl and stir in the mixed herbs, garlic and peppercorns.
6 Line a small plastic punnet or earthenware cheese mould with a double layer of damp cheesecloth, leaving a 5 cm (2 inch) overhang. Spoon in the curds and fold the cheesecloth over the top.
7 Invert the punnet or mould on to a wire rack placed over a shallow dish, cover tightly with cling film and chill for 18-24 hours.
8 To serve, unmould the cheese on to a plate, remove the cheesecloth and garnish with cucumber slices. Serve chilled with crusty bread rolls or crispbread.

TOMATO
AND HERB QUICHE

SERVES 4-6

225 g (8 oz) packet frozen shortcrust pastry, thawed	150 ml (¼ pint) single cream
350 g (12 oz) ripe tomatoes	15 ml (1 tbsp) chopped herbs, eg sage and thyme, or 10 ml (2 tsp) dried mixed herbs
3 eggs	
175 g (6 oz) Caerphilly cheese, grated	salt and pepper

1 Roll out the pastry on a floured surface and use to line a 23 cm (9 inch) flan tin placed on a baking sheet. Prick the base with a fork, line with foil and baking beans and bake blind in the oven at 200°C (400°F) mark 6 for 15 minutes.
2 Meanwhile, skin the tomatoes. Put them in a heatproof bowl, pour over boiling water and leave to stand for 2-3 minutes. Drain, plunge into ice-cold water, then remove them one at a time and peel off the skin with your fingers.
3 Remove the foil and beans from the pastry case and return to the oven for 5 minutes.
4 Meanwhile, lightly beat the eggs in a bowl. Add the cheese, cream, herbs and seasoning to taste and beat lightly again to mix.
5 Remove the pastry case from the oven. Slice the tomatoes and arrange half of them in the bottom of the pastry case. Slowly pour the egg and cheese mixture over the tomatoes, then arrange the remaining tomato on top.
6 Bake in the oven for 20-25 minutes until the filling is just set. Leave to stand for 15 minutes before serving.

MUSHROOM FLAN

SERVES 4

125 g (4 oz) wholemeal breadcrumbs	175 g (6 oz) mushrooms, sliced
300 ml (½ pint) natural yogurt	4 spring onions, chopped
salt and pepper	75 g (3 oz) Cheddar cheese, grated
4 eggs	watercress sprigs, to garnish
150 ml (¼ pint) milk	

1 Mix the breadcrumbs and 150 ml (¼ pint) of the yogurt to a paste. Add salt and pepper to taste.
2 Use the mixture to line a 23 cm (9 inch) flan dish or tin, pressing the paste into shape with the fingers. Set aside.
3 Whisk the eggs and milk together with the remaining yogurt and salt and pepper to taste.
4 Arrange the mushrooms, spring onions and half the cheese on the base of the flan. Pour the egg mixture over the top and then sprinkle with the remaining cheese.
5 Bake the flan in the oven at 180°C (350°F) mark 4 for about 30 minutes or until brown and set. Serve warm, garnished with watercress.

COOK'S TIP

The unusual base for this flan is made simply from wholemeal breadcrumbs and yogurt – less fattening than a conventional shortcrust pastry base – and with healthier ingredients. If you prefer a pastry base, either use a 225 g (8 oz) packet frozen shortcrust pastry, thawed; or shortcrust pastry made with 175 g (6 oz) flour - follow the recipe given in Tarte á l'Oignon (see page 80).

COURGETTE QUICHE

SERVES 4

FOR THE PASTRY	FOR THE FILLING
175 g (6 oz) plain flour	350 g (12 oz) courgettes
salt and pepper	3 eggs
125 g (4 oz) butter or margarine	150 ml (¼ pint) double cream
125 g (4 oz) Cheddar cheese, grated	10 ml (2 tsp) chopped basil
1 egg yolk, beaten	finely grated rind of 1 lime (optional)
	a little egg white

1 To make the pastry, sift the flour into a bowl with a pinch of salt. Rub in the butter until the mixture resembles fine breadcrumbs.
2 Stir in the cheese, then the egg yolk. Gather the mixture together with your fingers to make a smooth ball of dough. Wrap the dough and chill for 30 minutes.
3 Meanwhile, prepare the filling. Trim the courgettes, then cut into 2 cm (¾ inch) chunks. Plunge into boiling salted water, bring back to the boil, then simmer for 3 minutes. Drain and set aside.
4 Beat the eggs lightly with the cream. Stir in the basil, lime rind if using and season to taste. Set aside.
5 Roll out the chilled dough and use to line a 23 cm (9 inch) loose-bottomed flan tin. Chill for 15 minutes.
6 Prick the base of the dough with a fork, then line with foil and baking beans. Stand the tin on a preheated baking sheet and bake blind in the oven at 200°C (400°F) mark 6 for 10 minutes.
7 Remove the foil and beans and brush the pastry case with egg white. Return to the oven for 5 minutes.
8 Stand the courgette chunks upright in the pastry case and slowly pour in the egg and cream mixture. Return to the oven for 20 minutes.

WATERCRESS AND RICOTTA QUICHE

SERVES 6-8

Shortcrust Pastry made with 225 g (8 oz) flour (see page 79)	125 g (4 oz) Ricotta or curd cheese
50 g (2 oz) butter or margarine	300 ml (½ pint) single or double cream
1 bunch of spring onions, finely chopped	3 eggs, beaten
2 bunches of watercress	2.5 ml (½ tsp) freshly grated nutmeg
	salt and pepper

1   Roll out the pastry on a floured surface and use to line a 25 cm (10 inch) flan tin placed on a baking sheet. Prick the base with a fork, line with foil and baking beans and bake blind in the oven at 200°C (400°F) mark 6 for 15 minutes. Remove the foil and beans from the pastry case and return to the oven for 5 minutes.

2   To prepare the filling, melt the butter in a saucepan, add the spring onions and fry gently about 5 minutes until softened. Add the watercress and fry for a few minutes more, stirring frequently.

3   Transfer the contents of the pan to a blender or food processor. Add the cheese, cream, eggs and nutmeg with salt and pepper to taste and work until smooth and evenly blended.

4   Pour the filling into the baked flan case and bake in the oven at 190°C (375°F) mark 5 for 25-30 minutes until set. Serve warm or leave until cold.

VEGETABLE TARTS

MAKES 4

150 g (5 oz) plain flour	2 courgettes, sliced
salt and pepper	a little beaten egg white
175 g (6 oz) butter or margarine	150 g (5 oz) full-fat soft cheese with herbs and garlic
1 egg yolk	2 eggs, beaten
1 small onion, finely chopped	20 ml (4 tsp) chopped basil or 10 ml (2 tsp) dried

1   To make the pastry cases, sift the flour into a bowl with a pinch of salt. Add 125 g (4 oz) of the butter in pieces and work into the flour with your fingertips.

2   Add the egg yolk and 5-10 ml (1-2 tsp) cold water and work with a palette knife until the dough draws together.

3   Gather the dough into a ball, then wrap and chill in the refrigerator while making the filling.

4   Melt the remaining butter in a heavy-based frying pan, add the onion and fry gently for about 5 minutes until soft and lightly coloured. Add the courgettes and fry over a moderate heat for a few minutes, turning them frequently until they are light golden on all sides. Turn into a bowl and leave until cold.

5   Meanwhile, roll out the dough on a lightly floured surface and cut out 4 circles large enough to line 4 individual loose-bottomed 10 cm (4 inch) tartlet tins.

6   Place the pastry in the tins, prick the bases with a fork, then line with foil and beans. Bake 'blind' in the oven at 190°C (375°F) mark 5 for 10 minutes.

7   Remove the foil and beans, brush the pastry with the egg white and return to the oven for a further 5 minutes.

8   Put the cream cheese mixture in a bowl and beat with a wooden spoon until soft. Add the eggs and beat well, then add the courgettes, basil and salt and pepper to taste.

9   Divide the filling equally between the pastry cases. Return to the oven for a further 10-15 minutes, until the filling is set. Leave to stand for 15 minutes before serving.

ONION SOUFFLE QUICHE

SERVES 3-4

Sortcrust or Wholemeal Pastry made with 175 g (6 oz) flour (see page 80)	1 clove
2 medium onions, thinly sliced	25 g (1 oz) butter or margarine
300 ml (½ pint) milk	25 g (1 oz) plain wholemeal flour
1 bay leaf	2 eggs, separated
	salt and pepper

1 Roll out the pastry and use to line a 20 cm (8 inch) quiche tin or flan dish. Prick the base with a fork, then line with foil and baking beans. Bake in the oven at 200°C (400°F) mark 6 for 15 minutes. Remove the foil and beans and bake for a further 5 minutes.

2 Put the onions in a pan with the milk, bay leaf and clove. Cover and simmer for 25 minutes until the onion is tender. Discard the bay leaf and clove.

3 Melt the butter in a saucepan, add the flour and cook gently, stirring, for 1-2 minutes. Remove from the heat and gradually blend in the onion and milk mixture. Bring to the boil, stirring constantly, then simmer for 3 minutes until thick and smooth. Remove from the heat and beat in the egg yolks with salt and pepper to taste.

4 Whisk the egg whites until stiff but not dry. Gently fold into the onion mixture and spoon into the pastry case. Bake in the oven at 220°C (425°F) mark 7 for 30-35 minutes or until just set. Serve immediately.

PIZZA

SERVES 2-4

FOR THE PIZZA DOUGH	salt and pepper
450 g (1 lb) strong white or wholemeal flour	olive oil
5 ml (1 tsp) fast-action dried yeast	three 400 g (14 oz) cans chopped tomatoes

1 To make the pizza dough, put the flour, yeast and 5 ml (1 tsp) salt in a bowl and mix together. Make a well in the centre and add 300 ml (½ pint) tepid water with 30 ml (2 tbsp) olive oil. Beat thoroughly with your hand until the dough leaves the sides of the bowl clean. You may need to add more tepid water, particularly if using wholemeal flour.

2 Turn the dough on to a lightly floured surface and knead for about 10 minutes or until smooth and elastic. Roll out to make two 30 cm (12 inch) rounds or four thin 20 cm (8 inch) rounds; place on baking sheet(s). Spread with the tomatoes and add the topping(s) of your choice (see below). Season with salt and pepper and drizzle over a little olive oil. Leave in a warm place for 20-30 minutes or until the dough looks puffy around the edges.

3 Bake in the oven at 220°C (425°F) mark 7 for 20-30 minutes (depending on size) or until golden brown and bubbling. Serve hot.

TOPPINGS

Cheese
Most firm cheeses with good melting properties are suitable for topping pizzas. Mozzarella is traditional, but try Bel Paese, Fontina, Taleggio, Gruyère or Parmesan.

Vegetable
Almost any vegetable is good on a pizza. Try sliced fresh tomatoes; steamed fresh spinach (or well drained frozen leaf spinach); sliced canned artichokes; mushrooms, aubergine, courgettes or baby onions, cut into chunks or slices and sautéed in olive oil.

PIZZA WITH FOUR CHEESES

MAKES 4

1 quantity Pizza Dough (see page 63)	125 g (4 oz) Fontina or Gruyère cheese, diced
226 g (8 oz) can chopped tomatoes	125 g (4 oz) Taleggio cheese, diced
salt and pepper	20 ml (4 tsp) olive oil
125 g (4 oz) Mozzarella cheese, diced	20 ml (4 tsp) chopped mixed herbs or 10 ml (2 tsp) dried
125 g (4 oz) Bel Paese or Provolone cheese, diced	

1 Turn the pizza dough out on to a floured surface, roll out and cut into four 20 cm (8 inch) circles, making the edges slightly thicker than the centres.
2 Put the dough into oiled sandwich tins or flan rings placed on oiled baking sheets. Spread the tomatoes evenly over the dough, right to the edges. Season with salt and pepper to taste.
3 Mix the four cheeses together and sprinkle them evenly over the four pizzas. Sprinkle over the oil and herbs, with salt and pepper to taste.
4 Leave the pizzas to prove in a warm place for about 30 minutes, then bake in the oven at 220°C (425°F) mark 7 for 25 minutes or until the cheeses are melted and the dough is well risen. Swap over on the oven shelves halfway through the cooking time. Serve hot or cold.

PIZZA-IN-THE-PAN

SERVES 2

225 g (8 oz) self-raising flour	175 g (6 oz) Cheddar cheese, grated
salt and pepper	15 ml (1 tbsp) chopped herbs, eg parsley or basil
60 ml (4 tbsp) oil	few black olives
45 ml (3 tbsp) tomato purée	
400 g (14 oz) can chopped tomatoes, drained	

1 Sift the flour and seasoning into a bowl. Make a well in the centre and pour in 30 ml (2 tbsp) of the oil and 60 ml (4 tbsp) water. Mix to a soft dough – it will bind together very quickly, although you may need to add a little more water.
2 Knead the dough lightly on a floured surface, then roll out to a circle that will fit a medium frying pan.
3 Heat half the remaining oil in the pan. Add the circle of dough and fry gently for about 5 minutes until the base is cooked and lightly browned.
4 Turn the dough out onto a plate and flip it over.
5 Heat the remaining oil in the pan, then slide the dough back into the pan, browned side uppermost. Spread with the tomato purée, then top with the tomatoes and sprinkle with the grated cheese, herbs and black olives.
6 Cook for a further 5 minutes until the underside is done, then slide the pan under a preheated grill. Cook for 3-4 minutes until the cheese melts. Serve immediately.

FRIED POLENTA STICKS

SERVES 4

10 ml (2 tsp) salt	250-350 g (8-12 oz) Fontina cheese, to serve
225 g (8 oz) coarse-grain cornmeal or polenta flour	Tomato Sauce, to serve (see page 171)
oil, for frying	

1 To make the polenta sticks, put 1 litre (1¾ pints) water and the salt in a large pan and bring to simmering point.
2 Add the cornmeal in a very fine stream, stirring vigorously all the time with a long-handled wooden spoon. (Do not add the cornmeal all at once or it will become hard.)
3 When the mixture is smooth and thick, simmer for 20-30 minutes stirring until the polenta comes away from sides of pan.
4 Turn onto a wooden board and shape it into a cake about 5 cm (2 inches) high with a dampened wooden spoon. Leave for about 1 hour to cool.
5 When cold, divide the polenta into four sections, then cut each of the sections into 2.5 cm (1 inch) sticks.
6 Heat enough oil in a frying pan to come 2.5 cm (1 inch) up the sides of the pan. Fry the polenta sticks in batches for about 3 minutes on each side until crisp. Drain on absorbent kitchen paper. Serve hot, with the slices of cheese and the tomato sauce handed separately.

MACARONI CHEESE

SERVES 4

175 g (6 oz) short-cut macaroni	pinch of freshly grated nutmeg, or 2.5 ml (½ tsp) prepared mustard
40 g (1½ oz) butter or margarine	salt and pepper
60 ml (4 tbsp) plain flour	175 g (6 oz) mature Cheddar cheese, grated
600 ml (1 pint) milk	30 ml (2 tbsp) fresh breadcrumbs

1 Cook the macaroni in boiling salted water for 10 minutes, then drain well.
2 Meanwhile melt the butter in a saucepan, stir in the flour and cook gently for 1 minute. Remove from the heat and gradually stir in the milk. Bring to the boil and continue to cook, stirring, until the sauce thickens, then remove from the heat. Add the nutmeg or mustard and season to taste. Stir in 125 g (4 oz) cheese and the macaroni.
3 Pour into an ovenproof dish and sprinkle with the remaining cheese and the breadcrumbs. Place on a baking sheet and bake in the oven at 200°C (400°F) mark 6 for about 20 minutes or until golden and bubbling.

TAGLIATELLE WITH GORGONZOLA AND NUTS

SERVES 4

400 g (14 oz) wholewheat or green (spinach) tagliatelle	125 g (4 oz) walnuts, chopped
salt and pepper	5 ml (1 tsp) chopped sage
125 g (4 oz) Gorgonzola cheese	75 ml (5 tbsp) olive oil
	15 ml (1 tbsp) chopped parsley, to garnish

1 Cook the tagliatelle in a large saucepan of boiling salted water for 10 minutes or according to packet instructions, until al dente (tender but firm to the bite).
2 Meanwhile, crumble the cheese into a blender or food processor. Add two thirds of the walnuts and the sage. Blend to combine the ingredients.
3 Add the oil gradually through the funnel (as when making mayonnaise) and blend until the sauce is evenly incorporated.
4 Drain the tagliatelle well and return to the pan. Add the nut sauce and fold in gently to mix. Add seasoning to taste.
5 Transfer the pasta and sauce to a warmed serving bowl and sprinkle with the remaining walnuts. Serve immediately, garnished with chopped parsley.

SERVING SUGGESTION

Quick to make at the last-minute, this nutritious dish makes an unusual lunch or supper. Serve with a crisp green salad.

RICOTTA AND SPINACH RAVIOLI

SERVES-4

350 g (12 oz) fresh spinach, or 175 g (6 oz) frozen spinach	pinch of freshly grated nutmeg
175 g (6 oz) Ricotta or curd cheese	salt and pepper
125 g (4 oz) freshly grated Parmesan cheese	400 g (14 oz) large freshly made pasta sheets
1 egg, beaten	75 g (3 oz) butter, melted
	few sage leaves, chopped

1 To make the pasta stuffing, place the spinach in a saucepan with the water clinging to the leaves and cook gently for 5-10 minutes, or until thawed if using frozen spinach. Drain very well and chop the spinach finely.
2 Mix together the spinach, Ricotta or curd cheese, 65 g (2½ oz) Parmesan, the egg, nutmeg and seasoning.
3 Lay half of the pasta sheets out on a work surface and place teaspoonfuls of the filling evenly spaced at 4 cm (1½ inch) intervals across and down the sheet of dough.
4 With a pastry brush or your index finger, glaze the spaces between the filling with beaten egg or water.
5 Uncover the other sheet of the pasta, carefully lift this on the rolling pin (to avoid stretching) and unroll it over the first sheet, easing gently. Press down firmly around the pockets of filling and seal well.
6 With a ravioli cutter, serrated edged wheel or even a sharp knife, cut the ravioli into squares between the pouches. Leave to dry for about 1 hour before cooking.
7 Pour at least 2.3 litres (4 pints) water into a large saucepan and bring to the boil. Add 10 ml (2 tsp) salt. Cook the ravioli in batches at a gentle boil for about 5 minutes until just tender. Remove with a slotted spoon and place in a warmed buttered serving dish. Keep hot while cooking the remainder of the ravioli.
8 Toss the ravioli with the melted butter, remaining Parmesan and chopped sage. Serve immediately.

SPAGHETTI WITH RATATOUILLE SAUCE

SERVES 4

1 aubergine	3 medium courgettes, cut into thin strips
salt and pepper	350 g (12 oz) tomatoes, skinned and finely chopped
1 garlic clove, crushed	10 ml (2 tsp) chopped basil
1 onion, finely chopped	400 g (14 oz) wholewheat spaghetti
1 green pepper, seeded and cut into thin strips	freshly grated Parmesan cheese, to serve
1 red pepper, seeded and cut into thin strips	

1 Dice the aubergine, then spread out on a plate and sprinkle with salt. Leave for 30 minutes to dégorge.
2 Tip the diced aubergine into a sieve and rinse under cold running water. Put into a large, heavy-based saucepan with the garlic, vegetables and basil. Season to taste, cover and cook over a moderate heat for 30 minutes. Shake the pan and stir the vegetables frequently during this time, to encourage the juices to flow.
3 Meanwhile, cook the spaghetti in a large saucepan of boiling salted water for 12 minutes or according to packet instructions, until al dente (tender but firm to the bite).
4 Drain the spaghetti thoroughly and turn into a warmed serving dish. Taste and adjust the seasoning of the ratatouille sauce, then pour over the spaghetti. Serve immediately, with the Parmesan cheese.

SINGAPORE NOODLES

SERVES 4

225 g (8 oz) thin round egg noodles	2 carrots, thinly sliced
salt	handful of mustard greens, pak choi or 2 Chinese leaves, shredded
60 ml (4 tbsp) oil	125 g (4 oz) mangetouts
2 garlic cloves, crushed	4 spring onions, chopped
1 onion, chopped	5 ml (1 tsp) curry powder
2.5 cm (1 inch) piece fresh root ginger, peeled and chopped	30 ml (2 tbsp) light soy sauce
1 green chilli, seeded and chopped	30 ml (2 tbsp) hoisin sauce

1 Cook the noodles in boiling salted water following the instructions on the packet. Drain and toss in 15 ml (1 tbsp) of the oil.
2 Heat the remaining oil in a wok or very large frying pan. Add the garlic, onion, ginger and chilli and stir-fry for 2-3 minutes.
3 Add the vegetables and sprinkle with the curry powder. Stir-fry for 3-4 minutes or until the vegetables are softened but still crisp. Add the noodles with the soy and hoisin sauces and stir-fry for 1-2 minutes until hot.

VARIATION

Broccoli, green beans, baby sweetcorn, and water chestnuts are all suitable alternatives for any of the vegetables.

CELERIAC AU GRATIN

SERVES 4-6

15 ml (1 tbsp) lemon juice	150 ml (¼ pint) dry white wine
2 heads of celeriac, total weight about 900 g (2 lb)	175 g (6 oz) Gruyère cheese, grated
salt and pepper	75 g (3 oz) Parmesan cheese, freshly grated
125 g (4 oz) butter or margarine	

1   Fill a bowl with cold water and add the lemon juice. Peel the celeriac, then cut into chunky pieces. Place the pieces in the bowl of acidulated water as you prepare them, to prevent discolouration.
2   Drain the celeriac, then plunge quickly into a large pan of boiling salted water. Return to the boil and cook for 10 minutes. Drain thoroughly.
3   Melt the butter in a flameproof gratin dish. Add the celeriac and turn to coat in the butter. Stir in the wine. Mix together the Gruyère and Parmesan cheeses and sprinkle over the top of the celeriac, with salt and pepper to taste. Bake in the oven at 190°C (375°F) mark 5 for 30 minutes until the celeriac is tender when pierced with a skewer and the topping is golden brown.

SERVING SUGGESTION

Serve with a colourful tomato or red pepper salad, and hot garlic or herb bread.

COOK'S TIP

From the same family as celery, which it resembles in flavour, celeriac is an unusual, quite ugly-looking vegetable, sometimes called 'turnip-rooted celery', which is an apt description. Only buy small celeriac, very large specimens tend to be woody and lacking in flavour.

LENTIL AND CELERY STUFFED PEPPERS

SERVES 2

125 g (4 oz) red lentils	1 onion, finely chopped
salt and pepper	75 g (3 oz) celery, finely chopped
2 green peppers, about 175 g (6 oz) each	75 g (3 oz) full-fat soft cheese
25 g (1 oz) butter or margarine	1 egg

1   Cook the lentils in boiling salted water for 12-15 minutes until just tender.
2   Meanwhile, halve the peppers lengthwise and remove the cores and seeds. Place in a steamer and steam, covered, for about 15 minutes or until soft.
3   Melt the butter in a frying pan, add the onion and celery and fry gently for 2-3 minutes.
4   Drain the lentils and add to the onion and celery. Cook, stirring, for 1-2 minutes until heated through.
5   Remove the pan from the heat and beat in the cheese and egg with salt and pepper to taste.
6   Remove the peppers from the steamer and fill with the lentil mixture. Place under a hot grill for about 5 minutes or until golden brown. Serve hot.

COOK'S TIP

Serve these stuffed peppers for a tasty supper, accompanied by warm wholemeal bread and a tomato salad.

CATALAN RED PEPPERS

SERVES 2

2 red peppers	few mixed black and green stoned olives, chopped
olive oil	20 ml (4 tsp) capers
75 g (3 oz) mixed long-grain and wild rice	20 ml (4 tsp) white wine vinegar
salt and pepper	1 small garlic clove, crushed
4 tomatoes	lettuce, to serve
4 spring onions, chopped	

1 Rinse and dry the peppers, then place on a baking sheet and brush lightly with oil. Bake in the oven at 220°C (425°F) mark 7 for 15-20 minutes or until just tender. Cool, halve and remove the core and seeds. (The skin can also be removed, if wished, but the pepper will not hold its shape so well.) Pat dry with absorbent kitchen paper.
2 Meanwhile, cook the rice in boiling salted water according to the packet instructions until tender. Drain and rinse under cold running water, then drain well again. Quarter the tomatoes, discard the seeds and roughly chop the flesh. Mix into the rice with the spring onions, olives and capers.
3 Whisk together 30 ml (2 tbsp) olive oil, the vinegar and garlic, and season with salt and pepper. Stir into the rice mixture.
4 Pile the rice into the pepper halves and arrange on a serving plate. Cover and chill for 30 minutes before serving on a bed of lettuce.

COOK'S TIP

If you prefer to eat this hot, keep the peppers in the oven until the filling is ready. Rinse the rice with boiling, not cold, water, pile it into the hot peppers, pour over the dressing and serve immediately.

SPINACH AND FETA PUFFS

SERVES 4

25 g (1 oz) butter	pepper
50 g (2 oz) onion, finely chopped	two 20 cm (8 inch) ready-rolled squares puff pastry, thawed
125 g (4 oz) ready prepared fresh spinach, or 75 g (3 oz) frozen leaf spinach, thawed	50-75 g (2-3 oz) Feta cheese, sliced
freshly grated nutmeg	beaten egg or milk, to glaze

1 Melt the butter in a medium saucepan and sauté the onion for 2 minutes or until softened. Add the spinach with plenty of nutmeg. Cook for 3-4 minutes; or 2 minutes if using frozen spinach; stirring until the spinach is soft and the juices have evaporated. Season with pepper and cool slightly.
2 Cut each pastry square in half diagonally. Divide the spinach mixture between each triangle. Top with feta cheese. Dampen the edges of the pastry, fold over and seal well. Brush with beaten egg or milk to glaze.
3 Place on a baking sheet and cook in the oven at 200°C (400°F) mark 6 for about 15 minutes or until cooked through and golden brown. Serve immediately, with a mixed salad.

COOK'S TIP

Don't use too much filling or it will ooze out on cooking.

GARLIC MUSHROOM PARCELS

SERVES 4-6

15 ml (1 tbsp) olive oil	15 ml (1 tbsp) chopped thyme or 5 ml (1 tsp) dried
1 onion, finely chopped	pepper
1-2 garlic cloves, crushed	50 g (2 oz) cream cheese
225 g (8 oz) button mushrooms, chopped	6 sheets of filo pastry
	25 g (1 oz) butter, melted

1 Heat the oil in a medium saucepan, add the onion and garlic and cook gently for 3-5 minutes or until the onion has softened. Add the mushrooms, thyme and pepper to taste. Cook for 5-6 minutes, stirring.
2 Drain off any excess juices and add the cheese, stirring continuously until the cheese has melted. Cook for a further 2 minutes, then leave to cool.
3 To make the parcels, lay the first sheet of filo pastry lengthways on a work surface. Brush with butter, then lay a second sheet on top. Brush with butter, then cut into eight equal strips.
4 Place 5 ml (1 tsp) of the cooked filling in one corner of a strip of pastry. Fold this corner over to make a triangle, encasing the filling. Continue to fold in the shape of a triangle, brushing with a little extra melted butter just before the final fold. Repeat to make 24 parcels. Place on a greased baking sheet.
5 Bake in the oven at 200°C (400°F) mark 6 for 10-15 minutes or until golden brown and crisp, turning the parcels over halfway through cooking. Serve hot or cold.

SPINACH AND STILTON CREPES

SERVES 8

900 g (2 lb) fresh spinach	40 ml (8 tsp) plain flour
salt and pepper	150 ml (¼ pint) single cream
50 g (2 oz) butter	8 Crêpes (see page 158)
50 g (2 oz) salted peanuts, chopped	300 ml (½ pint) milk
2.5 ml (½ tsp) paprika	50 g (2 oz) Blue Stilton cheese, grated

1 Tear the stalks off the spinach and wash, but do not dry. Place in a large saucepan, sprinkle with salt, cover tightly and cook for 10 minutes. Drain well and chop.
2 Heat 25 g (1 oz) butter in a small saucepan, add the peanuts and paprika and fry gently for 1 minute. Stir in the spinach, 20 ml (4 tsp) flour and the cream. Season to taste. Bring to the boil and cook for 2-3 minutes, stirring. Divide the filling between the crêpes, roll up and place, side by side, in a buttered ovenproof dish.
3 Melt the remaining butter in a saucepan, stir in the remaining flour and cook for 1 minute, stirring. Remove from the heat and gradually stir in the milk. Bring to the boil, stirring all the time, until the sauce thickens. Stir in the cheese and season to taste. Pour over the crêpes, cover lightly with foil and bake in the oven at 180°C (350°F) mark 4 for 25-30 minutes.

VARIATION

Spinach and Ricotta Crêpes

Ricotta is a fragrant Italian cheese made from the whey left over when producing other cheeses. It has a delicate, smooth flavour and is often mixed with spinach in stuffings for ravioli or cannelloni. It would make an ideal substitute for Stilton in the above recipe.

TURMERIC AND WALNUT MUSHROOMS

SERVES 8

1.1 kg (2½ lb) button mushrooms	15 ml (1 tbsp) turmeric
300 ml (½ pint) olive oil	1 garlic clove, crushed
100 ml (4 fl oz) white wine vinegar	salt and pepper
5 ml (1 tsp) Dijon mustard	125 g (4 oz) walnut pieces
5 ml (1 tsp) sugar	350 g (12 oz) Emmental cheese, cubed
	chopped parsley, to garnish

1 Leave the small button mushrooms whole and cut any larger ones in half. Place in a serving dish.
2 In a jug, whisk together the oil, vinegar, mustard, sugar, turmeric and garlic until well blended. Add salt and pepper to taste.
3 Pour the dressing over the mushrooms and mix thoroughly to coat. Cover and leave to marinate in the refrigerator for at least 8 hours.
4 To serve, stir the mushrooms well and mix in the walnut and Emmental. Garnish with chopped parsley.

BULGAR STUFFED TOMATOES

SERVES 4

125 g (4 oz) bulgar wheat	30 ml (2 tbsp) Pesto (see page 172)
4 large beefsteak tomatoes, each about 175 g (6 oz)	45 ml (3 tbsp) chopped basil
25 g (1 oz) nuts, such as hazelnuts, peanuts or cashews, toasted and chopped	salt and pepper
	TO SERVE
	natural yogurt
50 g (2 oz) stoned black olives, roughly chopped	Pesto (see page 172), or Guacamole (see page 31)
	chopped basil

1 Put the bulgar wheat in a bowl and pour over 150 ml (¼ pint) boiling water. Leave to soak for 30 minutes or until the water has been absorbed and the bulgar has softened.
2 Cut the tops off the tomatoes and reserve. Scoop out the tomato centres with a spoon and finely chop half the tomato flesh. (Discard the remainder.)
3 Add the chopped tomato to the bulgar wheat with the remaining ingredients and season with salt and pepper. Use to fill the tomato shells.
4 To serve, top each tomato with a spoonful of yogurt and a little pesto or a spoonful of guacamole. Sprinkle with basil and replace the tomato tops.

SERVING SUGGESTION

Serve these stuffed tomatoes as part of a summer lunch with a selection of salads. They are equally delicious served hot.

GOLDEN BAKED POTATOES

SERVES 8

4 medium baking potatoes scrubbed and pricked	60 ml (4 tbsp) milk
oil, for brushing	125 g (4 oz) Cheddar cheese, grated
salt and pepper	few drops of Worcestershire sauce
25 g (1 oz) butter or margarine	parsley sprigs, to garnish
1 onion, finely chopped	

1 Scrub the potatoes. Brush with a little oil and sprinkle lightly with salt. Prick all over with a skewer or fork. Bake in the oven at 200°C (400°F) mark 6 for 1¼ hours or until tender.

2 Halve the potatoes and scoop out the insides, leaving a thin shell. Mash the potato flesh.

3 Heat the butter in a frying pan and lightly brown the onion, then add the milk and heat gently.

4 Beat this mixture into the mashed potato with half the cheese, the seasoning and Worcestershire sauce.

5 Pile the mixture back into the potato shells and scatter over the remaining grated cheese.

6 Return to the oven for about 20 minutes, until golden. Serve immediately, garnished with parsley.

COOK'S TIP

The best potatoes to use for baking are Maris Piper, Desirée and Pentland Squire, although King Edward and Pentland grown are almost as good.

BAKED POTATOES WITH CHICK PEAS

SERVES 4

4 baking potatoes, each weighing about 275 g (10 oz)	400 g (14 oz) can chick peas, drained
45 ml (3 tbsp) oil	60 ml (4 tbsp) chopped parsley
salt and pepper	150 ml (¼ pint) natural yogurt
1 onion, roughly chopped	chopped parsley, to garnish
2.5 ml (½ tsp) ground coriander	
2.5 ml (½ tsp) ground cumin	

1 Scrub the potatoes and pat dry. Brush them with 15 ml (1 tbsp) of the oil and sprinkle lightly with salt.

2 Place them directly on the oven shelf and bake in the oven at 200°C (400°F) mark 6 for 1¼ hours or until tender.

3 Meanwhile, heat the remaining oil in a large saucepan, add the onion, coriander and cumin and fry for 4 minutes, stirring occasionally. Add the chick peas and cook for a further 1-2 minutes, stirring all the time.

4 Halve the potatoes and scoop out the flesh, keeping the shells intact. Add the potato flesh to the chick pea mixture with the parsley and yogurt. Mash until smooth; add seasoning to taste.

5 Place the potato shells on a baking sheet and fill with the potato and chick pea mixture. Return to the oven and bake for a further 10-15 minutes. Serve hot, sprinkled with chopped parsley.

SERVING SUGGESTION

Serve these jacket potatoes with a salad of shredded cabbage, celery, apple and walnuts.

MEXICAN BAKED POTATOES

SERVES 4

4 medium baking potatoes	pinch of granulated sugar
30 ml (2 tbsp) oil	salt and pepper
1 onion, finely chopped	425 g (15 oz) can red kidney beans, drained
1 garlic clove, crushed	30 ml (2 tbsp) chopped parsley
400 g (14 oz) can tomatoes	
10 ml (2 tsp) tomato purée	50 g (2 oz) mature or farmhouse Cheddar cheese, coarsely grated
2.5 ml (½ tsp) chilli powder	

1   Scrub the potatoes. Brush with a little oil and sprinkle lightly with salt. Prick all over with a skewer or fork. Bake in the oven at 200°C (400°F) mark 6 for 1¼ hours or until tender.

2   Meanwhile, make the stuffing. Heat the remaining oil in a saucepan, add the onion and garlic and fry gently until soft.

3   Add the tomatoes with their juice and stir to break up with a wooden spoon. Add the tomato purée, chilli powder, sugar and salt and pepper to taste and bring to the boil, stirring. Simmer, uncovered, for about 20 minutes, stirring occasionally. Add the beans and parsley and heat through.

4   When the potatoes are cooked, slice off the top third of each one and reserve for lids. Scoop out some of the potato from the bottom third of each one and add to the chill bean mixture.

5   Place a potato on each serving plate and spoon the chilli bean mixture into each one. Sprinkle grated cheese on top, then replace the lids at an angle to serve.

SERVING SUGGESTION

This supper dish is hot, spicy and substantial. Serve accompanied by a crisp green salad.

SWISS STUFFED POTATOES

SERVES 4

4 medium baking potatoes	125 g (4 oz) full-fat soft cheese
50 g (2 oz) butter or margarine	1.25 ml (¼ tsp) freshly grated nutmeg
1 small onion, finely chopped	salt and pepper
450 g (1 lb) fresh spinach, chopped or 225 g (8 oz) frozen chopped spinach, thawed	50 g (2 oz) Gruyère or Emmental cheese, grated
	pinch of paprika or cayenne

1   Scrub the potatoes, then pat dry with absorbent kitchen paper.

2   With a sharp pointed knife, score a line in the skin around the middle of each potato.

3   Place the potatoes directly on the oven shelf and bake in the oven at 200°C (400°F) mark 6 for 1¼ hours or until tender.

4   About 15 minutes before the end of the cooking time, melt the butter in a heavy-based saucepan, add the onion and fry gently for about 5 minutes until soft and lightly coloured. Add the fresh spinach and cook gently for 2-3 minutes, stirring frequently. (If using frozen spinach, heat through.) Remove from the heat.

5   When the potatoes are cooked, slice in half lengthways. Scoop out the flesh into a bowl and add the spinach mixture, the soft cheese, nutmeg and salt and pepper to taste. Mix well.

6   Spoon the mixture into the potato shells, mounding it up in the centre. Stand the stuffed potatoes on a baking sheet. Sprinkle over the cheese and finally the paprika or cayenne. Return to the oven for 10-15 minutes, until the cheese topping is bubbling and golden. Serve hot.

BARBECUED BEANS

SERVES 4

350 g (12 oz) dried red kidney beans, soaked overnight in cold water	5 ml (1 tsp) vegetable yeast extract
1.1 litres (2 pints) tomato juice	15 ml (1 tbsp) mustard powder
1 large onion, sliced	15 ml (1 tbsp) honey
30 ml (2 tbsp) soy sauce	2.5 ml (½ tsp) chilli powder
60 ml (4 tbsp) cider vinegar	salt and pepper

1 Drain the beans and place in a saucepan. Cover with cold water, bring to the boil and boil rapidly for 10 minutes, then drain.

2 Put the tomato juice, onion, soy sauce, vinegar, yeast extract, mustard, honey and chilli powder in a flameproof casserole. Bring to the boil and add the beans.

3 Cover and cook in the oven at 140°C (275°F) mark 1 for about 4 hours until the beans are tender. Season with salt and pepper to taste.

MEXICAN RE-FRIED BEANS

SERVES 4-6

30 ml (2 tbsp) oil	1 green chilli, seeded and finely chopped
1 onion, finely chopped	two 425 g (15 oz) cans red kidney or pinto beans, drained
1 garlic clove, crushed	

1 Heat the oil in a large frying pan, add the onion and fry gently for about 5 minutes until soft and lightly coloured. Stir in the garlic and chilli and continue cooking for 1-2 minutes. Remove from the heat.

2 Mash the beans in a bowl with a potato masher or the end of a rolling pin. Add to the frying pan with 150 ml (¼ pint) water and stir well to mix.

3 Return the pan to the heat and fry for about 5 minutes, stirring constantly until the beans resemble porridge, adding more water if necessary. Take care that the beans do not catch and burn. Serve hot, topped with grated Cheddar cheese, if liked.

COOK'S TIP

Re-fried beans can be re-fried again and again, with the addition of a little more water each time. The flavour improves with each frying.

BOSTON BAKED BEANS

SERVES 6-8

450 g (1 lb) dried haricot beans, soaked overnight in cold water	450 ml (¾ pint) tomato juice
2 onions, chopped	450 ml (¾ pint) lager
30 ml (2 tbsp) Dijon mustard	60 ml (4 tbsp) tomato purée
30 ml (2 tbsp) dark brown sugar	60 ml (4 tbsp) Worcestershire sauce
75 ml (5 tbsp) black treacle	30 ml (2 tbsp) chilli sauce
	1 garlic clove, crushed
	salt and pepper

1 Drain the beans. Put them in a large flameproof casserole and add enough fresh cold water to cover. Bring to the boil and boil rapidly for 10 minutes, then simmer for 45 minutes. Drain and return to the casserole with the remaining ingredients. Mix thoroughly together, season with salt and pepper, cover with a tightly fitting lid and cook in the oven at 150°C (300°F) mark 2 for 4 hours or until the beans are very tender.

2 Check and stir the beans occasionally during cooking and add a little extra tomato juice or water, if necessary, to prevent them drying out. Taste and adjust the seasoning, if necessary, before serving.

COOK'S TIP

There are many versions of this classic dark, rich New England dish and they all vary enormously, so much so that haricot beans and black treacle or molasses seem to be the only constants. The chilli sauce and garlic are not particularly traditional and may be omitted if you prefer your beans less spicy. This recipe includes Worcestershire sauce, vegetarian brands of which are quite readily available. Check the label when buying.

TOFU BURGERS

MAKES 8

15 ml (1 tbsp) oil	225 g (8 oz) packet original tofu
1 large carrot, finely grated	25 g (1 oz) wholemeal breadcrumbs
1 large onion, finely grated	25 g (1 oz) mixed nuts, finely chopped
10 ml (2 tsp) coriander seeds, finely crushed (optional)	salt and pepper
1 garlic clove, crushed	oil, for frying or grilling
5 ml (1 tsp) curry paste	
5 ml (1 tsp) tomato purée	

1 Heat the 15 ml (1 tbsp) oil in a large frying pan. Add the carrot and onion and fry for 3-4 minutes or until the vegetables are softened, stirring all the time. Add the coriander seeds, if using, garlic, curry paste and tomato purée. Increase the heat and fry for 2 minutes, stirring all the time.

2 Mash the tofu with a potato masher, then stir into the vegetables with the breadcrumbs and nuts. Season with salt and pepper, and beat thoroughly until the mixture starts to stick together. With floured hands, shape the mixture into eight burgers.

3 Heat some oil in a frying pan and fry the burgers for 3-4 minutes on each side or until golden brown. Alternatively, to grill the burgers, brush them lightly with oil and cook under a hot grill for about 3 minutes on each side or until golden brown. Drain on absorbent kitchen paper and serve hot.

COOK'S TIP

Adding tofu to vegetarian burgers ensures that they remain moist. It also produces burgers that are lower in fat than those based entirely on nuts.

CURRIED NUT BURGERS

MAKES 6

90 ml (6 tbsp) oil	175 g (6 oz) granary breadcrumbs
1 onion, finely chopped	2 carrots, grated
15 ml (1 tbsp) Madras curry paste or powder	salt and pepper
175 g (6 oz) Edam cheese, diced	2 eggs
175 g (6 oz) chopped mixed nuts	30 ml (2 tbsp) wholemeal flour, for coating
	watercress sprigs, radicchio and cucumber, to garnish

1 Heat 30 ml (2 tbsp) of the oil in a small saucepan, add the onion and curry paste or powder and fry gently for 5 minutes until the onion is soft but not coloured.

2 Put the onion in a bowl with the cheese, 150 g (5 oz) of the nuts and 125 g (4 oz) of the breadcrumbs. Add the carrots and seasoning to taste, and stir well to mix. Bind with one of the eggs.

3 With floured hands, form the mixture into 6 burger shapes, coating them lightly with flour.

4 Beat the remaining egg in a shallow dish and dip the burgers in it to coat them lightly.

5 Mix the remaining nuts and breadcrumbs together on a flat plate. Coat the burgers in this mixture, pressing it on firmly with your hands. Chill the burgers in the refrigerator for 30 minutes to firm the coating.

6 Heat the remaining oil in a large frying pan, add the burgers and fry over moderate to high heat for 10 minutes on each side until golden brown and cooked through. Drain on absorbent kitchen paper before serving with the watercress, radicchio and cucumber.

SERVING SUGGESTION

Serve these burgers hot or cold, with wedges of lemon or lime. A natural yogurt, cucumber and mint salad would make a refreshing accompaniment, contrasting well with the spicy richness of the curried nut mixture.

LENTIL CROQUETTES

SERVES 4-8

225 g (8 oz) split red lentils	salt and pepper
2 celery sticks, finely chopped	30 ml (2 tbsp) wholemeal flour, for coating
1 onion, chopped	5 ml (1 tsp) paprika
1-2 garlic cloves, crushed	5 ml (1 tsp) turmeric
10 ml (2 tsp) garam masala	60 ml (4 tbsp) oil
1 egg, beaten	cucumber slices, to garnish

1 Place the lentils in a large saucepan with the celery, onion, garlic, garam masala and 600 ml (1 pint) water. Bring to the boil, stirring with a wooden spoon to mix.

2 Lower the heat and simmer gently for 30 minutes or until the lentils are tender and have absorbed all the liquid. Stir frequently to prevent the lentils sticking to the bottom of the pan.

3 Remove from the heat. Leave to cool for a few minutes, then beat in the egg and seasoning to taste.

4 Turn the mixture on to a board or flat plate and spread out evenly. Leave until cold, then chill in the refrigerator for 30 minutes to firm the mixture.

5 With floured hands, form the mixture into 8 triangular croquette shapes. Coat in the flour mixed with the paprika and turmeric. Chill again for 30 minutes.

6 Heat the oil in a large frying pan, add the croquettes and fry over moderate to high heat for 10 minutes, turning once until crisp and golden on both sides. Drain on absorbent kitchen paper. Serve hot, garnished with cucumber slices and accompanied by yogurt.

SERVING SUGGESTION

Serve these spicy croquettes for a tasty lunch dish with a side salad of tomato, onion and fennel. Allow 1 or 2 per person depending on appetite.

MAIN COURSES

These sustaining dishes require the simplest of accompaniments – often a crisp salad will suffice. Choose from tasty pies and flans; comforting vegetable hot pots and casseroles; delicious pasta and vegetables bakes; and spicy curries.

CHEESE FONDUE

SERVES 6

450 g (1 lb) Gruyère cheese	1 liqueur glass of kirsch (optional)
450 g (1 lb) Emmental cheese	pepper
30 ml (2 tbsp) cornflour	pinch of grated nutmeg
1 garlic clove	1 French loaf, cubed
450 ml (¾ pint) dry white wine	

1 Grate the Gruyère and Emmental cheeses and mix together with the cornflour.
2 Rub the inside of a heavy-based flameproof dish with the garlic. Put the cheese mixture in the dish and add the wine.
3 Heat gently, stirring all the time until the cheese has melted. Add the kirsch, if using, and season with freshly ground pepper and nutmeg. Stir well together.
4 When the mixture is of a thick creamy consistency, it is ready to serve. Pile the bread cubes into a basket and serve with the fondue.

VEGETABLE TOAD-IN-THE-HOLE

SERVES 4

350 g (12 oz) prepared mixed vegetables, such as carrots, courgettes and broccoli	pinch of salt
4 cherry tomatoes	1 egg
white vegetable fat	175 ml (6 fl oz) milk and water mixed
50 g (2 oz) plain flour	Tomato Sauce (see page171) or chutney, to serve

1 Cut the vegetables into chunks; steam or boil until just tender. Prick the tomatoes with a fork.
2 Put a knob of fat into each compartment of a four-hole Yorkshire pudding tin. Put the tin in the oven at 220°C (425°F) mark 7 for about 5 minutes to heat the fat.
3 Meanwhile, sift the flour and salt into a bowl and make a well in the centre. Break the egg into the well, then add half the liquid. Gradually mix the flour into the liquid to make a smooth, thick paste, then gradually work in the remaining liquid. Beat until smooth. If necessary, remove any lumps with a balloon whisk.
4 Divide the vegetables between the compartments in the pudding tin and pour over the batter. Bake on the top shelf in the oven for 30-35 minutes or until well risen and golden brown. Serve with tomato sauce or chutney.

MIXED VEGETABLE RING

SERVES 4

125 g (4 oz) butter	salt and pepper
1 large onion, sliced	215 ml (7½ fl oz) milk
50 g (2 oz) mushrooms	125 g (4 oz) plain flour
2 courgettes, sliced	3 eggs, beaten
175 g (6 oz) aubergine, quartered and sliced	40 g (1½ oz) walnut pieces, chopped
1 red pepper, seeded and sliced	125 g (4 oz) Double Gloucester cheese with chives, grated
3 tomatoes, skinned and chopped	

1 Melt 25 g (1 oz) of the butter in a large saucepan, add the onion and mushrooms and fry lightly for 5 minutes or until softened.

2 Add the courgettes, aubergine and red pepper and cook for 5 minutes, stirring occasionally. Add the tomatoes and season to taste.

3 Melt the remaining butter in a medium saucepan with the milk, then bring to the boil. Remove the pan from the heat, tip in all the flour and beat thoroughly with a wooden spoon. Allow to cool slightly, then beat in the eggs, a little at a time. Stir in the walnuts.

4 Pipe or spoon the mixture around the edge of a well-greased 900 ml (1½ pint) ovenproof serving dish. Fill the centre with the vegetables and bake in the oven at 200°C (400°F) mark 6 for 35-40 minutes or until the pastry is risen and golden. Sprinkle with the cheese, then return to the oven until the cheese has melted. Serve at once.

VEGETABLE JALOUSIE

SERVES 4

600 g (1¼ 1b) fresh broad beans, shelled, or 350 g (12 oz) frozen	125 g (4 oz) Caerphilly or Wensleydale cheese, grated
4 carrots, thinly sliced	45 ml (3 tbsp) freshly grated Parmesan cheese
3 leeks, thickly sliced	1.25 ml (¼ tsp) ground mace
salt and pepper	10 ml (2 tsp) chopped summer savory
25 g (1 oz) butter or margarine	400 g (14 oz) frozen puff pastry, thawed
50 g (2 oz) plain flour	beaten egg, to glaze
300 ml (½ pint) milk	

1 Parboil broad beans in boiling salted water for 4 minutes. Remove with a slotted spoon and set aside. Parboil the carrots for 2 minutes only; remove. Parboil the leeks for 1 minute; reserve 30 ml (2 tbsp) blanching water.

2 Melt the butter in a clean pan, add the flour and cook gently, stirring, for 1-2 minutes. Remove from heat and gradually blend in the milk. Bring to the boil, stirring, then simmer for 3 minutes until thick and smooth. Add the cheese, mace and salt and pepper to taste. Remove from heat and fold in the vegetables. Cover surface closely with greaseproof paper, then leave until cold.

3 Meanwhile, roll out half of the pastry thinly on a lightly floured surface to a 30 x 23 cm (12 x 9 inch) rectangle. Place on a wetted baking sheet.

4 Stir reserved blanching water and the savory into the cold filling, then spread over the pastry to within about 1 cm (½ inch) of the edges. Brush the edges with water.

5 Roll out remaining pastry to a slightly larger rectangle. Fold in half lengthways. With scissors, cut through the double thickness of the pastry at 5 cm (2 inch) intervals. Unfold the pastry and place over the filling. Press the edges firmly to seal, then flute or crimp. Brush with beaten egg, then bake in the oven at 220°C (425°F) mark 7 for 30 minutes until golden brown. Serve cut into slices.

SPINACH AND GARLIC TART

SERVES 8-10

FOR THE PASTRY	
225 g (8 oz) plain flour	450 g (1 lb) fresh spinach
2.5 ml (½ tsp) salt	40 g (1½ oz) freshly grated Parmesan cheese
125 g (4 oz) butter or margarine	150 ml (¼ pint) double cream
FOR THE FILLING	45 ml (3 tbsp) ground almonds
15 ml (1 tbsp) olive oil	1 egg yolk
1 large onion, chopped	freshly grated nutmeg
1-2 garlic cloves, crushed	15 g (½ oz) pine nuts

1 To make the pastry put the flour and salt in a bowl, then rub in the fat until the mixture resembles fine breadcrumbs. Stir in enough water to bind the mixture together. Knead lightly, then roll out on a floured surface. Use to line a shallow, loose-bottomed 25 cm (10 inch) fluted flan tin. Cover and chill for at least 30 minutes.
2 Meanwhile heat the oil in a large heavy-based saucepan. Add the onion and garlic and cook, stirring, for 1-2 minutes. Reduce the heat, cover and cook until the onion is very soft.
3 Add the spinach and stir to mix with the onion mixture. Re-cover the pan and cook for 4-5 minutes until the spinach is just cooked. Remove from the heat. Stir in half the grated Parmesan, the cream, almonds and egg yolk. Season generously with nutmeg, salt and pepper.
4 Line the pastry case with foil or greaseproof paper weighed down with baking beans and bake blind in the oven at 190°C (375°F) mark 5 for 15-20 minutes. Remove the baking beans and greaseproof paper and cook for a further 10 minutes or until the base is cooked through.
5 Spread the filling in the pastry case and top with the pine nuts. Stand the tart on a baking sheet and cook at 200°C (400°F) mark 6 for 10 minutes until filling is lightly set. Sprinkle with remaining cheese. Serve warm or cold.

GOAT'S CHEESE AND MINT FLAN

SERVES 6

Wholemeal or Shortcrust Pastry made with 175 g (6 oz) flour (see page 80)	300 g (10 oz) fromage frais
	2 eggs
175 g (6 oz) mild fresh creamy goat's cheese (chèvre)	salt and pepper
	small handful of mint leaves

1 Roll out the pastry on a lightly floured surface and use to line a greased shallow loose-bottomed 23 cm (9 inch) fluted flan tin. Cover and chill while making the filling.
2 To make the filling, beat the cheese until smooth. Gradually beat in the fromage frais, followed by the eggs. Season with salt and pepper.
3 Line the pastry case with foil or greaseproof paper weighed down with baking beans and bake blind in the oven at 200°C (400°F) mark 6 for 10-15 minutes, then remove the paper and beans and bake for a further 5 minutes until the pastry base is cooked through.
4 Stir the filling, then pour it into the pastry case. Sprinkle with the mint leaves and grind a little pepper over the top. Bake in the oven at 200°C (400°F) mark 6 for about 15 minutes or until firm to the touch. Brown under a hot grill for 2-3 minutes. Serve warm or cold.

SERVING SUGGESTION

This delicately flavoured, creamy tart is delicious served with a salad, or in thinner slices as a starter, garnished with extra mint leaves.

TARTE A L'OIGNON

SERVES 4-6

FOR THE PASTRY	700 g (1½ lb) onions, thinly sliced
175 g (6 oz) plain flour	2 eggs
1.25 ml (¼ tsp) salt	50 ml (2 fl oz) milk
75 g (3 oz) butter or margarine	150 ml (¼ pint) single cream
FOR THE FILLING	salt and pepper
50 g (2 oz) butter	pinch of freshly grated nutmeg

1 To make the pastry put the flour and salt in a bowl, then rub in the fat until the mixture resembles fine breadcrumbs. Stir in enough water to bind the mixture together. Knead lightly, then roll out on a floured surface. Use to line a 20 cm (8 inch) flan tin or ring placed on a baking sheet. Cover and chill for at least 30 minutes.
2 To make the filling, melt the butter in a large frying pan, add the onions, cover and cook gently for 20 minutes.
3 Beat together the eggs, milk and cream until smooth. Season to taste and add the nutmeg.
4 Pour a little of the egg mixture into the pastry case. Add the onions, then pour in the remaining egg mixture.
5 Bake in the oven at 200°C (400°F) mark 6 for 30 minutes or until golden brown and set.

VARIATION

For a wholemeal pastry case, replace half the plain flour with wholemeal flour.

CAULIFLOWER AND STILTON FLAN

SERVES 4-6

Shortcrust Pastry made with 175 g (6 oz) flour (see left)	225 g (8 oz) onions, chopped
	30 ml (2 tbsp) plain flour
450 g (1 lb) cauliflower florets	200 ml (7 fl oz) milk
	pepper
salt and pepper	125 g (4 oz) Blue Stilton cheese, crumbled
25 g (1 oz) butter or margarine	25 g (1 oz) Cheddar cheese, grated

1 Roll out the pastry on a lightly floured surface and use to line a 23 cm (9 inch) flan dish or ring placed on a baking sheet. Chill in the refrigerator for 10-15 minutes.
2 Prick the base with a fork, line with foil and baking beans and bake blind in the oven at 200°C (400°F) mark 6 for 10-15 minutes until set. Remove the foil and beans.
3 Cook the cauliflower florets in a saucepan of boiling salted water for 4-5 minutes until barely tender. Drain well and cool.
4 Melt the butter in a pan and sauté the onion until soft. Stir in the flour and cook gently for 2 minutes, stirring. Remove the pan from the heat and gradually stir in the milk. Bring to the boil and continue to cook, stirring, until the sauce thickens, then add pepper to taste.
5 Sprinkle the Stilton evenly over the base of the flan. Arrange the cauliflower on top. Spoon over the onion sauce and sprinkle with the Cheddar cheese.
6 Bake in the oven at 190°C (375°F) mark 5 for 25-30 minutes until golden and bubbling. Serve hot.

BROCCOLI FLAN

SERVES 4-6

FOR THE PASTRY	FOR THE FILLING
175 g (6 oz) plain wholemeal flour	50 g (12 oz) broccoli
50 g (2 oz) porridge oats	3 eggs
salt and pepper	300 ml (½ pint) milk
125 g (4 oz) butter	

1 To make the pastry, put the flour, oats and 2.5 ml (½ tsp) salt into a bowl. Rub in the butter until the mixture resembles fine breadcrumbs. Add enough cold water to bind the mixture together and form a firm dough.
2 Roll out the pastry on a lightly floured surface and use to line a 23 cm (9 inch) flan dish. Line with foil or greaseproof paper weighed down with baking beans and bake blind at 200°C (400°F) mark 6 for 10-15 minutes, until set but not too brown. Remove the foil and beans.
3 To make the filling, roughly chop the broccoli, then cook in boiling salted water until just tender. Drain well. Arrange in the flan case.
4 Whisk together the eggs, milk and seasoning to taste. Pour into the flan case, making sure the broccoli is covered.
5 Bake at 190°C (375°F) mark 5 for about 40 minutes, until lightly set. Serve warm.

COOK'S TIP

As well as heads of green broccoli, you will sometimes find purple sprouting broccoli in the shops. Whichever variety you choose, buy the freshest possible, with no yellowing leaves, and eat within a couple of days. The pastry in this recipe uses rolled oats for an unusual texture.

LEEK AND PEA FLAN

SERVES 4-6

FOR THE FILLING	FOR THE PASTRY
450 g (1 lb) leeks, sliced	175 g (6 oz) plain wholemeal flour
125 g (4 oz) fresh or frozen shelled peas	50 g (2 oz) Cheddar cheese, grated
salt and pepper	75 g (3 oz) butter
150 ml (¼ pint) milk	1 egg, beaten
150 ml (5 fl oz) natural yogurt	
2 eggs	
50 g (2 oz) Cheddar cheese, grated	

1 To make the filling, cook the leeks and peas in a little salted water in a tightly covered medium saucepan until tender. Drain well.
2 Purée the leeks, peas, milk and yogurt together in a blender or food processor.
3 Beat the eggs into the purée and season to taste.
4 To make the pastry, put the flour and cheese in a bowl. Rub in the butter until the mixture resembles fine breadcrumbs, then bind together with the egg.
5 Roll out the pastry on a lightly floured surface and use to line a 23 cm (9 inch) flan dish. Pour in the leek mixture and sprinkle over the cheese. Bake in the oven at 190°C (375°F) mark 5 for 50-55 minutes, until golden.

WHOLEMEAL VEGETABLE PIE

SERVES 4

3 medium leeks	175 g (6 oz) Cheddar cheese, grated
275 g (10 oz) swede	
225 g (8 oz) turnip	30 ml (2 tbsp) chopped herbs, eg parsley, chives, thyme, marjoram or 10 ml (2 tsp) dried
4 carrots	
100 g (4 oz) butter or margarine	
225 g (8 oz) large flat mushrooms, sliced	salt and pepper
	Wholemeal Pastry made with 175 g (6 oz) (see page 80)
25 g (1 oz) plain flour	
300 ml (½ pint) vegetable stock	beaten egg, to glaze

1 Cut the leeks into 2.5 cm (1 inch) lengths; cut the swede, turnip and carrots into bite-sized chunks.
2 Melt the butter in a large saucepan, add the prepared vegetables and fry over moderate heat for about 10 minutes until turning golden brown. Add the mushrooms and cook for a further 2-3 minutes.
3 Sprinkle in the flour and cook gently, stirring, for 1-2 minutes. Gradually blend in the vegetable stock. Bring to the boil, stirring constantly, then simmer for 5-10 minutes or until the vegetables are just tender.
4 Remove from the heat and stir in the cheese, herbs and salt and pepper to taste. Pour into a 1.1 litre (2 pint) pie dish and allow to cool completely for about 1 hour.
5 Roll out the pastry on a floured surface. Cut a strip long enough to go around the rim of the pie dish. Moisten the rim with water and place the strip of pastry on the rim.
6 Roll out the remaining pastry to cover the pie. Moisten the strip of pastry on the rim of the dish, place the lid on top, trim off any excess pastry and press to seal.
7 Knock up and flute or crimp the edge. Decorate the top with any pastry trimmings and brush with beaten egg.
8 Bake the pie in the oven at 190°C (375°F) mark 5 for 15-20 minutes until lightly browned. Serve hot.

LEEK AND CHEESE PIE

SERVES 4

3 large leeks, total weight about 450 g (1 lb)	175 g (6 oz) Gruyère cheese, grated
6 spring onions	pinch of cayenne
40 g (1½ oz) butter or margarine	freshly grated nutmeg
	salt and pepper
1 egg, plus 1 egg yolk	Wholemeal Pastry made with 225 g (8 oz) flour (see page 80)
30 ml (2 tbsp) double cream	

1 Cut the leeks into 1 cm (½ inch) slices; finely chop the spring onions.
2 Melt the butter in a frying pan, add the leeks and cook for 5 minutes, stirring occasionally. Add the spring onions and cook for 2 minutes or until the leeks and onions are soft but not coloured. Remove from heat and allow to cool for 5 minutes.
3 Mix the egg, egg yolk, cream and Gruyère cheese in a bowl. Stir in the leek mixture and add the cayenne with the nutmeg and salt and pepper to taste.
4 Cut the pastry into 2 pieces, one slightly larger than the other. Roll out the larger piece thinly until 2.5 cm (1 inch) larger than the top of a 20 cm (8 inch) pie dish.
5 Lift the pastry on to the pie dish taking care not to stretch it. Ease it into place by pressing with your fingertips, working outwards from the centre and up the sides. Spoon the leek and cheese filling into the lined dish, mounding it up slightly in the centre.
6 Roll out the remaining pastry for the lid until it is 1 cm (½ inch) larger than the circumference of the dish. Moisten the pastry round the rim of the dish, place the lid on top, trim off any excess pastry and press to seal.
7 Knock up and flute or crimp the edges. Decorate the top with any pastry trimmings and brush with beaten egg. Make a slash in the top of the pie to allow steam to escape.
8 Bake in the oven at 200°C (400°F) mark 6 for about 30 minutes or until lightly brown. Serve warm or cold.

BEAN AND POTATO PIE

SERVES 6

450 g (1 lb) floury potatoes, such as King Edward or Maris Piper, peeled and roughly chopped	150 g (5 oz) full-fat soft cheese with garlic and herbs
salt and pepper	225 g (8 oz) cooked black-eyed beans or one 425 g (15 oz) can black-eyed beans, drained and rinsed
30 ml (2 tbsp) oil	
1 large onion, chopped	freshly grated nutmeg
450 g (1 lb) leeks, sliced	two 370 g (13 oz) packets frozen puff pastry, thawed
225 g (8 oz) mushrooms, sliced	milk or beaten egg, to glaze
125 g (4 oz) fresh spinach	sesame seeds, for sprinkling

1 Cook the potatoes in boiling salted water for 10-15 minutes or until tender. Drain well and leave to cool.
2 Meanwhile, heat the oil in a large saucepan, add the onion and leeks and fry for 5-10 minutes or until soft. Add the mushrooms and continue cooking until the mushrooms are soft. Add the spinach and cook for 1 minute or until the spinach is just wilted. Add the full-fat soft cheese, the beans and potatoes and season generously with salt, pepper and nutmeg. Leave to cool.
3 Thinly roll out one packet of pastry on a lightly floured surface to a rectangle measuring about 33 cm (13 inches) long and 25 cm (10 inches) wide. Transfer the pastry to a baking sheet.
4 Spoon the filling on to the pastry, leaving a 2.5 cm (1 inch) border around the edges. Roll out the second piece of pastry and use to cover the first. Brush the edges with milk or beaten egg and press together to seal. Lightly mark squares on the pastry with the back of a knife. Brush with milk or beaten egg and sprinkle with sesame seeds. Bake in the oven at 200°C (400°F) mark 6 for 30-35 minutes or until well risen and golden brown. Serve with a mixed salad or steamed fresh vegetables.

VEGETABLE HOT POT

SERVES 4

450 g (1 lb) carrots, thinly sliced	bouquet garni
2 large onions, thinly sliced	salt and pepper
3 celery sticks, thinly sliced	425 g (15 oz) can butter beans, drained
450 g (1 lb) potatoes, peeled and sliced	125 g (4 oz) frozen peas
125 g (4 oz) swede, thinly sliced	175 g (6 oz) fresh breadcrumbs
450 ml (¾ pint) vegetable stock	175 g (6 oz) Cheddar cheese, grated

1 Layer the carrots, onions, celery, potatoes and swede in a 2.3 litre (4 pint) casserole.
2 Pour the vegetable stock into the casserole and add the bouquet garni. Season to taste.
3 Cover the casserole, and cook in the oven at 180°C (350°F) mark 4 for 1 hour.
4 Remove the bouquet garni. Add the beans and peas to the casserole. Mix the breadcrumbs and cheese together and spoon over the hot pot. Return to the oven and cook, uncovered, for about 20 minutes.

VARIATION

The vegetables used in this satisfying dish can be varied according to the season. Other root vegetables, such as parsnips or turnips could replace the swede, and any canned beans could be used instead of butter beans. When available, replace frozen peas with fresh ones.

ROOT VEGETABLE HOT POT

SERVES 4-6

1 onion	salt and pepper
225 g (8 oz) potatoes	300 ml (½ pint) vegetable stock
225 g (8 oz) swede	30 ml (2 tbsp) chopped parsley
4 medium carrots	
2 medium leeks	125 g (4 oz) mature Cheddar cheese, grated
10 ml (2 tsp) yeast extract	

1 To prepare the vegetables, finely chop the onion. Peel the potatoes and swede and cut into chunks. Slice the carrots thinly. Cut the leeks into thick rings.
2 Put the prepared vegetables in a flameproof casserole with the yeast extract and seasoning to taste. Pour in the stock and bring to the boil, stirring to mix all the ingredients together.
3 Cover the casserole and simmer for 30 minutes until the vegetables are tender. Stir in the parsley, then taste and adjust the seasoning.
4 Sprinkle the cheese over the top of the vegetables, then put under a moderate grill for 5 minutes until melted and bubbling. Serve hot, straight from the casserole.

SERVING SUGGESTION

Serve with chunky slices of wholemeal bread, or on a bed of brown rice.

BUCKWHEAT AND LENTIL CASSEROLE

SERVES 4

150 g (5 oz) buckwheat	225 g (8 oz) red lentils
salt and pepper, to taste	3 bay leaves
30 ml (2 tbsp) oil	30 ml (2 tbsp) lemon juice
1 red or green pepper, seeded and cut into strips	1 garlic clove, crushed
1 onion, finely chopped	2 rosemary sprigs
350 g (12 oz) courgettes, sliced	5 ml (1 tsp) cumin seeds
	600 ml (1 pint) vegetable stock
175 g (6 oz) mushrooms, sliced	chopped parsley, to garnish

1 Bring 450 ml (¾ pint) water to the boil in a saucepan, sprinkle in the buckwheat, add a pinch of salt and return to the boil. Boil rapidly for 1 minute. Lower the heat, cover and cook gently, without stirring, for 12 minutes or until the water has been absorbed. Transfer to a greased casserole.
2 Heat the oil in a flameproof casserole or saucepan and fry the pepper and onion for 5 minutes. Add the courgettes and mushrooms and fry for 5 minutes. Stir in the lentils, bay leaves, lemon juice, garlic, rosemary, cumin and stock. Add to the buckwheat and stir well.
3 Simmer for 45 minutes until the lentils are cooked, stirring occasionally. Adjust the seasoning and sprinkle with chopped parsley. Serve hot with boiled rice and grated cheese, if liked.

COOK'S TIP

Buckwheat consists of tiny, brown seeds. They are high in protein and contain most of the B vitamins. The grains are gluten free.

RED KIDNEY BEAN HOT POT

SERVES 4-6

225 g (8 oz) dried red kidney beans, soaked in cold water overnight	600 ml (1 pint) vegetable stock
50 g (2 oz) butter or margarine	salt and pepper
2 onions, sliced	225 g (8 oz) French beans, topped and tailed
225 g (8 oz) celery, sliced	225 g (8 oz) courgettes, sliced
225 g (8 oz) carrots, sliced	50 g (2 oz) wholemeal breadcrumbs
30 ml (2 tbsp) plain wholemeal flour	75 g (3 oz) Cheddar cheese, grated

1 Drain the soaked kidney beans and rinse well under cold running water. Put in a large saucepan, cover with plenty of fresh cold water and bring slowly to the boil.
2 Skim off any scum with a slotted spoon, then boil rapidly for 10 minutes. Half cover the pan with a lid and simmer for about 1½ hours, until the beans are tender.
3 Melt the butter in a large saucepan, add the onions and fry gently for about 5 minutes until softened. Add the celery and carrots. Cover and cook gently for 5 minutes.
4 Add the flour and cook gently, stirring, for 1-2 minutes. Remove from the heat and gradually blend in the stock. Bring to the boil, stirring constantly, then simmer for 5 minutes. Season with salt and pepper to taste.
5 Add the French beans and simmer for a further 5 minutes, then add the courgettes. Cook for a further 5-10 minutes, until the vegetables are tender but still with a bite.
6 Drain the kidney beans, add to the vegetables and heat through for about 5 minutes. Taste and adjust seasoning, then turn into a deep flameproof dish.
7 Mix the breadcrumbs and cheese together. Sprinkle on top of the bean mixture and brown under a preheated grill until crisp and crusty. Serve hot, with nutty brown rice or wholemeal bread, and a crisp green salad.

LENTIL HOT POT

SERVES 2

175 g (6 oz) green lentils	300 ml (½ pint) vegetable stock
salt and pepper	125 g (4 oz) French beans, topped and tailed
25 g (1 oz) butter or margarine	125 g (4 oz) courgettes, sliced
1 onion, chopped	25 g (1 oz) fresh breadcrumbs
2.5 ml (½ tsp) curry powder	75 g (3 oz) Cheddar cheese, grated
125 g (4 oz) celery, sliced	
125 g (4 oz) carrots, sliced	
15 ml (1 tbsp) plain flour	

1 Cook the lentils in boiling salted water for 20 minutes or until tender. Drain well.
2 Meanwhile, melt the butter in a large saucepan, add the onion and fry for about 5 minutes until soft but not coloured. Add the curry powder, celery and carrots, cover and cook gently for 5 minutes.
3 Stir in the flour and cook for 1 minute, then stir in the stock. Bring to the boil, stirring. Season with salt and pepper to taste and simmer for 5 minutes.
4 Add the French beans and simmer for a further 5 minutes, then add the courgettes. Continue cooking for about 10 minutes or until the vegetables are tender, but still have bite.
5 Drain the lentils and add to the vegetables. Heat through for 2-3 minutes. Taste and adjust seasoning, then turn into a deep ovenproof dish.
6 Mix the breadcrumbs and cheese together and sprinkle on top. Put under a preheated hot grill until crisp and golden brown. Serve hot.

VEGETARIAN ROAST

SERVES 4-6

175 g (6 oz) long-grain brown rice	125 g (4 oz) wholemeal breadcrumbs
15 g (½ oz) butter or margarine	125 g (4 oz) almonds, finely chopped
1 onion, chopped	125 g (4 oz) Cheddar cheese, grated
1 garlic clove, crushed	2 eggs
2 carrots, grated	salt and pepper
125 g (4 oz) button mushrooms, finely chopped	

1 Cook the rice in boiling salted water for 30-35 minutes or until tender. Drain well.

2 Meanwhile, heat the butter in a medium frying pan, add the onion, garlic, carrots and mushrooms and fry for 5-10 minutes or until softened, stirring frequently. Stir in the breadcrumbs, almonds, cooked rice, cheese and eggs. Season to taste and mix thoroughly together.

3 Pack the mixture into a greased 1.7 litre (3 pint) loaf tin and bake in the oven at 180°C (350°F) mark 4 for 1-1¼ hours or until firm to the touch and brown on top. Serve sliced, hot or cold.

VARIATION

Any type of chopped nuts can be used in the above recipe. Try substituting brazils or unsalted peanuts or cashews for the almonds.

CHEESE AND NUT ROAST

SERVES 4-6

40 g (1½ oz) butter or margarine	125 g (4 oz) unsalted peanuts, finely chopped
1 onion, finely chopped	125 g (4 oz) fresh brown breadcrumbs
125 g (4 oz) Sage Derby cheese, or Cheddar cheese plus 5 ml (1 tsp) rubbed sage	2 eggs
50 g (2 oz) hazelnuts, finely chopped	salt and pepper
50 g (2 oz) Brazil nuts, finely chopped	Tomato Sauce (see page 171), to serve

1 Grease and base-line a 900 ml (1½ pint) loaf tin.

2 Melt the butter in a saucepan, add the onion and fry gently for about 5 minutes or until soft and just beginning to brown. Transfer to a bowl.

3 Grate the cheese finely into the bowl. Stir to mix with the onion, adding the sage if needed. Add the nuts, breadcrumbs and eggs and mix well again. Season to taste with salt and pepper.

4 Press the nut mixture evenly into the prepared tin. Bake in the oven at 180°C (350°F) mark 4 for about 45 minutes, or until golden brown.

5 Leave the nut roast to cool in the tin for 2-3 minutes, then turn out on to a warmed serving dish. Cut into slices and serve hot, with the tomato sauce.

CHEESY POTATO PIE

SERVES 4

900 g (2 lb) potatoes, peeled and cut into chunks	1 large red pepper, seeded and roughly chopped
45 ml (3 tbsp) milk	450 g (1 lb) courgettes, thickly sliced
125 g (4 oz) Cheddar or Cotswold cheese, grated	225 g (8 oz) button mushrooms
50 g (2 oz) butter or margarine	10 ml (2 tsp) mild paprika
salt and pepper	25 g (1 oz) plain wholemeal flour
450 g (1 lb) leeks, sliced	300 ml (½ pint) vegetable stock

1 Cook the potatoes in boiling salted water for 15-20 minutes or until tender. Drain and mash with the milk, half the cheese and half the butter or margarine. Season to taste.
2 Meanwhile, heat the remaining butter in a large saucepan and fry the leeks and pepper for 4-5 minutes, until softened. Add the courgettes, mushrooms and paprika and fry for a further 2 minutes.
3 Sprinkle in the flour, then gradually add the stock and bring to the boil, stirring continuously. Cover and simmer for 5 minutes.
4 Spoon the vegetable mixture into an ovenproof serving dish and cover evenly with the cheesy potato. Sprinkle with the remaining cheese. Bake in the oven at 200°C (400°F) mark 6 for 20-25 minutes or until the top is crisp and golden brown.

COOK'S TIP

Buy maincrop potatoes rather than new ones for this recipe. Maris Piper is particularly good for mashing, or you could use Desirée, recognisable by its red skin. Cotswold cheese, a mixture of Double Gloucester cheese and chives, gives a lovely flavour to the crispy potato topping.

CELERIAC WITH TOMATO SAUCE

SERVES 4

60 ml (4 tbsp) olive oil	5 ml (1 tsp) ground cinnamon
1 large onion, finely chopped	1 bay leaf
3 garlic cloves, crushed	salt and pepper
350 g (12 oz) ripe tomatoes, skinned and finely chopped	2 heads celeriac, total weight about 900 g (2 lb)
15 ml (1 tbsp) tomato purée	5 ml (1 tsp) lemon juice
30 ml (2 tbsp) red wine or red wine vinegar	50 g (2 oz) dried wholemeal breadcrumbs
60 ml (4 tbsp) chopped parsley	50 g (2 oz) freshly grated Parmesan cheese

1 To prepare the tomato sauce, heat the oil in a heavy-based saucepan, add the onion and garlic and fry gently for about 10 minutes until very soft and lightly coloured.
2 Add the tomatoes, tomato purée, wine, parsley, cinnamon, bay leaf and salt and pepper to taste. Add 450 ml (¾ pint) hot water and bring to the boil, stirring with a wooden spoon to break up the tomatoes.
3 Lower the heat, cover and simmer the tomato sauce, uncovered, for 30 minutes, stirring occasionally.
4 Meanwhile peel the celeriac, then cut into chunky pieces. As you prepare the celeriac, place the pieces in a bowl of water to which the lemon juice has been added, to prevent discolouration.
5 Drain the celeriac, then plunge quickly into a large pan of boiling salted water. Return to the boil and blanch for 10 minutes.
6 Drain the celeriac well, then put in an ovenproof dish. Pour over the tomato sauce, discarding the bay leaf, then sprinkle the breadcrumbs and cheese evenly over the top.
7 Bake in the oven at 190°C (375°F) mark 5 for 30 minutes, until the celeriac is tender when pierced with a skewer and the topping is golden brown. Serve hot.

COURGETTE
AND TOMATO BAKE

SERVES 4

700 g (1½ lb) courgettes	15 ml (1 tbsp) chopped fresh marjoram or 5 ml (1 tsp) dried
salt and pepper	
about 150 ml (¼ pint) oil	two 170 g (6 oz) packets Mozzarella cheese, thinly sliced
1 onion, finely chopped	
450 g (1 lb) tomatoes, skinned and chopped	75 g (3 oz) freshly grated Parmesan cheese
1 large garlic clove, crushed	parsley sprigs, to garnish
30 ml (2 tbsp) tomato purée	

1 Cut the courgettes into 5 mm (¼ inch) thick slices. Put in a colander, sprinkling each layer generously with salt, and leave for at least 20 minutes.
2 Heat 30 ml (2 tbsp) of the oil in a saucepan, add the onion and fry for about 5 minutes or until just beginning to brown.
3 Stir in the tomatoes, garlic and tomato purée and season to taste. Simmer for about 10 minutes, stirring to break down the tomatoes. Stir in the marjoram and remove from the heat.
4 Rinse the courgettes and pat dry with absorbent kitchen paper. Heat half the remaining oil in a frying pan, add half the courgettes and fry until golden brown. Drain well on absorbent kitchen paper while frying the remaining courgettes in the remaining oil.
5 Layer the courgettes, tomato sauce and Mozzarella cheese in a shallow ovenproof dish, finishing with a layer of Mozzarella. Sprinkle with the Parmesan cheese.
6 Bake in the oven at 180°C (350°F) mark 4 for about 40 minutes or until brown and bubbling. Serve hot, garnished with parsley.

CAULIFLOWER
AND COURGETTE BAKE

SERVES 4

700 g (1½ lb) cauliflower	45 ml (3 tbsp) wholemeal flour
salt and pepper	
50 g (2 oz) butter or margarine	150 ml (¼ pint) milk
	3 eggs, separated
225 g (8 oz) courgettes, thinly sliced	15 ml (1 tbsp) freshly grated Parmesan cheese

1 Divide the cauliflower into small florets, trimming off thick stalks and leaves. Cook in boiling salted water for 10-12 minutes or until tender.
2 Meanwhile, in a separate pan, melt 25 g (1 oz) of the butter, add the courgettes and cook until beginning to soften. Remove from the pan with a slotted spoon and drain on absorbent kitchen paper.
3 Melt the remaining butter in the pan, stir in the flour and cook, stirring, for 1-2 minutes. Remove from the heat and add the milk, a little at a time, whisking constantly after each addition. Return to the heat and bring to the boil, stirring. Simmer until thickened.
4 Drain the cauliflower well and place in a blender or food processor with the warm sauce, egg yolks and plenty of seasoning. Blend together until evenly mixed, then turn into a large bowl.
5 Whisk the egg whites until stiff and carefully fold into the cauliflower mixture.
6 Spoon half the mixture into a 1.6 litre (2¾ pint) soufflé dish. Arrange the courgettes on top, reserving a few for garnish, then cover with the remaining cauliflower mixture. Top with the reserved courgettes.
7 Sprinkle over the Parmesan cheese and bake in the oven at 190°C (375°F) mark 5 for 35-40 minutes or until golden. Serve immediately.

88

JERUSALEM ARTICHOKE GRATIN

SERVES 4

VEGETABLE COUSCOUS

SERVES 6

900 g (2 lb) Jerusalem artichokes	1.25 ml (¼ tsp) freshly grated nutmeg
salt and pepper	3 medium leeks, thickly sliced
squeeze of lemon juice	225 g (8 oz) fresh or frozen peas
75 g (3 oz) butter or margarine	150 ml (¼ pint) double cream
15 ml (1 tbsp) olive oil	75 g (3 oz) Gruyère cheese, grated
225 g (8 oz) button onions, skinned	75 g (3 oz) Cheddar cheese, grated
2 garlic cloves, crushed	
150 ml (¼ pint) dry white wine or vegetable stock	50 g (2 oz) dried wholemeal breadcrumbs

1 Parboil the artichokes in salted water with the lemon juice added for 10 minutes. Remove with a slotted spoon and leave to cool.
2 Peel the artichokes and slice thickly. Set aside.
3 Heat 50 g (2 oz) butter with the oil in a saucepan, add the onions and garlic and toss until well coated.
4 Pour in the wine or stock and 150 ml (¼ pint) water and bring to the boil. Add the nutmeg, cover and simmer for 10 minutes. Add the artichokes, leeks and peas and continue simmering for 5 minutes or until tender. Transfer the vegetables to a flameproof gratin dish.
5 Boil the cooking liquid rapidly until reduced by about half, then lower the heat and stir in the cream.
6 Mix the two cheeses together. Stir half into the sauce, season and stir until melted.
7 Pour the cheese sauce over the vegetables. Mix the remaining cheese and breadcrumbs, then sprinkle on top.
8 Dot with the remaining butter, then bake in the oven at 220°C (425°F) mark 7 for 10 minutes or until golden.

225 g (8 oz) chick peas, soaked in cold water overnight	4 large tomatoes, skinned and chopped
450 g (1 lb) couscous	2 garlic cloves, crushed
4 courgettes, cut into 1 cm (½ inch) slices	1.1 litres (2 pints) vegetable stock
1 red pepper, seeded and diced	salt and pepper
1 green pepper, seeded and diced	25 g (1 oz) blanched almonds
	5 ml (1 tsp) turmeric
2 onions, diced	10 ml (2 tsp) paprika
2 carrots, diced	2.5 ml (½ tsp) ground coriander
225 g (8 oz) turnips, diced	25 g (1 oz) butter, melted
1 small cauliflower, cut into small florets	125 g (4 oz) dried apricots, soaked overnight

1 Drain the chick peas, place in a saucepan and cover with cold water. Bring to the boil, lower the heat, cover and simmer for 50 minutes or until tender; drain. Meanwhile place the couscous in a large bowl with 450 ml (¾ pint) tepid water and leave to soak for 10-15 minutes until the water is absorbed.
2 Place the prepared vegetables in a large saucepan with the garlic, stock, pepper to taste, chick peas, almonds and spices. Bring to the boil.
3 Drain the couscous and place in a steamer over the vegetables. Cover and cook for 40 minutes, then remove the steamer and cover the saucepan.
4 Drain and quarter the apricots; add them to the vegetables. Add the butter to the couscous, fork well to remove any lumps, return it to the steamer over the simmering vegetables, cover and cook for 20 minutes.
5 Season the vegetables and serve with the couscous.

VEGETARIAN MEDLEY

SERVES 4

25 g (1 oz) butter or margarine	15 ml (1 tbsp) chopped fresh sage or 5 ml (1 tsp) dried
2 carrots, sliced	125 g (4 oz) lentils, cooked
1 large onion, chopped	15 ml (1 tbsp) raisins
1 green pepper, seeded and sliced	30 ml (2 tbsp) unsalted peanuts
2 tomatoes, skinned and chopped	salt and pepper
1 large cooking apple, peeled and chopped	300 ml (10 fl oz) natural yogurt
1 garlic clove, crushed	25 g (1 oz) full-fat soft cheese
	sage leaves, to garnish

1   Melt the butter in a large frying pan and lightly fry the carrots, onion, green pepper, tomatoes, apple, garlic and sage for 15 minutes, until softened.

2   Add the lentils, raisins and peanuts. Season to taste.

3   Stir the yogurt into the soft cheese and mix well to blend. Stir into the vegetable mixture. Reheat gently for 5 minutes. Serve at once, garnished with sage.

STUFFED CABBAGE ROLLS

SERVES 4

8-10 large cabbage leaves, trimmed	450 ml (¾ pint) vegetable stock
30 ml (2 tbsp) oil	400 g (14 oz) can tomatoes
2 medium onions, finely chopped	5 ml (1 tsp) Worcestershire sauce
125 g (4 oz) mushrooms, chopped	2.5 ml (½ tsp) dried basil
50 g (2 oz) long-grain brown rice	salt and pepper
	50 g (2 oz) hazelnuts, skinned and chopped

1   Blanch the cabbage leaves in boiling water for 3-4 minutes. Drain thoroughly.

2   Heat 15 ml (1 tbsp) of the oil in a frying pan and fry half the onions with the mushrooms for 5 minutes until browned. Add the rice and stir well.

3   Add 300 ml (½ pint) of the stock to the rice. Cover and cook for about 40 minutes until the rice is tender and the stock has been completely absorbed.

4   Meanwhile, make a tomato sauce. Heat the remaining oil in a pan and fry the remaining onion for about 5 minutes until golden. Add the tomatoes, remaining stock, Worcestershire sauce, basil and salt and pepper to taste. Bring to the boil, stirring, and simmer for 8 minutes. Purée in a blender or food processor until smooth.

5   Stir the hazelnuts into the rice with salt and pepper to taste, then remove from the heat. Divide the rice mixture between the cabbage leaves and roll up to make neat parcels.

6   Arrange the cabbage parcels in an ovenproof dish. Pour over the tomato sauce. Cover and cook in the oven at 180°C (350°F) mark 4 for about 1 hour until tender.

STUFFED PEPPERS WITH PINE NUTS

SERVES 6

3 green peppers	125 g (4 oz) mushrooms, sliced
3 red peppers	salt and pepper
50 g (2 oz) butter or margarine	75 g (3 oz) pine nuts or flaked almonds, roasted and chopped
1 onion, finely chopped	
125 g (4 oz) long-grain rice	10 ml (2 tsp) soy sauce
450 ml (¾ pint) vegetable stock	30 ml (2 tbsp) oil
15 ml (1 tbsp) tomato purée	

1 Cut a 2.5 cm (1 inch) lid from the stem end of the peppers. Scoop out the seeds and membrane. Blanch the shells and lids in boiling water for about 2 minutes. Drain and cool.

2 Melt the butter in a saucepan and gently fry the onion for 5 minutes until softened. Stir in the rice and cook for 1-2 minutes.

3 Add the stock, tomato purée and mushrooms. Bring to the boil and simmer for 13-15 minutes until the rice is tender and all the stock absorbed.

4 Season well and stir in the nuts and soy sauce. Use this mixture to fill the peppers.

5 Replace lids, then place the peppers in a deep oven-proof dish and pour over the oil. Cover and cook in the oven at 190°C (375°F) mark 5 for 30 minutes until tender.

SERVING SUGGESTION

With their filling of rice, mushrooms and nuts, these stuffed peppers are substantial enough to serve on their own. Alternatively, serve with wholemeal or garlic bread.

CHEESY STUFFED AUBERGINES

SERVES 4

2 medium aubergines	15 ml (1 tbsp) tomato purée
salt and pepper	125 g (4 oz) long-grain rice
75 ml (5 tbsp) olive oil	50 g (2 oz) chopped mixed nuts
1 onion, finely chopped	
1-2 garlic cloves, crushed	30 ml (2 tbsp) chopped parsley
1 red or green pepper, seeded and finely diced	125 g (4 oz) Cheddar cheese, grated
175 g (6 oz) button mushrooms, finely chopped	75 g (3 oz) fresh wholemeal breadcrumbs
4 ripe tomatoes, skinned and finely chopped	

1 Slice the aubergines in half lengthways. Scoop out and reserve the flesh, leaving a shell inside the skin so that the aubergines will hold their shape.

2 Sprinkle the insides of the aubergine shells with salt and stand upside down to drain for 30 minutes.

3 Dice the aubergine flesh, then place in a colander, sprinkling each layer with salt. Cover with a plate, place heavy weights on top and leave to dégorge for 30 minutes.

4 Meanwhile, heat 60 ml (4 tbsp) oil in a heavy-based pan. Add the onion and garlic; fry gently for 5 minutes until soft. Add the pepper and fry gently for 5 minutes.

5 Rinse the diced aubergine under cold running water, then pat dry with absorbent kitchen paper. Add to the pan with mushrooms, tomatoes and tomato purée. Simmer for 5 minutes, then add the rice, nuts, parsley and seasoning.

6 Rinse the aubergine cases and pat dry with absorbent kitchen paper. Brush a baking dish with the remaining oil, then stand the aubergine cases in the dish. Fill with the stuffing mixture.

7 Mix the grated cheese and breadcrumbs together, then sprinkle evenly on top of the aubergines. Bake uncovered in the oven at 180°C (350°F) mark 4 for 45 minutes. Serve hot, with extra boiled rice, and Tomato Sauce (page 171).

IMAM BAYILDI

SERVES 6

6 small aubergines	60 ml (4 tbsp) chopped parsley
salt and pepper	3.75 ml (¾ tsp) ground allspice
200 ml (7 fl oz) olive oil	5 ml (1 tsp) sugar
450 g (1 lb) onions, finely sliced	30 ml (2 tbsp) lemon juice
3 garlic cloves, crushed	chopped parsley, to garnish
400 g (14 oz) can tomatoes, drained or 450 g (1 lb) tomatoes, skinned and chopped	

1   Halve the aubergines lengthways. Scoop out the flesh and reserve, leaving a substantial shell.
2   Sprinkle the insides of the aubergine shells with salt and put upside-down on a plate. Leave for 30 minutes to drain away the juices.
3   Heat 45 ml (3 tbsp) olive oil in a saucepan, add the onions and garlic and fry gently for about 15 minutes or until soft but not coloured. Add the tomatoes, reserved aubergine flesh, parsley and allspice. Season with salt and pepper. Simmer gently for about 20 minutes or until the mixture has reduced.
4   Rinse the aubergines and pat dry with absorbent kitchen paper. Spoon the filling into each half and place them side by side in a shallow ovenproof dish. They should fit quite closely together.
5   Mix the remaining oil with 150 ml (¼ pint) water, the sugar and lemon juice. Season with salt and pepper. Pour around the aubergines, cover and bake in the oven at 150°C (300°F) mark 2 for about 1 hour or until tender. Serve warm or chilled, garnished with parsley.

SERVING SUGGESTION

This traditional Turkish dish is usually served cold, but it could be served warm if you prefer. Serve with crusty bread or toasted pitta bread, and perhaps a salad.

SOUTHERN BAKED BEANS

SERVES 4

275 g (10 oz) dried haricot beans, soaked in cold water overnight	15 ml (1 tbsp) mustard powder
15 ml (1 tbsp) oil	30 ml (2 tbsp) treacle
2 onions, chopped	300 ml (½ pint) tomato juice
225 g (8 oz) carrots, chopped	45 ml (3 tbsp) tomato purée
	300 ml (½ pint) beer
	salt and pepper

1   Drain the beans and place in a saucepan of water. Bring to the boil and simmer for 25 minutes, then drain.
2   Meanwhile heat the oil in a flameproof casserole and fry the onions and carrots for 5 minutes until light golden.
3   Remove from the heat, add the mustard, treacle, tomato juice and purée, beer and beans. Stir well.
4   Bring to the boil, cover and cook in the oven at 140°C (275°F) mark 1 for about 5 hours, stirring occasionally, until the beans are tender and the sauce is the consistency of syrup. Season with salt and pepper to taste.

VARIATION

Use pinto or black-eyed beans instead of haricot beans.

TOFU AND VEGETABLES IN A SPICY SAUCE

SERVES 4

75 g (3 oz) creamed coconut	2.5 ml (½ tsp) chilli powder
225 g (8 oz) firm or pressed tofu	30 ml (2 tbsp) soy sauce
oil for deep-frying, plus 45 ml (3 tbsp)	4 carrots, cut into matchstick strips
6 spring onions, trimmed and finely chopped	225 g (8 oz) cauliflower florets, separated into small sprigs
2.5 cm (1 inch) piece fresh root ginger, peeled and finely chopped	175 g (6 oz) French beans, topped and tailed
1 garlic clove, crushed	175 g (6 oz) beansprouts
2.5 ml (½ tsp) turmeric	salt and pepper

1 To make the coconut milk, cut the creamed coconut into small pieces and place in a measuring jug. Pour in boiling water to the 900 ml (1½ pint) mark. Stir until dissolved, then strain through a muslin-lined sieve. Set aside.

2 Drain the tofu and cut into cubes. Pat thoroughly dry with absorbent kitchen paper. Heat the oil to 190°C (375°F) in a wok or deep-fat fryer. Deep-fry the cubes of tofu in the hot oil until golden brown on all sides, turning them frequently with a slotted spoon. Remove and drain on absorbent kitchen paper.

3 Heat the 45 ml (3 tbsp) oil in a heavy-based saucepan or flameproof casserole. Add the spring onions, ginger and garlic and fry gently for about 5 minutes until softened.

4 Add the turmeric and chilli powder and stir fry for 1-2 minutes, then add the coconut milk and soy sauce and bring to the boil, stirring all the time. Add the carrots and simmer, uncovered, for 10 minutes.

5 Add the cauliflower and French beans. Simmer for a further 5 minutes, then add the tofu and beansprouts and heat through. Season to taste, then turn into a warmed serving dish. Serve immediately, with rice or noodles.

SPICED CHICK PEAS WITH TOMATOES

SERVES 4

225 g (8 oz) dried chick peas, soaked in cold water over-night, or two 425 g (15 oz) cans chick peas, drained	15 ml (1 tbsp) ground cumin
4 garlic cloves, crushed	15 ml (1 tbsp) ground coriander
60 ml (4 tbsp) oil	5 ml (1 tsp) garam masala
2 onions, finely chopped	4 tomatoes, roughly chopped
2 small green chillies, seeded and finely chopped	30 ml (2 tbsp) chopped coriander
5 ml (1 tsp) turmeric	15 ml (1 tbsp) chopped mint
5 ml (1 tsp) paprika	salt and pepper
	chopped mint or parsley, to garnish

1 Drain the dried chick peas if using, and place in a large saucepan with half of the garlic. Cover with plenty of water, bring to the boil, cover and simmer for 2-3 hours until tender. Drain well and set aside.

2 Heat the oil in a heavy-based saucepan or flameproof casserole, add the remaining garlic and the onions and fry gently for about 5 minutes until soft and lightly coloured. Add the chillies, turmeric, paprika, cumin, coriander and garam masala and fry, stirring, for a further 1-2 minutes.

3 Add the tomatoes, coriander and mint and cook, stirring, for 5-10 minutes until reduced to a pulp.

4 Add the cooked or canned chick peas and stir well. Simmer gently for another 5 minutes or until the chick peas are heated through. Add salt and pepper to taste, then turn into a warmed serving dish. Sprinkle with chopped mint or parsley. Serve hot.

SPICED LENTIL CROQUETTES

SERVES 4

225 g (8 oz) moong dal	salt
5 ml (1 tsp) caraway seeds, crushed	about 60 ml (4 tbsp) ghee or oil
2.5 ml (½ tsp) chilli powder	300 ml (½ pint) natural yogurt
5 ml (1 tsp) garam masala	30 ml (2 tbsp) chopped mint
2.5 ml (½ tsp) turmeric	pepper

1 Pick over the dal and remove any grit or discoloured pulses. Rinse and drain well.
2 Put the dal in a bowl and cover with cold water. Leave to soak for 24 hours.
3 Drain the dal, then work in batches in a food processor until ground to a fine paste. Add the spices and 2.5 ml (½ tsp) salt and work again until thoroughly mixed in.
4 Heat a little ghee in a heavy-based frying pan until smoking hot. Add spoonfuls of the croquette mixture and fry for 2-3 minutes on each side until lightly coloured.
5 Remove the croquettes with a slotted spoon, then drain well on absorbent kitchen paper while frying the remainder. Add more ghee to the pan as necessary.
6 Put the yogurt in a blender or food processor with the mint and salt and pepper to taste. Work to a thin sauce.
7 Put the hot lentil cakes in a shallow serving dish and pour over the yogurt sauce. Cover the dish and chill for at least 2 hours before serving. Serve chilled.

COOK'S TIP

The moong dal in these croquettes is not cooked before being ground to a paste. For this reason it is absolutely essential to soak the dal for the full 24 hours or it will not be soft enough to grind.

DAL WITH AUBERGINE AND MUSHROOMS

SERVES 6-8

350 g (12 oz) masoor dal	45 ml (3 tbsp) oil
5 ml (1 tsp) turmeric	5 ml (1 tsp) cumin seeds
2 garlic cloves, crushed	5 ml (1 tsp) black mustard seeds
1 aubergine	2.5 ml (½ tsp) fennel seeds
225 g (8 oz) mushrooms, halved	5 ml (1 tsp) garam masala
5-10 ml (1-2 tsp) salt	chopped coriander, to garnish
2.5 ml (½ tsp) sugar	

1 Pick over the dal and remove any grit or discoloured pulses. Put into a sieve and wash thoroughly under cold running water. Drain well.
2 Put the dal in a large saucepan with the turmeric and garlic. Cover with 1.4 litres (2½ pints) water. Bring to the boil and simmer for about 25 minutes.
3 Meanwhile, wash the aubergine and pat dry with absorbent kitchen paper. Cut into 2.5 cm (1 inch) cubes.
4 Add the aubergine and mushrooms to the dal with the salt and sugar. Continue simmering gently for 15-20 minutes until all the vegetables are tender.
5 Heat the oil in a separate small saucepan, add the remaining spices and fry for 1 minute or until the mustard seeds begin to pop.
6 Stir the spice mixture into the dal, cover pan tightly with the lid and remove from the heat. Leave to stand for 5 minutes, for the flavours to develop. Turn into a warmed serving dish and garnish with coriander. Serve hot.

COOK'S TIP

The Indian word *dal* means pulse. There are hundreds of different kinds used in Indian cookery – go to an Indian specialist store or health food shop for the best choice. They are all extremely nutritious, with a high vitamin content.

MIXED VEGETABLE CURRY

SERVES 3-4

900 g (2 lb) mixed vegetables (eg potatoes, cauliflower, okra, carrots, beans, peas)	2 onions, sliced
60 ml (4 tbsp) oil	2.5 ml (½ tsp) turmeric
15 ml (1 tbsp) mustard seeds	salt
5 ml (1 tsp) ground cumin	2 tomatoes, skinned and chopped
2.5 ml (½ tsp) ground fenugreek	juice of ½ lemon

1 Cut the vegetables into similar-sized pieces. Blanch the vegetables in boiling water: potatoes for 10 minutes; cauliflower, okra and carrots for 3 minutes; beans and peas for 2 minutes. Drain and set aside.

2 Heat the oil in a flameproof casserole and add the mustard seeds, cumin and fenugreek. Cover the casserole and fry gently for 2-3 minutes, shaking the casserole constantly so that the spices do not scorch.

3 Add the onions and turmeric to the spices and fry gently for 5 minutes until the onions soften.

4 Add the vegetables to the pan with salt to taste and moisten with a few spoonfuls of water. Cover the casserole and cook gently for about 5 minutes, stirring occasionally, until the vegetables are tender but still crisp.

5 Add the tomatoes and lemon juice and taste and adjust seasoning. Cook for 1 minute more and then turn into a warmed serving dish. Serve hot, with boiled rice and a bowl of yogurt and grated cucumber, if liked.

THREE BEAN VEGETABLE CURRY

SERVES 6

125 g (4 oz) dried red kidney beans	30 ml (2 tbsp) plain wholemeal flour
125 g (4 oz) dried soya beans	10 ml (2 tsp) sugar
125 g (4 oz) dried black beans	20 ml (4 tsp) ground coriander
700 g (1½ lb) cauliflower	10 ml (2 tsp) ground cumin
1 medium onion	5 ml (1 tsp) turmeric
½ green pepper, seeded	2.5 ml (½ tsp) chilli powder
450 g (1 lb) courgettes	15 ml (1 tbsp) tomato purée
30 ml (2 tbsp) oil	900 ml (1½ pints) vegetable stock
125 g (4 oz) button mushrooms	salt and pepper
1 small piece fresh root ginger, crushed	

1 Soak the beans separately in cold water overnight. Next day, drain beans and rinse well under cold running water. Put the kidney beans in a large saucepan, cover with plenty of cold water and bring slowly to the boil.

2 Skim off any scum with a slotted spoon, then boil rapidly for 10 minutes. Add the soya beans, half cover the pan with a lid and simmer for 30 minutes. Add the black beans and continue cooking for 1 hour, until tender.

3 Meanwhile, divide cauliflower into small florets. Slice onion and green pepper thinly. Slice courgettes thickly.

4 Heat the oil in a large saucepan, add the onion and pepper and fry gently for 5-10 minutes until lightly browned. Stir in the mushrooms and courgettes and cook for a further 5 minutes.

5 Stir in the ginger, flour, sugar, coriander, cumin, turmeric, chilli powder and tomato purée. Cook, stirring, for 1-2 minutes, then blend in the stock.

6 Drain beans and add to pan with the cauliflower and salt and pepper to taste. Cover and simmer for 20 minutes until the vegetables are tender. Serve hot.

CHANNA DAL WITH GINGER

SERVES 4

225 g (8 oz) channa dal	1 garlic clove, crushed
25 g (1 oz) fresh root ginger	10 ml (2 tsp) turmeric
15 ml (1 tbsp) black peppercorns	about 1 litre (1¾ pints) vegetable stock
60 ml (4 tbsp) ghee or oil	salt
1 onion, chopped	

1 Pick over the dal and remove any grit or discoloured pulses. Rinse and drain well.

2 Peel the root ginger and chop the flesh finely. Crush the peppercorns with a pestle and mortar.

3 Heat the ghee in a heavy-based saucepan or flameproof casserole, add the onion and fry gently for about 5 minutes until soft and lightly coloured. Stir in the ginger, garlic, turmeric, peppercorns and dal. Stir over gentle heat for 2-3 minutes.

4 Add the stock and bring to the boil. Cover and simmer for about 1 hour, stirring frequently, until the dal is tender but still quite mushy in consistency. Add salt to taste before serving.

SERVING SUGGESTION

Serve with any rice dish, Sag Aloo (page 138), natural yogurt and a selection of pickles and relishes.

MOONG DAL AND SPINACH

SERVES 6

225 g (8 oz) moong dal (split, washed moong beans)	1 garlic clove, crushed
900 g (2 lb) fresh spinach washed and trimmed, or 450 g (1 lb) frozen chopped spinach	10 ml (2 tsp) ground coriander
	5 ml (1 tsp) ground turmeric
45 ml (3 tbsp) oil	2.5 ml (½ tsp) chilli powder
1 onion, finely chopped	1.25 ml (¼ tsp) asafoetida (optional)
15 g (½ oz) fresh root ginger, finely chopped	salt and pepper
	lemon wedges and parsley sprigs, to garnish

1 Rinse the dal under cold running water. Place in a bowl, cover with cold water and leave to soak for about 2 hours, then drain.

2 Place the fresh spinach in a saucepan with only the water that clings to the leaves. Cover and cook gently for about 5 minutes or until tender. Drain well and chop roughly. If using frozen spinach, place in a saucepan and cook for 7-10 minutes to thaw and to remove as much liquid as possible.

3 Heat the oil in a large sauté pan, add the onion, ginger and garlic and fry for 2-3 minutes.

4 Stir in the coriander, turmeric, chilli powder, asafoetida (if using) and the dal. Fry, stirring, for 2-3 minutes.

5 Pour in 300 ml (½ pint) water, season to taste and bring to the boil. Cover and simmer for about 15 minutes or until the dal is almost tender. Add a little more water if necessary, but the mixture should be almost dry.

6 Stir in the spinach and cook, stirring, for 2-3 minutes or until heated through. Taste and adjust the seasoning before serving, garnished with lemon wedges and parsley.

VEGETABLE BIRYANI

SERVES 4

350 g (12 oz) basmati rice	5 ml (1 tsp) turmeric
salt and pepper	2.5 ml (½ tsp) chilli powder
50 g (2 oz) ghee or clarified butter	3 carrots, thinly sliced
1 large onion, chopped	225 g (8 oz) French beans, halved
2.5 cm (1 inch) piece fresh root ginger, peeled and grated	225 g (8 oz) small cauliflower florets
1-2 garlic cloves, crushed	5 ml (1 tsp) garam masala
5 ml (1 tsp) ground coriander	juice of 1 lemon
10 ml (2 tsp) ground cumin	hard-boiled egg slices and coriander sprigs, to garnish

1 Put the rice in a sieve and rinse under cold running water until the water runs clear.

2 Put the rice in a saucepan with 600 ml (1 pint) water and 5 ml (1 tsp) salt. Bring to the boil, then reduce the heat and simmer for 10 minutes or until only just tender.

3 Meanwhile, melt the ghee in a large heavy-based saucepan, add the onion, ginger and garlic and fry gently for 5 minutes or until soft but not coloured. Add the coriander, cumin, turmeric and chilli powder and fry for 2 minutes, stirring constantly to prevent the spices burning.

4 Remove the rice from the heat and drain. Add 90 ml (1½ pints) water to the onion and spice mixture and season with salt and pepper. Stir well and bring to the boil. Add the carrots and beans and simmer for 15 minutes, then add the cauliflower and simmer for a further 10 minutes. Add the rice, fold in gently and simmer until reheated.

5 Stir the garam masala and lemon juice into the biryani and simmer for a few minutes more to reheat and allow the flavours to develop. Taste and adjust the seasoning, if necessary, then turn into a warmed serving dish. Garnish with egg slices and coriander and serve immediately, with Curry Sauce (see page 171).

MUTTAR PANEER

SERVES 3-4

275 g (10 oz) paneer	2.5 ml (½ tsp) chilli powder
oil, for frying	350 g (12 oz) shelled fresh or frozen peas
2 onions, roughly chopped	4 small tomatoes, skinned and finely chopped
2.5 cm (1 inch) piece fresh root ginger, peeled and roughly chopped	125 ml (4 fl oz) vegetable stock
1 garlic clove, crushed	salt
5 ml (1 tsp) turmeric	30 ml (2 tbsp) chopped coriander
5 ml (1 tsp) garam masala	

1 Cut the paneer into small cubes. Heat a little oil in a deep, heavy-based frying pan until very hot.

2 Add the cubes of paneer to the oil and fry until golden on all sides, turning once. Remove from the oil and drain on absorbent kitchen paper.

3 Pour off all but about 60 ml (4 tbsp) of the oil. Add the onions, ginger and garlic and fry gently, stirring frequently, for 10 minutes. Add the turmeric, garam masala and chilli powder and fry for a further 2 minutes.

4 Add the peas and tomatoes to the pan and stir to combine with the spiced onion mixture. Add the stock, season with salt, then cover tightly and simmer gently for 15 minutes or until the peas are tender.

5 Add the paneer and chopped coriander. Shake the pan gently to mix the cheese with the peas. Simmer for a further 5 minutes before serving, accompanied by Indian bread and a dal dish.

COOK'S TIP

Paneer is an Indian curd cheese, available from specialist Asian food stores.

MACARONI PIE

SERVES 6

125 g (4 oz) butter or margarine	75 g (3 oz) plain wholemeal flour
30 ml (2 tbsp) olive oil	600 ml (1 pint) milk
1 small onion, finely chopped	75 g (3 oz) Gruyère cheese, grated
2 garlic cloves, crushed	1.25 ml (¼ tsp) freshly grated nutmeg
400 g (14 oz) can tomatoes	
5 ml (1 tsp) chopped basil or 2.5 ml (½ tsp) dried	60 ml (4 tbsp) freshly grated Parmesan cheese
salt and pepper	45 ml (3 tbsp) dried wholemeal breadcrumbs
225 g (8 oz) large wholewheat macaroni	

1 To make the tomato sauce, melt 50 g (2 oz) of the butter in a heavy-based saucepan with the olive oil. Add the onion and garlic and fry gently for 5 minutes until soft but not coloured.
2 Add the tomatoes and their juices with the basil and salt and pepper to taste, then stir with a wooden spoon to break up the tomatoes. Bring to the boil, then lower the heat and simmer for 10 minutes, stirring occasionally.
3 Meanwhile, cook the macaroni in a large pan of boiling salted water for 10 minutes or until just tender.
4 For the cheese sauce, melt the remaining butter in a saucepan, add the flour and cook stirring, for 2 minutes. Remove from the heat and gradually blend in the milk, stirring after each addition. Bring to the boil slowly, stirring all the time until the sauce thickens. Add the Gruyère, nutmeg and salt and pepper to taste; stir until melted.
5 Drain the macaroni and mix with the tomato sauce. Arrange half of this mixture in a large greased ovenproof dish. Pour over half of the cheese sauce. Repeat the layers, then sprinkle evenly with the Parmesan cheese and breadcrumbs.
6 Bake in the oven at 190°C (375°F) mark 5 for 15 minutes, then brown under a preheated grill. Serve hot.

WHOLEWHEAT MACARONI BAKE

SERVES 4-6

175 g (6 oz) wholewheat macaroni	5 ml (1 tsp) dried mixed herbs
salt and pepper	5 ml (1 tsp) dried oregano
30 ml (2 tbsp) oil	30 ml (2 tbsp) plain wholemeal flour
1 onion, chopped	300 ml (½ pint) milk
225 g (8 oz) button mushrooms	125 g (4 oz) cream cheese
350 g (12 oz) tomatoes, skinned and roughly chopped	1 egg, beaten
	5 ml (1 tsp) English mustard powder
300 ml (½ pint) vegetable stock	30 ml (2 tbsp) wholemeal breadcrumbs
15 ml (1 tbsp) tomato purée	30 ml (2 tbsp) freshly grated Parmesan cheese

1 Cook the macaroni in plenty of boiling salted water for 10 minutes; drain. Heat the oil in a saucepan and fry the onion for 5 minutes.
2 Cut the small mushrooms in half and slice the larger ones. Add to the pan and cook with the onion for 1-2 minutes.
3 Add the tomatoes and stock and bring to the boil, stirring constantly. Lower the heat, add the tomato purée and herbs and season to taste. Simmer for 10 minutes.
4 Put the flour and milk in a blender and blend for 1 minute. Transfer to a pan and simmer, stirring constantly, for 5 minutes or until thick. Remove from the heat and beat in the cheese, egg and mustard. Season.
5 Mix the macaroni with the mushroom and tomato sauce, then pour into a baking dish. Pour over the cheese sauce and sprinkle with breadcrumbs and Parmesan.
6 Bake in the oven at 190°C (375°F) mark 5 for 20 minutes or until golden brown and bubbling. Serve hot.

LEEK AND
MACARONI BAKE

SERVES 4

125 g (4 oz) short-cut macaroni	600 ml (1 pint) milk
50 g (2 oz) butter or margarine	175 g (6 oz) Double Gloucester cheese with chives, grated
275 g (10 oz) leeks, roughly chopped	salt and pepper
25 g (1 oz) plain flour	25 g (1 oz) breadcrumbs
	30 ml (2 tbsp) chopped chives

1 Cook the macaroni in plenty of boiling salted water for 10 minutes or until just tender. Drain well.
2 Melt the butter in a frying pan, add the leeks and sauté for 2 minutes. Stir in the flour and cook gently for 1 minute, stirring. Remove the pan from the heat and gradually stir in the milk. Bring to the boil and continue to cook, stirring, for 2 minutes. Remove from the heat and stir in the macaroni and all but 30 ml (2 tbsp) cheese. Season to taste.
3 Spoon the mixture into a buttered 1.1 litre (2 pint) shallow ovenproof dish. Mix together the breadcrumbs, chives and remaining cheese and sprinkle evenly in lines across the dish.
4 Bake in the oven at 190°C (375°F) mark 5 for 30-35 minutes or until golden. Serve immediately.

MACARONI
AND BROCCOLI CHEESE

SERVES 2

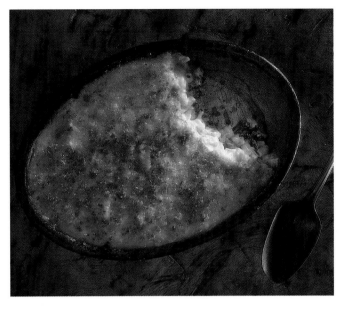

75 g (3 oz) wholewheat macaroni	300 ml (½ pint) milk
salt and pepper	75 g (3 oz) Red Leicester cheese, grated
25 g (1 oz) butter or margarine	100 g (4 oz) broccoli florets
25 g (1 oz) wholemeal plain flour	15 ml (1 tbsp) wholemeal breadcrumbs

1 Cook the macaroni in plenty of boiling salted water for 10 minutes or until just tender. Drain.
2 Put the butter or margarine, flour and milk in a saucepan. Heat, whisking continuously, until the sauce boils, thickens and is smooth. Simmer for 1-2 minutes.
3 Remove pan from the heat, add most of the cheese and stir until melted. Season to taste.
4 Blanch the broccoli in boiling water for 7 minutes or until tender. Drain well.
5 Put the broccoli in the base of a 900 ml (1½ pint) flameproof serving dish. Cover with the macaroni and cheese sauce. Sprinkle with remaining cheese and breadcrumbs. Brown under a hot grill.

COOK'S TIP

This version of ever-popular macaroni cheese uses Red Leicester cheese, wholewheat pasta, and broccoli. If you have never used wholewheat pasta before you will find the flavour is stronger and nuttier than the plain kind.

RATATOUILLE PASTA BAKE

SERVES 4-6

30 ml (2 tbsp) olive oil	30 ml (2 tbsp) chopped basil or 5 ml (1 tsp) dried
1 large onion, thinly sliced	pinch of sugar
1 red pepper, seeded and cut into strips	salt and pepper
1 yellow pepper, seeded and cut into strips	450 ml (¾ pint) vegetable stock
225 g (8 oz) courgettes, cut into strips	350 g (12 oz) mixed coloured pasta twists
450 g (1 lb) ripe tomatoes, skinned and chopped	50 g (2 oz) butter
2 garlic cloves, crushed	175 g (6 oz) mature Cheddar cheese, grated
30 ml (2 tbsp) tomato purée	

1 Heat the oil in a large pan, add the onion and peppers, and cook for 5 minutes or until softened, stirring. Add the courgettes and cook for 5 minutes.
2 Stir in the tomatoes, garlic, tomato purée, basil and sugar. Season to taste and simmer for 25-30 minutes, stirring occasionally and gradually adding the stock.
3 Meanwhile, bring a large saucepan of salted water to the boil and add the pasta twists. Cook for 10-12 minutes, until just tender. Drain, then return to the pan, add the butter, toss well and season to taste. Transfer to a deep flameproof dish.
4 Pour the ratatouille sauce over the pasta and sprinkle over the cheese. Grill until golden.

VEGETABLE LASAGNE

SERVES 6

30 ml (2 tbsp) olive oil	2 large courgettes, sliced
1 garlic clove, crushed	two 400 g (14 oz) cans chopped tomatoes
1 carrot, chopped	30 ml (2 tbsp) tomato purée
1 large onion, sliced	2 bay leaves
1 red pepper, seeded and chopped	about 350 g (12 oz) fresh lasagne or 225g (8 oz) dried
15 ml (1 tbsp) mild paprika	salt and pepper
10 ml (2 tsp) dried oregano or marjoram	900 ml (1½ pints) Béchamel Sauce (see page172)
1 large aubergine, cut into large chunks	freshly grated Parmesan cheese (optional), to finish
225g (8 oz) button mushrooms, sliced	

1 Heat the oil in a large saucepan. Add the garlic, carrot, onion and pepper and fry for 1-2 minutes or until beginning to soften. Add the paprika, herbs and aubergine and fry for a few minutes more.
2 Add the remaining vegetables to the pan with the tomatoes, tomato purée and bay leaves. Bring to the boil, then reduce the heat, cover and simmer for 30 minutes.
3 Meanwhile, if using dried lasagne that needs pre-cooking, cook it in boiling salted water according to packet instructions. Drain and leave to dry on a clean tea-towel.
4 Spread a small amount of the tomato sauce in the base of a 2.8 litre (5 pint) ovenproof dish. Cover with a layer of lasagne and top with a layer of Béchamel Sauce. Continue layering in this way, ending with a layer of Béchamel Sauce that covers the pasta completely. Sprinkle with the cheese, if using.
5 Bake the lasagne in the oven at 200°C (400°F) mark 6 for 45 minutes-1 hour or until piping hot and well browned. Serve with a crisp green salad.

SALADS

Side salads and main course salads for all seasons are featured here.
Experiment with your own combinations of salad vegetables, fruits, nuts, seeds, pasta
and pulses, too – tossed with one of the dressings on page 173.

EGG, CHICORY AND CELERY SALAD

SERVES 4-6

1 eating apple, cored and chopped	2.5 ml ($\frac{1}{2}$ tsp) prepared English mustard
1 head of celery, trimmed and sliced	2.5 ml ($\frac{1}{2}$ tsp) sugar
1 cooked beetroot, peeled and sliced	60 ml (4 tbsp) single cream
2 heads of chicory, sliced	10 ml (2 tsp) white wine vinegar
1 punnet of mustard and cress, trimmed	salt and pepper
	3 eggs, hard-boiled and cut into wedges

1 Lightly mix the apple, celery, beetroot and chicory together with the cress in a large salad bowl.
2 To make the dressing, whisk the mustard, sugar, cream and vinegar together. Season to taste. Pour over the salad and toss together so that everything is coated in the dressing. Add the eggs, then serve at once.

CRUNCHY WINTER SALAD

SERVES 4

2 eating apples	1 small onion, finely sliced
finely grated rind and juice of $\frac{1}{2}$ lemon	2 celery sticks, sliced
45 ml (3 tbsp) oil	125 g (4 oz) Cheddar cheese, diced
150 ml ($\frac{1}{4}$ pint) natural yogurt	125 g (4 oz) natural unsalted peanuts
salt and pepper	grapefruit segments and celery leaves, to garnish
225 g (8 oz) red cabbage, finely sliced	

1 Quarter and core the apples, then cut into chunks. Toss in 30 ml (2 tbsp) of the lemon juice.
2 To make the dressing, in a bowl, whisk the remaining lemon juice with the rind, oil, yogurt and salt and pepper to taste until well emulsified.
3 Put the cabbage, onion, celery, apple, cheese and peanuts in a large bowl, pour over the dressing and toss well. Garnish with grapefruit segments and celery leaves.

COLESLAW WITH CHEESE AND BRAZIL NUTS

SERVES 6

225 g (8 oz) hard white cabbage	60 ml (4 tbsp) mayonnaise
175 g (6 oz) shelled Brazil nuts	juice of 1 lemon
225 g (8 oz) Edam or Gouda cheese, grated	30 ml (2 tbsp) oil
	30 ml (2 tbsp) chopped parsley
2 large carrots, peeled and grated	2.5-5 ml ($\frac{1}{2}$-1 tsp) caraway seeds, according to taste
60 ml (4 tbsp) natural yogurt	salt and pepper

1   Shred the cabbage finely with a sharp knife or grater. Place in a bowl. Chop the nuts roughly. Add the nuts to the cabbage, reserving 30 ml (2 tbsp) for the garnish. Add two thirds of the cheese to the bowl with the carrots.

2   In a separate bowl, mix the yogurt with the mayonnaise, lemon juice, oil, parsley and caraway seeds. Add salt and pepper to taste.

3   Pour the dressing over the salad ingredients, then toss well to mix. Sprinkle with the reserved nuts and the remaining cheese. Cover and chill in the refrigerator for 30 minutes. Taste and adjust seasoning before serving.

INDONESIAN SALAD

SERVES 4

1 small pineapple	30 ml (2 tbsp) crunchy peanut butter
$\frac{1}{2}$ cucumber	
175 g (6 oz) young carrots, peeled	20 ml (4 tsp) soy sauce
	60 ml (4 tbsp) olive oil
1 crisp green eating apple	juice of $\frac{1}{2}$ lemon
125 g (4 oz) beansprouts	salt and pepper

1   Cut the top and bottom off the pineapple. Stand the fruit upright on a board. Using a large, sharp knife, slice downwards in sections to remove the skin and 'eyes' of the fruit. Slice off the pineapple flesh, leaving the core, then discard the core.

2   Cut the pineapple flesh into small cubes, then cut the cucumber and carrots lengthways into thin matchstick shapes. Quarter and core the apple (but do not peel), then chop roughly. Combine all the fruit and vegetables together in a bowl with the beansprouts.

3   To make the dressing, put the peanut butter in a bowl, then gradually whisk in the remaining ingredients with a fork. Season.

4   Pour the dressing over the salad and toss well to mix. Cover and leave to stand for 30 minutes before serving.

CHEESE, BEANSPROUT AND PINEAPPLE SALAD

SERVES 4

225 g (8 oz) carrots, peeled	275 g (10 oz) beansprouts
225 g (8 oz) Edam cheese	10 ml (2 tsp) wine vinegar
227 g (8 oz) can pineapple slices in natural juice	salt and pepper

1 Cut the carrots into 2.5 cm (1 inch) matchstick thin strips. Coarsely grate the cheese.
2 Drain the pineapple, reserving the juice. Cut the pineapple into thin strips.
3 In a large bowl, mix together the beansprouts, carrot, cheese and pineapple.
4 To make the dressing, whisk the pineapple juice and vinegar together with seasoning to taste.
5 Just before serving, pour the dressing over the salad and toss well to mix.

VARIATION

Replace the cheese with the same quantity of tofu – cut into cubes. Tofu is available from the chilled cabinet of health food stores and large supermarkets.

BEAN, CHEESE AND AVOCADO SALAD

SERVES 4

425 g (15 oz) can red kidney beans, drained	1 small onion, finely chopped
90 ml (6 tbsp) olive oil	2 celery sticks, finely chopped
finely grated rind and juice of 1 lemon	2 tomatoes, skinned and chopped
1.25 ml (¼ tsp) Tabasco sauce	1 ripe avocado
salt and pepper	celery leaves, to garnish
175 g (6 oz) Edam cheese, diced	

1 Rinse the kidney beans, drain well and put in a bowl. Add the oil, lemon rind and juice, Tabasco and seasoning. Toss well.
2 Add the cheese, onion, celery and tomatoes to the beans and toss again to mix the ingredients together. Cover and chill in the refrigerator until required.
3 When ready to serve, peel the avocado, cut in half and remove the stone. Chop the flesh into chunky pieces. Fold the avocado pieces gently into the bean salad and taste and adjust seasoning. Garnish with celery leaves and serve.

ORIENTAL SALAD

SERVES 8

1 large cucumber	30 ml (2 tbsp) soy sauce
salt and pepper	15 ml (1 tbsp) peanut butter
1 small head Chinese leaves	30 ml (2 tbsp) sesame oil
1 red pepper	30 ml (2 tbsp) rice or wine vinegar
125 g (4 oz) button mushrooms	50 g (2 oz) shelled unsalted peanuts
225 g (8 oz) beansprouts	

1 Cut the cucumber in half lengthways and scoop out the seeds. Cut the halves into 5 cm (2 inch) sticks, leaving the skin on.

2 Shred the Chinese leaves. Halve the red pepper and remove the core and seeds; cut the flesh into thin strips. Wipe and slice the mushrooms. Trim the beansprouts.

3 Just before serving, mix the soy sauce in a large bowl with the peanut butter, oil, vinegar and salt and pepper to taste. Add the salad ingredients and the peanuts and toss together. Transfer to a serving bowl.

COOK'S TIP

Chinese leaves are an extremely versatile vegetable and can be lightly braised, steamed or served raw in salads. Look for Chinese leaves also under the name of Chinese cabbage or Chinese celery cabbage; it has long white stems and should not be confused with a similar-looking vegetable called 'bok choy', which has dark green stems.

GADO-GADO

SERVES 4

oil, for shallow-frying	8 small waxy new potatoes
125 g (4 oz) unsalted peanuts	4 small young carrots
1 small onion, very finely chopped	125 g (4 oz) cauliflower florets
2 garlic cloves, crushed	125 g (4 oz) green cabbage or spring greens
2.5-5 ml (½-1 tsp) chilli powder	125 g (4 oz) French beans
5 ml (1 tsp) sugar	125 g (4 oz) beansprouts
juice of 1 lemon	lettuce leaves, cucumber slices and hard-boiled egg, to garnish
25 g (1 oz) creamed coconut, roughly chopped (optional)	

1 To make the peanut sauce, heat the oil in a wok and fry the peanuts for about 5 minutes until well browned. Remove with a slotted spoon; drain on absorbent kitchen paper.

2 Pour off all but 30 ml (2 tbsp) of the oil, add the onion and garlic to the wok and fry for 5 minutes until soft.

3 Add the chilli powder and stir-fry for 1-2 minutes, then add 350 ml (12 fl oz) water, the sugar, lemon juice and creamed coconut, if using. Bring to the boil.

4 Grind the peanuts in a food processor. Add to the sauce and simmer, stirring, until thickened; set aside.

5 Scrub the potatoes. Slice the carrots thinly. Divide the cauliflower into small sprigs. Shred the cabbage leaves. Top and tail the French beans.

6 Boil the potatoes in salted water for about 20 minutes until tender; remove. Add the carrots to the water and parboil for 4 minutes; remove. Blanch the cauliflower and beans in the water for 3 minutes; remove. Blanch the cabbage and beansprouts for 1 minute only, then drain. Skin the potatoes, then slice into rings.

7 Line a large shallow serving dish or platter with lettuce leaves. Arrange the vegetables on top, then garnish with the slices of cucumber and hard-boiled egg. Serve immediately, with the peanut sauce handed separately.

GOAT'S CHEESE WITH PEAR AND WALNUTS

SERVES 2

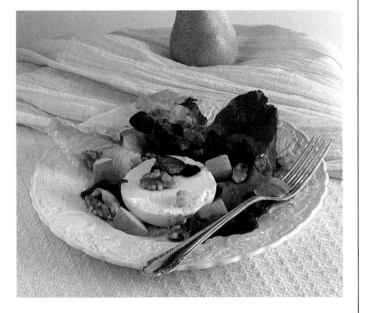

few salad leaves, such as Webb's lettuce and radicchio, torn into pieces	50 g (2 oz) walnuts, chopped
125 g (4 oz) goat's cheese, halved into 2 discs	½ bunch watercress
	30 ml (2 tbsp) lemon juice
2 ripe pears, cored and cut into chunks	45 ml (3 tbsp) oil

1 Arrange the salad leaves on two serving plates and top with the goat's cheese. Mix together the pears, walnuts and watercress.
2 Blend the lemon juice and oil together, add to the pear mixture and toss to coat. Spoon on to the cheese to serve.

VARIATION

If you prefer not to use goat's cheese, Caerphilly makes a delicious substitute, as do other white cheeses, such as Lancashire, Wensleydale or white Stilton.

VEGETABLE SALAMAGUNDY

SERVES 8

50 g (2 oz) green lentils	1 yellow pepper, seeded and cut into strips
1 bay leaf	½ small head of celery, trimmed and sliced
salt and pepper	
225 g (8 oz) French beans, trimmed	50 g (2 oz) lamb's lettuce, trimmed
225 g (8 oz) mangetout, trimmed	1 small onion, thinly sliced
225 g (8 oz) beef tomatoes, sliced	2 Cox's apples, sliced
	few black olives
225 g (8 oz) cherry tomatoes	120 ml (4 fl oz) Vinaigrette Dressing (see page 173)

1 Cook the lentils in boiling salted water with the bay leaf, until just tender. Drain and leave to cool. Blanch the beans and mangetout in boiling salted water for 2 minutes. Drain, rinse under cold running water and drain.
2 Arrange all the ingredients on one or two large platters in a symmetrical pattern. Sprinkle with the dressing to serve.

COOK'S TIP

Salamagundy is an old English supper dish which dates back to the eighteenth century. It originally contained a varied mixture of meats. Here we make the most of fresh colourful vegetables. Use others in season if you prefer. Add hard-boiled quail's eggs, or nuts, if liked.

GREEK SALAD

SERVES 4

½ large cucumber	125 g (4 oz) feta cheese, cut into cubes
salt and pepper	
450 g (1 lb) firm ripe tomatoes	60 ml (4 tbsp) olive oil
	15 ml (1 tbsp) lemon juice
1 medium red onion	good pinch of dried oregano
18 black olives	

1 Peel the cucumber and slice thinly. Put into a colander or sieve, sprinkle with a little salt and leave to stand for about 15 minutes.
2 Slice the tomatoes thinly. Slice the onion into thin rings. Rinse the cucumber under cold running water, drain and pat dry with absorbent kitchen paper.
3 Arrange the cucumber, tomatoes and onion in a serving dish. Scatter the olives and cubed cheese over the top.
4 In a bowl, whisk together the oil, lemon juice, oregano and salt and pepper to taste. Spoon the dressing over the salad. Serve with warm pitta bread.

GRAPE, WATERCRESS AND STILTON SALAD

SERVES 4-6

175 g (6 oz) black grapes	5 ml (1 tsp) poppy seeds
1 bunch of watercress	pinch of sugar
45 ml (3 tbsp) oil	salt and pepper
15 ml (1 tbsp) lemon juice	225 g (8 oz) Stilton cheese

1 Halve the grapes and remove the pips. Place in a bowl, cover and chill in the refrigerator. Trim the watercress of any tough stalks.
2 In a jug, whisk together the oil, lemon juice, poppy seeds, sugar and salt and pepper to taste.
3 Cut the Stilton into 2 cm (¾ inch) cubes. Toss well in the prepared dressing to coat completely. Cover and chill for 1 hour.
4 To serve, toss together the grapes, watercress, Stilton and dressing. Serve immediately.

PEASANT SALAD

SERVES 8

700 g (1½ lb) potatoes	1 yellow pepper, seeded and chopped
salt	chopped parsley
3 eggs	2 courgettes, very thinly sliced
450 g (1 lb) asparagus, trimmed	50 g (2 oz) green or black olives
1 avocado	45 ml (3 tbsp) capers
2 small red onions, halved and thinly sliced	45 ml (3 tbsp) mayonnaise
1 red pepper, seeded and chopped	1 quantity Mustard and Parsley Dressing (see page 173)

1 Cook the potatoes in boiling salted water for about 15 minutes or until tender. Cook the eggs in boiling water for about 10 minutes or until hard-boiled. Drain, cover with cold water and leave to cool.

2 Stand the asparagus, tied in a bundle, tips upwards, in about 5 cm (2 inches) of simmering salted water in a saucepan. Cover the tips with a tent of foil and cook for 5-8 minutes depending on the thickness of the asparagus; the stems cook in the simmering water, while the delicate tips are gently steamed. Drain thoroughly.

3 Drain the potatoes. Leave to cool slightly, then peel off the skins, if preferred. Cut the potatoes into large chunks. Cut off the asparagus tips and reserve; chop the stems into 2.5 cm (1 inch) pieces. Shell the eggs and cut into wedges. Peel and stone the avocado, and cut the flesh into chunks.

4 Mix all the ingredients together in a serving bowl. Whisk the mayonnaise into the dressing and pour over the salad. Toss together and serve immediately.

SERVING SUGGESTION

This hearty, colourful salad makes a meal in itself.

GRILLED VEGETABLE SALAD

SERVES 4-6

	FOR THE DRESSING
1 red pepper	10 ml (2 tsp) balsamic or garlic vinegar
1 green pepper	5 ml (1 tsp) thin honey
350 g (12 oz) courgettes	5 ml (1 tsp) Dijon mustard
6 whole garlic cloves	75 ml (5 tbsp) olive oil
1 bunch of asparagus	salt and pepper
olive oil, for brushing	
few cherry tomatoes	
chopped herbs, eg marjoram, basil, parsley and chives	

1 Halve the peppers and remove the seeds and cores. Cut each half into four. Thickly slice the courgettes on the diagonal. Remove the loose, papery outer skins from the garlic cloves, but leave the inner skins attached.

2 Pour enough water into a saucepan to come to a depth of about 5 cm (2 inches) and bring to the boil. When the water is boiling fast, add the peppers and the garlic. Bring back to the boil and boil for 1 minute.

3 Remove the peppers with a slotted spoon (leaving the garlic in the water), refresh under cold running water and leave to drain. Repeat this process with the courgettes, using the same water. Remove garlic from the pan; drain.

4 Steam the asparagus until just tender. Drain, arrange on a serving plate and leave to cool. Brush the blanched peppers, courgettes and garlic with a little olive oil and cook under a hot grill until flecked with brown. Turn them over, brush with more oil and cook the second side. Let cool, then arrange on the serving plate with the asparagus. Halve the tomatoes and scatter over the vegetables.

5 To make the dressing, put the vinegar, honey and mustard in a small bowl, and whisk together with a fork until well blended. Gradually whisk in the olive oil to make a very thick dressing. Season with salt and pepper.

6 Just before serving, drizzle the dressing over the vegetables and sprinkle with herbs.

CELERIAC AND BEAN SALAD

SERVES 4-6

225 g (8 oz) dried flageolet beans, soaked in cold water overnight	15 ml (1 tbsp) wholegrain mustard
1 large green pepper	1 garlic clove, crushed
finely grated rind and juice of 1 lemon	45 ml (3 tbsp) chopped parsley
60 ml (4 tbsp) oil	salt and pepper
	225 g (8 oz) celeriac

1 Drain the soaked beans and rinse well under cold running water. Put the beans in a large saucepan and cover with plenty of fresh cold water. Bring slowly to the boil, then skim off any scum with a slotted spoon. Half cover the pan with a lid and simmer gently for about 1 hour, or until the beans are just tender.

2 Meanwhile, halve the pepper and remove the core and seeds. Cut the flesh into cubes.

3 In a bowl, whisk together the grated lemon rind, about 30 ml (2 tbsp) lemon juice, the oil, mustard, garlic, parsley and salt and pepper to taste.

4 Just before the beans are ready, peel the celeriac and chop roughly into 2.5 cm (1 inch) cubes. Blanch in boiling salted water for 5 minutes. Drain well.

5 Drain the beans well and place in a bowl. Add the celeriac and toss all the salad ingredients together while the beans and celeriac are still hot. Leave to cool for 20 minutes, then cover and chill in the refrigerator for at least 1 hour before serving.

WINTER CABBAGE AND CAULIFLOWER SALAD

SERVES 4

225 g (8 oz) hard white cabbage	90 ml (6 tbsp) mayonnaise
225 g (8 oz) cauliflower florets	90 ml (6 tbsp) natural yogurt
2 large carrots	10 ml (2 tsp) French mustard
75 g (3 oz) mixed shelled nuts, roughly chopped	30 ml (2 tbsp) oil
50 g (2 oz) raisins	juice of ½ lemon
60 ml (4 tbsp) chopped parsley or coriander	salt and pepper
	3 red-skinned eating apples

1 Shred the cabbage finely with a sharp knife and place in a large bowl. Divide the cauliflower florets into small sprigs and add to the cabbage. Mix the vegetables gently with your hands.

2 Grate the carrots into the bowl, then add the nuts, raisins and parsley. Mix the vegetables together again until evenly combined.

3 Put the remaining ingredients except the apples in a jug. Whisk well to combine, then pour over the vegetables in the bowl and toss well.

4 Core and chop the apples, but do not peel them. Add to the salad and toss again to combine with the other ingredients. Cover the bowl and chill the salad in the refrigerator for about 1 hour before serving.

RED CABBAGE
AND APPLE SALAD

SERVES 8

½ red cabbage, about 900 g (2 lb), finely shredded	120 ml (4 fl oz) oil
3 dessert apples, peeled, cored and sliced	60 ml (4 tbsp) cider vinegar
	60 ml (4 tbsp) natural yogurt
1 small garlic clove, crushed	salt and pepper

1 Blanch the cabbage for 2-3 minutes in boiling salted water; do not over-blanch as it will lose its crisp texture. Drain and cool.
2 Combine the apples with the cabbage in a bowl. Put the rest of the ingredients in a screw-top jar; shake well. Pour at once over the cabbage and toss to mix.
3 Cover the salad and refrigerate overnight. Toss again to mix well before serving.

VARIATION

Add 50 g (2 oz) crumbled Danish Blue cheese to the salad with the dressing.

WALDORF
SALAD

SERVES 4

450 g (1 lb) eating apples	½ head celery, trimmed and sliced
juice of 1 lemon	
2.5 ml (½ tsp) sugar	50 g (2 oz) walnut halves
90 ml (3 fl oz) mayonnaise	lettuce leaves, to serve

1 Core the apples, but do not peel. Slice one and dice the rest. Dip the slices in some of the lemon juice to prevent discolouration.
2 In a large bowl, toss the diced apples in 30 ml (2 tbsp) lemon juice, the sugar and 15 ml (1 tbsp) mayonnaise. Leave to stand for about 30 minutes.
3 Just before serving, add the sliced celery, chopped walnuts and the remaining mayonnaise, and toss together.
4 Serve the salad in a bowl lined with lettuce leaves and garnish with the apple slices.

LEMONY BEAN SALAD

SERVES 4

125 g (4 oz) dried flageolet beans, soaked in cold water overnight	50 g (2 oz) black olives
90 ml (6 tbsp) olive oil	30 ml (2 tbsp) chopped mixed fresh herbs, eg basil, marjoram, lemon balm, chives
finely grated rind and juice of 1 lemon	4 large firm tomatoes
1-2 garlic cloves, crushed	about 1.25 ml (¼ tsp) sugar
salt and pepper	lemon slices, to garnish

1 Drain and rinse the beans, then place in a saucepan with plenty of water. Bring to the boil, then lower the heat, half cover with a lid and simmer for about 1 hour until tender.

2 Drain the beans, transfer to a bowl and immediately add the oil, lemon rind and juice, garlic and salt and pepper to taste. Stir well to mix, then cover and leave for at least 4 hours to allow the dressing to flavour the beans.

3 Stone the olives, then chop roughly. Add to the salad with the herbs.

4 To skin the tomatoes, put them in a bowl, pour over boiling water and leave for 2 minutes. Drain, then plunge into a bowl of cold water. Remove the tomatoes one at a time and peel off the skin with your fingers.

5 Slice the tomatoes thinly, then arrange on 4 serving plates. Sprinkle with the sugar and salt and pepper to taste. Pile the bean salad on top of each plate. Serve chilled, garnished with lemon slices.

CAULIFLOWER, BEAN AND CAPER SALAD

SERVES 4

175 g (6 oz) dried red kidney beans, soaked in cold water overnight	salt and pepper
1 small onion, finely chopped	225 g (8 oz) cauliflower
1-2 garlic cloves, crushed	60 ml (4 tbsp) natural yogurt
45 ml (3 tbsp) olive oil	60 ml (4 tbsp) mayonnaise
15 ml (1 tbsp) red wine vinegar	30 ml (2 tbsp) roughly chopped capers
5 ml (1 tsp) French mustard	30 ml (2 tbsp) chopped parsley

1 Drain and rinse the kidney beans, then place in a saucepan with plenty of water. Bring to the boil and boil rapidly for 10 minutes. Lower the heat, half cover with a lid and simmer for 1½ hours or until the beans are tender.

2 Drain the beans, transfer to a bowl and immediately add the onion, garlic, olive oil, vinegar, mustard and salt and pepper to taste. Stir well to mix, then cover and leave for at least 4 hours to allow the dressing to flavour the beans.

3 Divide the cauliflower into small sprigs, cutting away all tough stalks. Wash the florets thoroughly under cold running water, then blanch in boiling water for 1 minute only. Drain thoroughly.

4 Add the cauliflower florets to the bean salad with the yogurt, mayonnaise, capers and parsley. Mix well and chill in the refrigerator for about 30 minutes before serving.

THREE BEAN SALAD

SERVES 4-6

75 g (3 oz) dried red kidney beans, soaked in cold water overnight	100 ml (4 fl oz) Vinaigrette Dressing (see page 173)
75 g (3 oz) dried black-eyed beans, soaked in cold water overnight	15 ml (1 tbsp) chopped coriander
	1 small onion, sliced into rings
75 g (3 oz) dried pinto or borlotti beans, soaked in cold water overnight	salt and pepper
	coriander sprig, to garnish

1 Drain the beans and put in a saucepan of water. Bring to the boil and boil rapidly for 10 minutes, then boil gently for 1½ hours until tender.
2 Drain the cooked beans thoroughly and place them in a large salad bowl.
3 Combine the vinaigrette dressing and coriander, and pour over the beans while they are still warm.
4 Toss thoroughly and cool for 30 minutes. Mix the onion into the beans, add salt and pepper to taste and chill for 2-3 hours before serving, garnished with coriander.

FLAGEOLET AND TOMATO SALAD

SERVES 4

90 ml (6 tbsp) olive oil	4 tomatoes, skinned and chopped
30 ml (2 tbsp) lemon juice	1 small onion, finely chopped
30 ml (2 tbsp) mayonnaise	2 garlic cloves, finely chopped
45 ml (3 tbsp) chopped mixed fresh herbs, eg parsley, chervil, chives, marjoram, basil	TO SERVE
	lettuce leaves
salt and pepper	snipped chives and lemon twists, to garnish
400 g (14 oz) can flageolet beans	

1 Put the olive oil, lemon juice, mayonnaise, herbs and seasoning in a bowl and whisk until thick.
2 Rinse the beans under cold running water. Drain and add to the dressing with the tomatoes, onion and garlic.
3 Toss well, cover and chill for 30 minutes. Serve on individual plates lined with lettuce leaves. Garnish with chives and lemon twists.

TABOULEH

SERVES 6-8

225 g (8 oz) bulgar wheat	finely grated rind and juice of 1½ lemons
4 spring onions	salt and pepper
1 large bunch parsley, total weight about 125 g (4 oz)	few vine leaves or Cos lettuce leaves
3 large mint sprigs	lemon wedges and mint sprigs, to garnish
60 ml (4 tbsp) olive oil	

1 Put the bulgar wheat in a bowl and add cold water to cover by about 2.5 cm (1 inch). Soak for 30 minutes. Drain well in a sieve, then spread it out on a tea-towel and leave to dry.
2 Meanwhile finely chop the spring onions. Using a blender or food processor, chop the parsley and mint.
3 Mix the bulgar wheat, spring onions, parsley and mint together in a bowl, add the olive oil, lemon rind and juice and salt and pepper to taste.
4 To serve, place the salad on a serving dish lined with lettuce or vine leaves. Garnish with lemon wedges and mint sprigs.

COOK'S TIP

Bulgar wheat is available at health food stops. It is wholewheat grain which has been boiled and baked then cracked. It does not need cooking, simply soaking in cold water for 30 minutes until the grains swell.

WHOLEWHEAT, APRICOT AND NUT SALAD

SERVES 6-8

225 g (8 oz) wholewheat grain, soaked in cold water overnight	50 g (2 oz) unsalted peanuts
3 celery sticks	60 ml (4 tbsp) olive oil
125 g (4 oz) dried apricots	30 ml (2 tbsp) lemon juice
125 g (4 oz) Brazil nuts, roughly chopped	salt and pepper
	coriander and cucumber slices, to garnish

1 Drain the wholewheat grain, then tip into a large saucepan of boiling water. Simmer gently for 25 minutes or until the grains are cooked but have a little bite left.
2 Drain the wholewheat in a colander and rinse under cold running water. Tip into a large serving bowl and set aside.
3 Cut the celery into small diagonal pieces with a sharp knife. Stir into the wholewheat.
4 Using kitchen scissors, snip the apricots into small pieces over the wholewheat. Add the nuts and stir well to mix.
5 Mix the oil and lemon juice together with salt and pepper to taste. Pour over the salad and toss well. Chill in the refrigerator for 2 hours. Toss again just before serving, garnished with coriander and cucumber.

COOK'S TIP

You can buy the wholewheat grain for this recipe in any good health food shop. Sometimes it is referred to as 'kibbled' wheat, because the grains are cracked in a machine called a 'kibbler', which breaks the grain into little pieces. Do not confuse wholewheat grain with bulgar wheat (sometimes also called bulghar or burghul), which is cooked wheat which has been dried and cracked, used extensively in the cooking of the Middle East. Although different, the two kinds of wheat can be used interchangeably in most recipes.

WHOLEWHEAT BRAZIL SALAD

SERVES 4-6

75 g (3 oz) dried black-eyed beans, soaked in cold water overnight	½ cucumber, diced
125 g (4 oz) wholewheat grain, soaked in cold water overnight	225 g (8 oz) tomatoes, skinned and roughly chopped
90 ml (6 tbsp) natural yogurt	125 g (4 oz) Cheddar cheese, grated
30 ml (2 tbsp) olive oil	125 g (4 oz) Brazil nuts, roughly chopped
45 ml (3 tbsp) lemon juice	lettuce leaves, to serve
45 ml (3 tbsp) chopped mint	mint sprigs, to garnish
salt and pepper	

1 Drain the beans and place in a saucepan of water. Bring to the boil and simmer gently for 1½ hours or until tender.
2 Meanwhile, drain the wholewheat and place in a saucepan of water. Bring to the boil and simmer gently for 20-25 minutes or until tender. Drain, rinse well with cold water and cool for 30 minutes. When the beans are cooked, drain and cool for 30 minutes.
3 Whisk the yogurt and olive oil together with the lemon juice, mint and seasoning to taste.
4 Put the wholewheat, beans, cucumber, tomatoes, cheese and Brazil nuts in a bowl. Pour over the dressing and mix well.
5 Line a salad bowl with lettuce leaves and pile the wholewheat salad on top. Garnish with mint and chill before serving.

AVOCADO, LEMON AND OMELETTE SALAD

SERVES 4-6

4 eggs	5 ml (1 tsp) coriander seeds
50 g (2 oz) Cheddar cheese, grated	90 ml (6 tbsp) olive or sunflower oil
salt and pepper	45 ml (3 tbsp) lemon juice
25 g (1 oz) butter or margarine	2 ripe avocados
5 ml (1 tsp) black peppercorns	parsley sprigs, to garnish

1 Put the eggs in a bowl with the cheese and 15 ml (1 tbsp) water. Season with salt and pepper to taste and whisk together.
2 Melt a quarter of the butter in an omelette pan or small non-stick frying pan. When foaming, pour in a quarter of the egg mixture. After a few seconds, push the set egg mixture into the centre of the pan and tilt the pan to allow the egg to run to the edges. Cook until just set.
3 Brown the omelette under a preheated hot grill. Turn out on to a plate. Repeat with the remaining egg mixture to make another three omelettes.
4 While the omelettes are still warm, roll them up loosely. Wrap in greaseproof paper and leave to cool.
5 Meanwhile, crush the peppercorns and coriander seeds coarsely with a pestle and mortar, or with the end of a rolling pin in a strong bowl.
6 Whisk together the oil, lemon juice and crushed spices and season to taste. Halve, stone and peel the avocados, then slice thickly into the dressing. Toss gently to coat.
7 Slice the rolled omelettes thinly. Arrange the omelette rings and avocado slices in individual serving plates. Spoon over the dressing and garnish with sprigs of parsley. Serve immediately.

MOZZARELLA, AVOCADO AND TOMATO SALAD

SERVES 4

2 ripe avocados	4 medium tomatoes, thinly sliced
120 ml (8 tbsp) Vinaigrette Dressing (see page 173)	chopped parsley and mint sprigs, to garnish
175 g (6 oz) Mozzarella cheese, thinly sliced	

1 Halve the avocados lengthways and carefully remove the stones. Then peel and cut the avocados into slices.
2 Pour the dressing over the avocado slices. Stir to coat the slices thoroughly and prevent discolouration.
3 Arrange slices of Mozzarella, tomato and avocado on 4 individual serving plates. Spoon over the dressing and garnish with chopped parsley and a sprig of mint.

COOK'S TIP

Mozzarella is an Italian curd cheese, pale-coloured and egg-shaped. When fresh it is very soft and dripping with whey. Traditionally made from water buffalo's milk, Mozzarella is now also made from cow's milk. It should be eaten fresh, as the cheese ripens quickly and is past its best in a few days. Mozzarella is now readily available from delicatessens and supermarkets and can be used in salads, pizzas etc.

SALAD ELONA

SERVES 4

½ medium cucumber	45 ml (3 tbsp) oil
salt	15 ml (1 tbsp) balsamic or wine vinegar
225 g (8 oz) ripe strawberries	few lettuce leaves, to serve
10 ml (2 tsp) green peppercorns in brine	

1 Score the skin of the cucumber lengthways with a canelle knife or the prongs of a fork. Slice the cucumber very thinly, then place on a plate and sprinkle with salt. Leave to stand for about 30 minutes to draw out the excess moisture.
2 Meanwhile, prepare the strawberries. Reserve a few small ones for garnish. Hull the remaining strawberries, and slice in half lengthways.
3 Drain the peppercorns and pat dry with absorbent kitchen paper. Crush them with the back of a metal spoon in a small bowl. Add the oil and vinegar and whisk with a fork until well combined.
4 Rinse and drain the cucumber, pat dry with absorbent kitchen paper. Shred the lettuce, then arrange on serving plates. Arrange the cucumber slices and halved strawberries on the lettuce, alternating rings of each. Sprinkle over the dressing, then garnish the centre with the reserved whole strawberries. Serve as soon as possible.

COOK'S TIP

The combination of sweet and sour in this salad is unusual, but most refreshing. Do not use malt vinegar as it is too strong. Wine vinegar can be used, but if you are able to buy balsamic vinegar from a good delicatessen, it is perfect. It is also excellent in dressings for green salads.

CHERRY TOMATO AND BEAN SALAD

SERVES 8

225 g (8 oz) broad beans (shelled weight)	30 ml (2 tbsp) lemon juice
salt and pepper	45 ml (3 tbsp) chopped basil
225 g (8 oz) French beans, topped and tailed	125 g (4 oz) Mozzarella cheese, diced
150 ml (¼ pint) olive oil	700 g (1½ lb) cherry tomatoes, halved
1 garlic clove, crushed	basil leaves, to garnish
30 ml (2 tbsp) dry white wine	

1 Cook the broad beans in boiling salted water for about 3 minutes. Drain and remove the skins, if wished. Cook the French beans in boiling water for 7-10 minutes. Drain.
2 Place the oil, garlic, wine and lemon juice in a food processor and blend to an emulsion; alternatively shake in a screw-topped jar to mix. Stir in the chopped basil and seasoning.
3 Mix together the beans, Mozzarella and tomatoes. Pour over the dressing and stir to coat completely. Cover and leave to marinate for at least 1 hour. Garnish with basil leaves, to serve.

COOK'S TIP

Broad beans are better if skinned. You could use frozen broad beans or a 400 g (14 oz) can of lima beans, if preferred.

ROCKET, TOMATO AND SNAP PEA SALAD

SERVES 8

350 g (12 oz) sugar snap peas, topped and tailed	15 ml (1 tbsp) cider vinegar or lemon juice
225 g (8 oz) rocket (roquette)	5 ml (1 tsp) wholegrain mustard
450 g (1 lb) cherry tomatoes	salt and pepper
FOR THE DRESSING	pinch of sugar
60 ml (4 tbsp) olive and sunflower oil, mixed	

1 Bring a pan of salted water to the boil and add the sugar snap peas. Boil for 4 minutes, then drain and refresh in cold water to stop the cooking process and keep the colour. Pat dry on absorbent kitchen paper.
2 Mix the sugar snap peas, rocket and tomatoes together, halving the cherry tomatoes, if liked.
3 Whisk all the dressing ingredients together and pour over the salad, tossing to coat. Serve immediately.

COOK'S TIP

A crisp and colourful salad to freshen the palate! If you can't find rocket - a peppery salad leaf much loved in Italy - use watercress for a similar flavour.

TOMATO, AVOCADO AND PASTA SALAD

SERVES 4

175 g (6 oz) small wholemeal pasta shells	2 ripe avocados
salt and pepper	2 red onions
105 ml (7 tbsp) olive oil	16 black olives
45 ml (3 tbsp) lemon juice	225 g (8 oz) ripe cherry tomatoes, if available, or small salad tomatoes
5 ml (1 tsp) wholegrain mustard	basil leaves, to garnish
30 ml (2 tbsp) chopped basil	

1 Cook the pasta in plenty of boiling salted water for about 12-15 minutes until just tender. Drain in a colander and rinse under cold running water to stop the pasta cooking further. Cool for 20 minutes.

2 Meanwhile, whisk the oil in a bowl with the lemon juice, mustard, chopped basil and salt and pepper to taste.

3 Halve and stone the avocados then peel off the skins. Chop the avocado flesh into large pieces and fold gently into the dressing.

4 Slice the onions thinly into rings. Stone the olives. Halve the tomatoes and mix them with the onion rings, the olives and the cold pasta shells.

5 Spoon the pasta and tomato on to 4 individual serving plates. Spoon over the avocado and dressing and garnish with basil leaves. Serve immediately.

TOMATO AND OKRA VINAIGRETTE

SERVES 8

450 g (1 lb) okra	pinch of sugar
150 ml (¼ pint) oil	salt and pepper
30 ml (2 tbsp) lemon juice	450 g (1 lb) tomatoes, skinned
5 ml (1 tsp) tomato purée	

1 Trim off the tops and tails of the okra. Cook in boiling salted water for about 4 minutes or until just tender. Drain well and place in a bowl.

2 In a jug, whisk together the oil, lemon juice, tomato purée, sugar and salt and pepper to taste. Pour over the warm okra and fold gently to mix.

3 Slice the tomatoes thinly. Arrange in a serving bowl with the okra and vinaigrette. Cover and chill for at least 30 minutes before serving.

MARINATED MUSHROOM SALAD

SERVES 4

90 ml (6 tbsp) olive oil	225 g (8 oz) firm button mushrooms
30 ml (2 tbsp) lemon juice	30 ml (2 tbsp) chopped parsley, to garnish
salt and pepper	

1 First make the dressing. In a medium bowl, mix together the olive oil, lemon juice and salt and pepper to taste.
2 Slice the mushrooms finely, then add to the dressing and mix well to coat evenly. Cover and leave to stand in a cool place for at least 2 hours.
3 To serve, arrange on individual plates and garnish with the chopped parsley.

SPINACH AND MUSHROOM SALAD

SERVES 6

225 g (8 oz) fresh spinach, washed and trimmed	1 garlic clove, crushed (optional)
2 large slices of wholemeal bread	90 ml (6 tbsp) sunflower oil
2 oranges	30 ml (2 tbsp) lemon juice
10 ml (2 tsp) wholegrain mustard	salt and pepper
	2 avocados
	225 g (8 oz) button mushrooms, sliced

1 Tear the spinach leaves into small pieces and place in a bowl. Set aside.
2 To make the 'croûtons', cut the crusts off the slices of bread, then cut the bread into 5 mm (¼ inch) cubes or into shapes with a small cutter. Toast until evenly browned.
3 Peel the oranges using a serrated knife, cutting away all the skin and pith. Cut the oranges into segments, removing the membrane. Discard any pips.
4 Whisk together the mustard, garlic, sunflower oil, lemon juice and seasoning to taste until well emulsified.
5 Halve the avocados and remove the stones. Peel the avocados and chop the flesh into even-sized chunks.
6 Place the oranges, avocados and mushrooms on top of the spinach and pour over the dressing. Mix carefully and sprinkle with the croûtons. Serve immediately.

BEETROOT
SALAD WITH MINT

SERVES 4-6

120 ml (8 tbsp) chopped mint	5 ml (1 tsp) sugar
700 g (1½ lb) cooked beetroot	salt and pepper
150 ml (¼ pint) malt vinegar	2 onions, finely sliced into rings

1 Put 90 ml (6 tbsp) of the mint in a bowl and pour over 150 ml (¼ pint) boiling water. Leave to stand for 2-3 minutes.

2 Peel the beetroot and slice thinly. Place in a large shallow dish. Add the vinegar and sugar to the mint and water, with salt and pepper to taste. Pour over the beetroot. Cover and chill for 2-3 hours or overnight.

3 To serve, place alternate layers of beetroot and onion in a serving dish. Pour over the mint dressing and garnish with the remaining chopped mint. Serve chilled.

CUCUMBER
SALAD

SERVES 4

1 large cucumber	2.5 ml (½ tsp) dried dill
salt and pepper	150 ml (¼ pint) soured cream
45 ml (3 tbsp) white wine vinegar	150 ml (¼ pint) thick-set natural yogurt
25 g (1 oz) sugar	30 ml (2 tbsp) snipped chives

1 Using a cannelle knife or vegetable peeler, peel lengthways strips off the cucumber. Slice the cucumber thinly into rings.

2 Put the cucumber slices in a colander, sprinkling each layer liberally with salt. Cover with a plate, then leave for 30 minutes.

3 Meanwhile make the dressing. Put the vinegar, 45 ml (3 tbsp) water, and the sugar in a saucepan and heat gently. Boil for 1 minute, remove from the heat and leave to cool.

4 Rinse the cucumber slices quickly under cold running water, then pat dry; place in a bowl. Stir the dill into the dressing with plenty of pepper, then pour over the cucumber. Cover and chill for 4 hours or overnight, turning the slices occasionally.

5 Mix the soured cream and yogurt with the chives; season to taste. Arrange the cucumber on a serving plate; spoon the dressing in the centre. Serve chilled.

FENNEL AND CUCUMBER SALAD

SERVES 4

½ or 1 small cucumber	15 ml (1 tbsp) chopped mint
2 small fennel bulbs	pinch of sugar
90 ml (6 tbsp) olive oil	salt and pepper
30 ml (2 tbsp) lemon juice	sliced large radishes or tomatoes, to serve
1 garlic clove, crushed	

1 Peel the cucumber and halve lengthways. Scoop out the seeds and discard. Dice the flesh.

2 Trim the fennel, reserving a few feathery tops for the garnish. Grate the fennel into a bowl, add the diced cucumber and mix together.

3 Whisk together the oil, lemon juice, garlic, mint, sugar and salt and pepper to taste. Pour over the fennel and cucumber and toss lightly.

4 Line a shallow serving dish with radish or tomato slices then pile the salad in the centre. Garnish with the reserved fennel tops.

VARIATION

Add 1 bunch of watercress, trimmed and divided into sprigs.

FENNEL AND TOMATO SALAD

SERVES 6

90 ml (6 tbsp) oil, or half oil and half walnut oil	12 black olives, halved and stoned
45 ml (3 tbsp) lemon juice	450 g (1 lb) Florence fennel
salt and pepper	450 g (1 lb) ripe tomatoes

1 In a bowl, whisk together the oil(s), lemon juice and salt and pepper to taste. Add the olives to the dressing.

2 Snip off the feathery ends of the fennel and refrigerate them in a polythene bag until required.

3 Halve each bulb of fennel lengthways, then slice thinly crossways, discarding the roots. Blanch in boiling water for 2-3 minutes, then drain. While still warm, stir into the dressing.

4 Leave to cool, cover and refrigerate until required. Meanwhile skin and slice the tomatoes and refrigerate, covered.

5 Just before serving, arrange the tomatoes and fennel mixture on individual serving plates and snip the fennel tops over them.

VARIATION

To make a simple tomato salad, thinly slice really ripe tomatoes. Arrange in a large shallow dish, sprinkle with olive oil and a little raspberry or white wine vinegar, salt, pepper and chopped basil, chervil or tarragon.

FENNEL
A LA GRECQUE

SERVES 4

90 ml (6 tbsp) olive or sunflower oil	10 ml (2 tsp) tomato purée
1 large onion, finely chopped	1 bay leaf
1 garlic clove, finely chopped	5 ml (1 tsp) coriander seeds, crushed
150 ml (¼ pint) dry white wine	5 ml (1 tsp) sugar
4 ripe tomatoes, skinned and chopped	2.5 ml (½ tsp) chopped basil
	salt and pepper
juice of ½ lemon	2 medium bulbs of fennel

1 Heat the oil in a large saucepan, add the onion and garlic and fry gently for about 10 minutes or until they are soft but not coloured.

2 Add the wine, tomatoes, lemon juice, tomato purée, bay leaf, crushed coriander, sugar, basil and salt and pepper to taste. Bring to the boil, stirring, then cover and simmer for 20 minutes.

3 Meanwhile, trim off any green feathery tops from the fennel and set aside for the garnish.

4 Halve the bulbs of fennel, and slice them thinly.

5 Bring a large saucepan of salted water to the boil, add the fennel and blanch for 5 minutes. Drain the fennel well, add to the tomato sauce, cover and simmer gently for about 30 minutes.

6 Leave to cool for 30 minutes, then cover and chill in the refrigerator for at least 1 hour.

7 Before serving, chop the reserved fennel tops finely. Taste and adjust the seasoning of the tomato sauce. Turn into a serving dish and garnish with the chopped fennel. Serve chilled.

RADICCHIO
AND ALFALFA SALAD

SERVES 4-6

2 heads of radicchio	15 ml (1 tbsp) single cream (optional)
50-75 g (2-3 oz) alfalfa sprouts	1 small garlic clove, crushed
90 ml (6 tbsp) olive or sunflower oil	1.25 ml (¼ tsp) sugar
30 ml (2 tbsp) white wine vinegar	salt and pepper

1 Tear the radicchio into bite-sized pieces. Mix the alfalfa and radicchio together in a serving bowl.

2 In a jug, whisk together the oil, vinegar, cream if using, garlic and sugar, with salt and pepper to taste. Just before serving, pour the dressing over the radicchio and alfalfa and toss together.

SERVING SUGGESTION

Serve as a side salad whenever a colourful and crunchy accompaniment is required, or serve with a selection of cheeses and granary bread for a nutritious lunch.

ENDIVE, AVOCADO AND PEANUT SALAD

SERVES 4

½ small head curly endive, separated into sprigs	45 ml (3 tbsp) orange juice
2 oranges, peeled and segmented	15 ml (1 tbsp) olive oil
	salt and pepper
30 ml (2 tbsp) natural roasted peanuts	1 garlic clove, crushed
	15 ml (1 tbsp) chopped mint
¼ cucumber, halved, seeded and chopped	1 ripe avocado

1 Put the endive into a serving bowl and add the orange segments, peanuts and cucumber.
2 To make the dressing, mix the orange juice, olive oil, seasoning, garlic and mint together in another bowl.
3 Halve the avocado and remove the stone, peel and cut into thin slices. Toss gently in the dressing, then add with the dressing to the salad. Toss lightly together and serve.

COOK'S TIP

The peanuts and avocado provide a range of amino acids, making this salad a good source of protein.

SUMMER HERB SALAD

SERVES 8

few large handfuls of mixed herb leaves, eg Good King Henry, rocket, sorrel, lamb's lettuce, dandelion, salad burnet	15 ml (1 tbsp) dry mustard
	10 ml (2 tsp) clear honey
	60 ml (4 tbsp) lemon juice
handful of chervil sprigs	2.5 ml (½ tsp) paprika
handful of parsley sprigs	60 ml (4 tbsp) sunflower oil
	30 ml (2 tbsp) walnut oil
few herb flowers – sweet violet, marigold (if available)	salt and pepper

1 Wash and dry the leaves carefully. Shred them roughly with the hands and place them in a bowl with the chervil and parsley sprigs. Sprinkle the herb flowers over the top.
2 Blend the mustard powder with the honey until smooth. Add the lemon juice, paprika, sunflower and walnut oils and seasoning, and mix well.
3 Pour the dressing over the salad and toss lightly about 10 minutes before serving.

COOK'S TIP

Fresh herbs will last for several days provided they're kept cool, wrapped in a polythene bag. If they're really sad, stand the stems in a jug of water, tie a polythene bag over the whole thing and leave for an hour or two; most herbs will revive their spirits.

BEANSPROUT AND SESAME SALAD

SERVES 8

	FOR THE DRESSING
175 g (6 oz) beansprouts	90 ml (6 tbsp) oil
125 g (4 oz) mooli (daikon), cut into matchsticks	1 large garlic clove, crushed
½ onion, thinly sliced lengthways	15 ml (1 tbsp) finely chopped fresh root ginger
6 spring onions, cut into thin slivers	30 ml (2 tbsp) dry white wine
1 red or green pepper, seeded and thinly sliced	30 ml (2 tbsp) malt vinegar
4 celery sticks, cut into thin matchsticks	5 ml (1 tsp) caster sugar
	5 ml (1 tsp) hot mustard
125 g (4 oz) button mushrooms, sliced	2.5 ml (½ tsp) sesame oil
2 bamboo shoots, cut into matchsticks	30 ml (2 tbsp) toasted sesame seeds

1 Soak the beansprouts in cold water for 10 minutes, then drain and dry on absorbent kitchen paper. Put into a large bowl. Add the remaining prepared vegetables and mix together. Cover and chill for at least 1 hour before serving.
2 To prepare the dressing, place all the ingredients in a bowl or screw-topped jar and whisk or shake together until well blended.
3 Whisk or shake the dressing ingredients together once again until well blended and pour over the prepared vegetables. Toss the ingredients together lightly until coated in dressing. Turn the salad into a serving dish and sprinkle with the toasted sesame seeds. Serve immediately.

COOK'S TIP

The dressing improves in flavour if it is made several hours in advance.

MANGETOUT AND GREEN PEPPER SALAD

SERVES 8

350 g (12 oz) mangetouts, trimmed	grated rind and juice of 1 lemon
2 bunches spring onions, finely shredded	small pinch of caster sugar
4 green peppers, seeded and finely shredded	90 ml (3 fl oz) olive oil
	salt and coarsely ground pepper

1 Cook the mangetout in boiling salted water for 1-2 minutes or until just tender. Drain and refresh under cold water. Toss with the spring onions and peppers in a bowl.
2 Whisk together the grated rind and strained lemon juice, the sugar, olive oil and seasoning. Stir into the salad before serving.

COOK'S TIP

It's worth taking the time to shred the spring onions and peppers finely; use a very sharp knife to make it easier.

VARIATION

Replace the mangetouts with fine asparagus spears.

NEW POTATO SALAD

SERVES 8

1.4 kg (3 lb) small new potatoes, preferably Jersey Royals	150 ml (¼ pint) soured cream
	salt and pepper
300 ml (½ pint) mayonnaise	chopped herbs, eg chives or parsley

1 Clean the potatoes, but do not peel. Cut any large potatoes in half. Cook them gently in lightly salted boiling water until just tender. Drain and cool.
2 Mix the mayonnaise and cream together and season to taste with salt and pepper. Toss the potatoes in the dressing. Sprinkle with herbs to serve.

VARIATION

Flavour the dressing with 15-30 ml (1-2 tbsp) wholegrain mustard.

CHILLI POTATO SALAD

SERVES 6

900 g (2 lb) even-sized new potatoes	15 ml (1 tbsp) chilli seasoning
1 green pepper	salt and pepper
1 red pepper	1 onion, chopped
200 ml (7 fl oz) oil	30 ml (2 tbsp) sesame seeds
75 ml (5 tbsp) garlic vinegar	coriander, to garnish

1 Scrub the potatoes and boil in their skins until tender; about 20 minutes.
2 Meanwhile, halve the peppers, then remove the seeds and chop. Blanch them in boiling water for 1-2 minutes. Drain well. In a large bowl, whisk together the oil, vinegar, chilli seasoning and salt and pepper to taste.
3 Drain the potatoes well. Halve them if large, but do not peel them. While still hot, stir into the dressing with the onion and peppers. Cool, cover and chill for about 2 hours.
4 Toast the sesame seeds under the grill, leave to cool, then stir through the salad. Taste and adjust the seasoning before serving, garnished with coriander.

RICE SALAD

SERVES 4

275 g (10 oz) long-grain brown rice	90 ml (6 tbsp) corn or sunflower oil
salt and pepper	finely grated rind and juice of 1 large orange
1 head of fennel	175 g (6 oz) beansprouts
1 red pepper	few orange segments, to garnish
75 g (3 oz) cashew nuts, roughly chopped	

1 Cook the brown rice in plenty of boiling salted water for 30 minutes (or according to packet instructions), until tender but firm to the bite.
2 Meanwhile, prepare the remaining ingredients. Trim the fennel, reserving a few feathery tops for the garnish. Chop the fennel finely. Halve, core and seed the red pepper, then chop finely.
3 In a jug, whisk the oil, orange rind and juice together, with salt and pepper to taste.
4 Drain the rice thoroughly, then turn into a bowl. Add the dressing while the rice is still hot and toss well to combine. Leave to stand for about 1 hour, or until the rice is cold.
5 Add the fennel, red pepper, beansprouts and nuts to the rice and toss well to mix. Taste and adjust the seasoning. Turn the salad into a serving bowl and garnish with the reserved fennel tops and the orange segments. Serve at room temperature.

ORIENTAL RICE RING

SERVES 4

225 g (8 oz) brown rice	5 ml (1 tsp) clear honey
salt and pepper	2 carrots, finely grated
40 g (1½ oz) creamed coconut	1 red pepper, seeded and cut into thin strips
105 ml (7 tbsp) sunflower oil	75 g (3 oz) beansprouts
15 ml (1 tbsp) soy sauce	25 g (1 oz) unsalted peanuts, chopped
15 ml (1 tbsp) wine vinegar	15 ml (1 tbsp) lemon juice

1 Cook the brown rice in plenty of boiling salted water until tender: about 30 minutes or according to packet instructions.
2 Meanwhile, grate the creamed coconut into a bowl. Add 60 ml (4 tbsp) of the oil, the soy sauce, vinegar and honey and beat well to mix.
3 Drain the rice well and tip into the bowl of dressing. Stir quickly to mix, add seasoning to taste, then spoon into a lightly oiled 900 ml (1½ pint) ring mould. Press down well, cover and chill in the refrigerator for at least 4 hours, or overnight if more convenient.
4 Combine the carrots, red pepper, beansprouts and peanuts with the remaining oil and the lemon juice. Add seasoning to taste.
5 Turn the rice ring out on to a flat serving plate. Pile the salad in the centre just before serving.

SERVING SUGGESTION

This attractive salad can be served as a nutritious lunch with granary bread rolls, cheese and a green salad.

ACCOMPANIMENTS

Interesting accompaniments can transform a simple vegetarian meal into something rather special. Stir-fries and sautés, vegetables in creamy sauces, bakes, gratins and curry accompaniments are all included here.

BROCCOLI WITH ALMONDS

SERVES 4

700 g (1½ lb) broccoli florets, trimmed	25 g (1 oz) butter or margarine
salt and pepper	50 g (2 oz) flaked almonds
	juice of ½ lemon

1 Cook the broccoli in boiling salted water for about 10 minutes, until just tender.
2 Meanwhile, melt the butter in a small saucepan and cook the almonds over a gentle heat until golden brown. Stir in the lemon juice and season with pepper to taste.
3 Drain the broccoli well, then toss with the almonds. Serve at once.

COOK'S TIP

The delicious crunch of almonds makes broccoli into something quite special. Broccoli does not keep well, so buy it as fresh as possible, without any signs of yellowing. Beware of overcooking it – some crispness should be retained.

CAULIFLOWER AND POTATO BAKE

SERVES 4

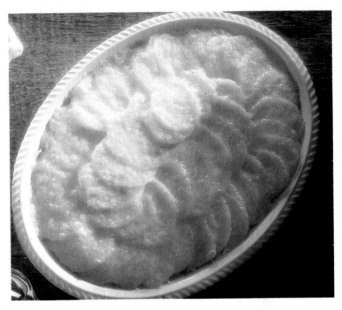

450 g (1 lb) new potatoes, thinly sliced	pinch of freshly grated nutmeg
salt and pepper	150 ml (¼ pint) milk
1 small cauliflower, broken into florets	50 g (2 oz) Cheddar cheese, grated
1 garlic clove, crushed	

1 Cook the potatoes in boiling salted water for 5 minutes. Drain well.
2 Layer the potatoes and cauliflower in a lightly oiled 1.1 litre (2 pint) ovenproof serving dish. Stir the garlic and nutmeg into the milk and pour over the potatoes and cauliflower.
3 Sprinkle with the cheese, cover and bake in the oven at 180°C (350°F) mark 4 for 45-50 minutes, until the vegetables are tender. Uncover and place under a medium grill until lightly browned. Serve at once.

COOK'S TIP

Cauliflower is available all year round and is often eaten with a sauce, as in this recipe. Freshly grated nutmeg and garlic add flavour to the sauce, which is soaked up deliciously by the potatoes.

TRIO OF VEGETABLE PUREES

SERVES 4

450 g (1 lb) carrots, roughly chopped	pinch of granulated sugar
450 g (1 lb) parsnips or turnips, roughly chopped	40 g (1½ oz) butter or margarine
salt and pepper	45 ml (3 tbsp) single or double cream
350 g (12 oz) frozen peas	1.25 ml (¼ tsp) ground coriander
few mint sprigs	good pinch of freshly grated nutmeg
5 ml (1 tsp) lemon juice	

1 Cook the carrots and parsnips or turnips in separate pans of boiling salted water for about 20 minutes or until tender. At the same time, cook the frozen peas in boiling salted water according to packet instructions, with the mint sprigs, lemon juice and sugar.

2 Drain the vegetables, keeping them separate. Put the peas and mint in a blender or food processor with one third of the butter and 15 ml (1 tbsp) of the cream. Work to a smooth purée, then add salt and pepper to taste.

3 Rinse out the machine, then add the carrots, another third of the butter, 15 ml (1 tbsp) cream and the coriander. Work to a smooth purée, then add salt and pepper to taste.

4 Repeat puréeing with the parsnips or turnips, the remaining butter and cream and the nutmeg. Add salt and pepper to taste.

5 Return all 3 purées to individual pans and reheat gently, stirring all the time. Spoon into 3 warmed serving bowls or in sections in a large bowl. Serve immediately.

AUBERGINES WITH MUSTARD AND YOGURT

SERVES 6

3 medium aubergines, total weight about 900 g (2 lb)	60 ml (4 tbsp) chopped coriander
60 ml (4 tbsp) ghee or oil	5 ml (1 tsp) salt
30 ml (2 tbsp) black mustard seeds, ground	300 ml (½ pint) natural yogurt
2.5 ml (½ tsp) chilli powder	

1 Grill the aubergines for about 15 minutes, turning occasionally, until the skins are charred and the flesh soft. Leave until just cool enough to handle, then peel off the skins and discard. Chop the flesh roughly and set aside.

2 Heat the ghee in a heavy-based frying pan. Add the ground mustard seeds, aubergine flesh and the chilli powder. Stir over moderate heat for about 5 minutes or until thoroughly hot, then add the coriander.

3 Beat the salt into the yogurt, then stir into the aubergine until evenly blended. Turn into a warmed serving dish and serve immediately.

CAULIFLOWER IN CURRY SAUCE

SERVES 4

1 large cauliflower	5 ml (1 tsp) salt
90 ml (6 tbsp) ghee or oil	5 ml (1 tsp) turmeric
5 ml (1 tsp) black mustard seeds	3 tomatoes, skinned and finely chopped
5 ml (1 tsp) cumin seeds	1 small green chilli, seeded and finely chopped
5 cm (2 inch) piece fresh root ginger, peeled and finely chopped	2.5 ml (½ tsp) sugar
1 small onion, finely chopped	30 ml (2 tbsp) chopped coriander

1 Divide the cauliflower into small florets, discarding the green leaves and tough stalks.
2 Heat the ghee in a heavy-based saucepan or flameproof casserole. Add the mustard seeds and, when they begin to pop, stir in the cumin seeds, ginger, onion, salt and turmeric. Fry for 2-3 minutes, stirring constantly.
3 Add the cauliflower and mix well to coat with the spice mixture. Stir in the tomatoes, chopped green chilli, sugar and half of the chopped coriander. Cover the pan tightly with a lid and cook gently for 15 minutes or until the cauliflower is tender but not mushy.
4 Uncover the pan and boil rapidly for 1-2 minutes to reduce and thicken the sauce. Turn into a warmed serving dish and sprinkle with the remaining chopped coriander. Serve immediately.

VARIATIONS

This curry sauce can be used for other vegetables besides cauliflower. Potatoes are one of the best vegetables to curry, and peas, okra, mushrooms, carrots and aubergines are also good. They can all be cooked in the same way as the cauliflower in this recipe, although the cooking time in step 3 will vary according to the type of vegetable used. Why not choose three or four different vegetables and make a mixed vegetable curry?

OKRA WITH ONION AND CHILLI

SERVES 4

450 g (1 lb) okra or two 425 g (15 oz) cans okra in brine, drained	1 onion, finely sliced
	2 small green chillies
45 ml (3 tbsp) ghee or oil	10 ml (2 tsp) ground cumin
	salt and pepper

1 Wash the fresh okra and trim the ends. Dry well on absorbent kitchen paper. If using canned okra, rinse, drain and dry well.
2 Heat the ghee in a large heavy-based frying pan or wok, add the onion and fry over moderate heat, stirring constantly, for about 5 minutes until turning golden.
3 Trim the ends off the green chillies and cut the flesh into fine rings. Remove as many seeds as you like, according to how hot you like the dish is to be.
4 Add the okra, chillies and cumin, with salt and pepper to taste. Continue cooking over moderate heat, stirring constantly, for about 10-15 minutes. The fresh okra should be cooked but still quite crisp and the onions a deeper brown. The canned okra will become slightly sticky. Taste and adjust the seasoning, then turn into a warmed serving dish. Serve immediately.

BROAD BEANS IN PARSLEY SAUCE

SERVES 6

1.8 kg (4 lb) broad beans, shelled	salt and pepper
50 g (2 oz) butter	2 egg yolks
75 ml (5 tbsp) flour	90 ml (6 tbsp) single cream
400 ml (¾ pint) vegetable stock	45 ml (3 tbsp) chopped parsley
	30 ml (2 tbsp) lemon juice

1   Cook the broad beans in a large pan of boiling salted water for about 15 minutes until tender. Drain and place in a vegetable dish. Keep warm, covered.

2   Meanwhile, prepare the sauce. Melt the butter in a pan, stir in the flour and cook gently for 1 minute, stirring. Remove from the heat and gradually stir in the stock.

3   Bring to the boil, and continue to cook, stirring, until the sauce thickens. Season and simmer for about 5 minutes.

4   Beat the egg yolks with the cream in a small basin, add about 90 ml (6 tbsp) hot sauce and stir until blended.

5   Remove the pan from the heat, add the egg mixture and stir well. Cook over a low heat without boiling until the sauce thickens a little more. Remove from the heat and stir in the parsley and lemon juice. Adjust seasoning and pour the sauce over the broad beans to serve.

CARROTS IN LEMON CREAM SAUCE

SERVES 4

50 g (2 oz) butter	pinch of freshly grated nutmeg
700 g (1½ lb) carrots, thinly sliced	50 g (2 oz) sultanas
juice of ½ lemon	150 ml (¼ pint) soured cream
	chopped parsley, to garnish

1   Melt the butter in a pan and add the carrots. Cover and sauté gently for about 20 minutes, until just tender, shaking the pan occasionally to prevent sticking.

2   Stir in the lemon juice, nutmeg, sultanas and soured cream, season to taste and heat through gently. Serve immediately, garnished with chopped parsley.

CARROTS WITH MINT AND LEMON

SERVES 4

700 g (1½ lb) small new carrots, trimmed and scrubbed	5 ml (1 tsp) light soft brown sugar
salt and pepper	15 g (½ oz) butter
finely grated rind and juice of ½ lemon	30 ml (2 tbsp) chopped mint

1 Cook the carrots in boiling salted water for about 10 minutes, until just tender. Drain.

2 Return the carrots to the pan with the remaining ingredients and toss together over a high heat until the butter melts. Serve at once.

COOK'S TIP

Tender young carrots, in the shops during spring and early summer, have a lovely sweet flavour which is brought out to the full by the sugar and lemon juice in this recipe. Unwashed carrots, which sometimes still have their feathery foliage, keep better than those sold washed and prepacked.

FRENCH BEANS IN SOURED CREAM

SERVES 4

700 g (1½ lb) French beans	salt and pepper
25 g (1 oz) butter or margarine	150 ml (¼ pint) vegetable stock
1 small onion, chopped	90 ml (3 fl oz) soured cream or smetana
5 ml (1 tsp) paprika	

1 Top and tail the French beans and cut them into 2.5 cm (1 inch) lengths. Melt the butter in a pan, add the onion and cook gently for 5 minutes until soft and golden, but do not brown.

2 Stir in 2.5 ml (½ tsp) paprika, the beans, seasoning and stock. Bring to the boil, cover and simmer for 5-10 minutes until the French beans are tender.

3 Stir the cream into the pan and reheat without boiling. Turn into a heated serving dish and dust the top with the remaining paprika.

CELERY
BAKED IN CREAM
SERVES 4

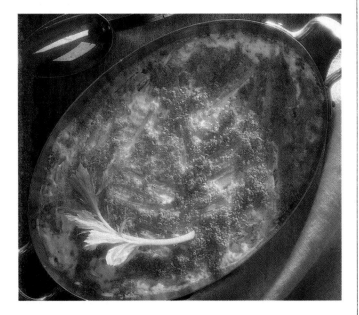

1 large head of celery	300 ml (½ pint) single cream
1.25 ml (¼ tsp) ground allspice	salt and pepper
2 garlic cloves, crushed	25 g (1 oz) fresh wholemeal breadcrumbs

1 Reserve a few celery leaves to garnish, then cut the sticks lengthways into thin strips. Cut each strip into 5 cm (2 inch) lengths and put into an ovenproof serving dish.
2 Mix the allspice, garlic and cream together and season to taste. Pour over the celery. Sprinkle with the breadcrumbs.
3 Bake in the oven at 200°C (400°F) mark 6 for about 1¼ hours or until the celery is tender. Serve hot, garnished with the reserved celery leaves.

COOK'S TIP

Both white and green celery are available and either variety can be used for this recipe.

SALSIFY
AU GRATIN
SERVES 4

450 g (1 lb) salsify	2.5 ml (½ tsp) mustard powder
300 ml (½ pint) vegetable stock	175 g (6 oz) mature Cheddar cheese, grated
25 g (1 oz) butter or margarine	salt and pepper
45 ml (3 tbsp) plain wholemeal flour	50 g (2 oz) fresh wholemeal breadcrumbs

1 Cut the salsify into 2.5 cm (1 inch) lengths and put in a saucepan with the stock. Bring to the boil, cover and simmer gently for 15-20 minutes until tender. Drain, reserving the stock, and put the salsify into an ovenproof dish.
2 Melt the butter in a saucepan, add the flour and mustard powder and cook over a low heat, stirring with a wooden spoon, for 2 minutes. Remove the pan from the heat and gradually blend in the reserved stock, stirring after each addition.
3 Bring to the boil slowly, then simmer for 2-3 minutes, stirring. Add half the cheese and salt and pepper to taste and pour over the salsify.
4 Mix the remaining cheese with the breadcrumbs and sprinkle over the dish. Bake in the oven at 190°C (375°F) mark 5 for 20-25 minutes until the top is golden brown. Serve hot.

AUBERGINE GALETTE

SERVES 4

1.4 kg (3 lb) aubergines	5 ml (1 tsp) sugar
salt and pepper	15 ml (1 tbsp) chopped basil or 5 ml (1 tsp) dried
900 g (2 lb) fresh tomatoes, skinned and quartered, or two 400 g (14 oz) cans tomatoes, drained	olive oil, for frying
	200 g (7 oz) Mozzarella cheese, thinly sliced
30 ml (2 tbsp) tomato purée	50 g (2 oz) freshly grated Parmesan cheese
1 garlic clove, crushed	
50 ml (2 fl oz) olive oil	basil sprig, to garnish

1 Slice the aubergines into 5 mm (¼ inch) slices and place in a colander or large sieve. Sprinkle with salt and set aside for 30 minutes to remove the bitter juices.

2 Meanwhile, make the tomato sauce. Put the tomatoes, tomato purée, garlic, olive oil, sugar and basil in a saucepan. Stir well and simmer gently for 20 minutes until the liquid is reduced by half. Season with salt and pepper to taste.

3 Rinse the aubergine slices thoroughly under cold running water, drain, then pat dry with absorbent kitchen paper. Heat a little olive oil in a frying pan and fry, a few at a time, adding more oil as required, until golden brown on both sides. Drain on absorbent kitchen paper.

4 Layer the aubergine slices, tomato sauce, Mozzarella cheese and half the Parmesan cheese in a greased shallow ovenproof dish, finishing with a layer of aubergine. Scatter over the remaining Parmesan and drizzle over some olive oil.

5 Bake in the oven at 180°C (350°F) mark 4 for 50-60 minutes until the cheese is golden and bubbling. Garnish with a sprig of basil.

SAUTEED AUBERGINES AND COURGETTES

SERVES 8

4 small aubergines	15 ml (1 tbsp) toasted sesame seeds
salt and pepper	
450 g (1 lb) small courgettes	oregano or marjoram sprigs, to garnish
45 ml (3 tbsp) olive oil	

1 Cut the aubergines lengthways into 2.5 cm (1 inch) slices. Cut the slices across into 1 cm (½ inch) wide fingers. Put the aubergines in a colander and sprinkle generously with salt. Leave to dégorge for at least 30 minutes.

2 Rinse the aubergines and dry thoroughly. Trim the courgettes and cut into pieces about the same size as the aubergine.

3 Heat the oil in a large heavy-based frying pan and sauté the aubergines for 3 minutes. Add the courgettes and continue cooking for 3-4 minutes or until just tender but not soggy. Season with salt and pepper. Sprinkle with the sesame seeds and garnish with oregano or marjoram.

COOK'S TIP

Aubergines can contain bitter juices, especially when mature. Salting and draining before cooking helps to remove these juices and also reduces the aubergine's tendency to absorb large quantities of oil during cooking. This process is known by the French term dégorger. Courgettes and cucumber may also be treated in this way. Choose small aubergines in preference to the larger plump variety, as they are less bitter.

COURGETTES WITH MUSHROOMS

SERVES 8

1.1 kg (2½ lb) courgettes	225 g (8 oz) button mushrooms
50 g (2 oz) butter or margarine	90 ml (3 fl oz) soured cream
salt and pepper	basil sprig, to garnish

1 Cut the courgettes into 5 mm (¼ inch) slices.
2 Melt the butter in a roasting tin, add the courgettes and turn to coat; season well with salt and pepper.
3 Bake the courgette slices in the oven at 200°C (400°F) mark 6 for about 15 minutes.
4 Meanwhile, slice the mushrooms. Stir into the courgettes and return to the oven for a further 10-15 minutes.
5 Stir the soured cream into the vegetables and heat through on top of the stove; make sure that the cream does not boil or it might curdle. To serve, adjust the seasoning and spoon the vegetables into a serving dish. Garnish with the basil.

VARIATION

French beans or young broccoli or cauliflower florets can be used instead of the courgettes.

FENNEL AU GRATIN

SERVES 4-6

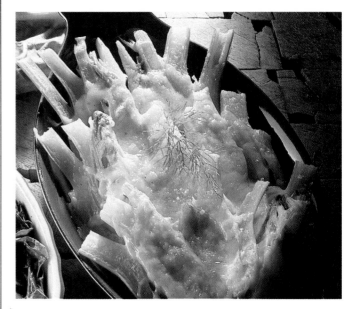

4 small bulbs of fennel	50 g (2 oz) Fontina cheese, grated
salt and pepper	45 ml (3 tbsp) freshly grated Parmesan cheese
30 ml (2 tbsp) olive oil	
25 g (1 oz) butter	

1 Using a sharp knife, carefully cut each bulb of fennel into quarters lengthways.
2 Cook the fennel quarters in a large pan of boiling salted water for 20 minutes until just tender. Drain thoroughly.
3 Heat the oil with the butter in a flameproof gratin dish. Add the fennel and toss to coat in the oil and butter.
4 Turn the fennel quarters cut side up in the dish. Sprinkle with the two cheeses and seasoning.
5 Grill under a preheated hot grill for 5 minutes or until the cheeses are melted and bubbling. Serve hot.

COOK'S TIP

The Fontina cheese in this recipe is a hard, mountain cheese with a sweet, nutty flavour. If difficult to obtain, use Gruyère or Emmental instead.

SAUTEED CUCUMBER WITH ROSEMARY

SERVES 4-6

1 medium cucumber	15 ml (1 tbsp) chopped rosemary
salt and pepper	2.5 ml (½ tsp) sugar
50 g (2 oz) butter or margarine	60 ml (4 tbsp) soured cream
1 small onion, finely chopped	

1 Score the cucumber lengthwise with a canelle knife or the prongs of a fork. Cut into 5 cm (2 inch) lengths, then cut each lengthways into quarters. Remove seeds. Put in a colander and sprinkle with salt. Cover with a plate and leave for 30 minutes. Press to extract liquid, rinse and pat dry with absorbent kitchen paper.
2 Melt the butter in a frying pan. Add the onion and fry for 5 minutes. Add the cucumber, rosemary, sugar and pepper to taste and fry for 5 minutes only, stirring. Remove from the heat and stir in the cream. Serve hot.

BAKED CHERRY TOMATOES

SERVES 8

32 cherry tomatoes, about 700 g (1½ lb) total weight	30 ml (2 tbsp) chopped parsley
50 g (2 oz) butter or margarine	salt and pepper
	parsley sprigs, to garnish

1 Make a small slash in the skin of each tomato. Place in a large bowl and pour over enough boiling water to cover. Leave for 1 minute, drain and refresh under cold running water.
2 Peel each tomato and place in a large ovenproof dish.
3 Melt the butter and stir in the parsley. Brush over the tomatoes and season well.
4 Bake in the oven at 220°C (425°F) mark 7 for about 10 minutes or until hot and just beginning to soften. Garnish with parsley to serve.

COOK'S TIP

It's not absolutely essential to peel the tomatoes but it does give a better finish.

TOMATOES AU GRATIN

SERVES 6

900 g (2 lb) large Marmande or Beefsteak tomatoes	salt and pepper
50 g (2 oz) butter or margarine, softened	300 ml (½ pint) double cream
2-3 garlic cloves, chopped	50 g (2 oz) dried wholemeal breadcrumbs
5 ml (1 tsp) sugar	25 g (1 oz) freshly grated Parmesan cheese
20 ml (4 tsp) chopped basil or 10 ml (2 tsp) dried	

1 Skin the tomatoes: put them in a large bowl, pour over boiling water and leave for 10 seconds. Drain, then plunge the tomatoes into a bowl of cold water. Peel off the skin with your fingers, then slice the tomatoes thinly.

2 Brush the inside of an ovenproof dish liberally with some of the butter. Arrange a layer of tomato slices in the bottom of the dish, sprinkle with a little of the garlic, sugar and basil, then add salt and pepper to taste. Pour over a thin layer of cream.

3 Repeat these layers until all the ingredients are used up. Mix the breadcrumbs and Parmesan together, then sprinkle over the top of the tomatoes and cream. Dot with the remaining butter.

4 Bake in the oven at 180°C (350°F) mark 4 for 40 minutes until the topping is golden brown. Serve hot.

PEPERONATA

SERVES 6

60 ml (4 tbsp) olive oil	700 g (1½ lb) ripe tomatoes, skinned and roughly chopped
1 large onion, finely sliced	
6 red peppers, seeded and sliced into strips	15 ml (1 tbsp) chopped parsley
2 garlic cloves, crushed	salt and pepper
	parsley sprigs, to garnish

1 Heat the oil in a frying pan, add the onion and fry gently for 5 minutes until soft but not coloured.

2 Add the peppers and garlic to the pan, cook gently for 2-3 minutes, then add the tomatoes, parsley and salt and pepper to taste.

3 Cover and cook gently for 30 minutes until the mixture is quite dry. If necessary, remove the lid about 10 minutes before the end of cooking to allow the liquid to evaporate. Taste and adjust the seasoning.

4 Garnish with parsley before serving, either hot or cold.

STIR-FRIED MIXED VEGETABLES

SERVES 8

4 large fat carrots, peeled	30 ml (2 tbsp) oil
1 bunch of spring onions	225 g (8 oz) French beans
½ head of Chinese leaves	225 g (8 oz) mangetouts

1 Run a sharp potato peeler along the length of each carrot to peel off long, thin, ribbon-like strips. Cut the onions into long strips and the cabbage into large chunks.
2 Heat the oil in a large wok, add the beans and fry for 3-4 minutes, stirring all the time. Add the cabbage and carrots and stir-fry for a further 2 minutes, then add the mangetouts and cook for 1 minute. Pile onto a hot serving dish and serve immediately.

COOK'S TIP

Vegetable stir-fries are delicious made with whatever vegetables you have to hand, though it's important to cut them into small pieces of a similar size. Add tougher, slower-cooking vegetables, such as baby corn, carrots, green beans, onions, peppers, celery, fennel and radish, first. Delicate fast-cooking vegetables, such as beansprouts, Chinese leaves, pak choi and spinach, need only 2-3 minutes in the hot oil. Once you've grasped the basic technique, it has endless possibilities. When cooked, the vegetables should be served right away, so make sure that any accompanying noodles or rice are almost cooked when you begin stir-frying.

ORIENTAL VEGETABLE, FRUIT AND NUT STIR-FRY

SERVES 8

FOR THE SAUCE	5 cm (2 inch) piece fresh root ginger, peeled and cut into matchsticks
1-2 green chillies, seeded and chopped	
15 ml (1 tbsp) dark soft brown sugar	6 carrots, cut into matchsticks
juice of 1 lime or lemon	3 red peppers, seeded and sliced
10 ml (2 tsp) cornflour	225 g (8 oz) fine green beans, halved
30 ml (2 tbsp) crunchy peanut butter	225 g (8 oz) mangetouts, halved
60 ml (4 tbsp) soy sauce	1 small pineapple, peeled, cored and cut in chunks
FOR THE STIR-FRY	75 g (3 oz) dry roasted peanuts, coarsely chopped
45 ml (3 tbsp) oil	
1 bunch spring onions, cut into 2.5 cm (1 inch) lengths	125 g (4 oz) beansprouts
2 garlic cloves, shredded	salt and pepper

1 To make the sauce, pound the chillies in a mortar with the sugar and lime juice. Dissolve the cornflour in a little cold water. Stir in the chilli mixture, peanut butter and soy sauce, then 150 ml (¼ pint) cold water.
2 Heat a wok. Add 30 ml (2 tbsp) oil and heat until hot but not smoking. Add the spring onions, garlic and ginger and stir-fry for about 5 minutes to flavour the oil. Remove from the pan with a slotted spoon and drain.
3 Heat the remaining oil in the wok, add the carrots and stir-fry for 3 minutes, then add the peppers and stir-fry for 2-3 minutes. Add the beans and mangetouts and stir-fry for 2-3 minutes. Remove all vegetables from the wok.
4 Pour the sauce into the wok. Stir over high heat until thickened and dark, then return all the vegetables to the wok. Add the pineapple, beansprouts and two thirds of the peanuts and stir-fry for a few minutes. Season to taste. Sprinkle with the remaining peanuts to serve.

ROASTED OATMEAL VEGETABLES

SERVES 6

450 g (1 lb) carrots	175 g (6 oz) coarse oatmeal
450 g (1 lb) parsnips	5 ml (1 tsp) paprika
450 g (1 lb) onions	salt and pepper
120 g (8 tbsp) oil	

1 Peel the carrots and parsnips and cut into large chunks; quarter the onions, keeping the root end intact.
2 Put the carrots and parsnips in a saucepan of water, bring to the boil and cook for 2 minutes. Drain well.
3 Put 30 ml (2 tbsp) of the oil in the saucepan and add the carrots and parsnips. Add the onions, oatmeal, paprika and salt and pepper to taste. Stir gently to coat the vegetables.
4 Put the remaining oil in a large roasting tin and heat in the oven at 200°C (400°F) mark 6. When very hot, add the vegetables and any remaining oatmeal and baste to coat.
5 Roast in the oven for about 1 hour, or until the vegetables are just tender and golden brown, basting occasionally during cooking. Spoon into a warmed serving dish and sprinkle over any oatmeal 'crumbs'. Serve hot.

VARIATION

Replace the carrots and parsnips with swede and turnips.

WATERCRESS AND OATMEAL CROQUETTES

MAKES 12

700 g (1½ lb) floury potatoes	15 ml (1 tbsp) plain wholemeal flour
15 g (½ oz) butter or margarine, softened	50 g (2 oz) fresh wholemeal breadcrumbs
1 bunch of watercress	50 g (2 oz) medium oatmeal
2 eggs	oil, for deep-frying
salt and pepper	

1 Scrub the potatoes and boil in their skins until tender, about 20 minutes. Drain well, peel, then sieve them into a large bowl or mash very well. Beat in the butter.
2 Finely chop the watercress. Add to the bowl with 1 egg and salt and pepper; mix well. Mould the potato mixture into 12 cork-shaped croquettes. Coat each lightly in flour.
3 Break the remaining egg on to a plate and beat lightly. Combine the breadcrumbs and oatmeal on another plate.
4 Dip the croquettes into the beaten egg, then coat in the breadcrumb mixture, pressing it on firmly. Chill for at least 30 minutes or until required.
5 To serve, heat the oil in a deep-fat fryer to 190°C (375°F). Deep-fry the croquettes for about 4 minutes or until golden brown on all sides. Drain on absorbent kitchen paper before serving.

BAKED PEPPERS WITH WILD RICE FILLING

SERVES 4

175 g (6 oz) mixed long-grain and wild rice	50 g (2 oz) butter or margarine
salt and pepper	1 onion, chopped
2 small red peppers	175 g (6 oz) button mushrooms, sliced
2 small green peppers	good pinch of cayenne pepper
a little oil, for brushing	

1 Cook the rice in a large saucepan of boiling water for about 15 minutes or until tender. Drain well and rinse with boiling water, then drain well again.

2 Cut the peppers in half lengthways. Leave the stalks in place but discard the seeds and pith. Blanch the peppers in boiling water for 5 minutes; drain, then plunge into cold water and leave until cold. Drain and pat dry, then brush with oil.

3 Melt the butter in a saucepan and fry the onion and mushrooms until lightly golden. Stir in the rice, salt and pepper and cayenne. Remove from the heat and spoon the mixture into the prepared peppers. Arrange in a greased shallow ovenproof dish. Cover with lightly greased foil.

4 Bake in the oven at 190°C (375°F) mark 5 for 30-35 minutes or until the peppers are tender and the filling is heated through. Uncover, then fluff up the rice with a fork. Serve hot.

COOK'S TIP

Despite its name, wild rice is an aquatic grass native to Canada and North America. It has a fragrant, nutty flavour and a crunchy texture.

SAUTEED ARTICHOKES WITH ORANGE

SERVES 4

900 g (2 lb) Jerusalem artichokes	30 ml (2 tbsp) oil
salt and pepper	25 g (1 oz) butter or margarine
squeeze of lemon juice	chopped parsley (optional)
1 orange	

1 Scrub the artichokes. If small, leave them whole; if not, cut them into large chunks about the size of golf balls.

3 Put the artichokes in a saucepan and cover with salted water acidulated with lemon juice. Bring to the boil, then reduce the heat, cover and simmer for 8-10 minutes or until the artichokes are barely tender. Finely grate the orange rind and segment the flesh, discarding all pith.

3 Drain the artichokes and refresh under cold running water. Peel off the skins and divide the flesh into good-sized chunks.

4 Heat the oil and butter in a frying pan and add the artichokes with the orange rind. Fry over a moderate heat, turning frequently, until golden brown.

5 Stir in the orange segments and parsley, if wished. Adjust the seasoning, if necessary, before serving.

COOK'S TIP

Jerusalem artichokes are knobbly little roots looking rather like root ginger. They have a soft, sweet, almost earthy flavour. They're quite delicious, but should only be eaten in moderate quantities as they have a well-founded reputation for causing flatulence!

FRIED MASALA POTATOES

SERVES 4-6

900 g (2 lb) new potatoes	4 garlic cloves, chopped
oil, for deep-frying	2 onions, chopped
10 ml (2 tsp) cumin seeds	45 ml (3 tbsp) ghee or oil
15 ml (1 tbsp) coriander seeds	5 ml (1 tsp) chilli powder
7.5 ml (1½ tsp) garam masala	2.5 ml (½ tsp) turmeric
2.5 cm (1 inch) piece fresh root ginger, peeled and roughly chopped	5 ml (1 tsp) salt
	300 ml (½ pint) natural yogurt

1 Wash the potatoes and scrub clean if necessary. Cut into 2.5 cm (1 inch) pieces and pat dry with absorbent kitchen paper.
2 Heat the oil in a deep-fat fryer to 180°C (350°F) and deep-fry the potatoes in batches for 10 minutes or until golden brown. Remove from the oil and drain on absorbent kitchen paper.
3 Place the cumin and coriander seeds in a blender or food processor with the garam masala, ginger, garlic and onions. Work until smooth, adding a little water if necessary.
4 Heat the ghee in a heavy-based frying pan, add the masala paste and fry gently for about 5 minutes. Add the chilli, turmeric and salt and fry for a further 1 minute.
5 Pour in the yogurt, then add the potatoes. Stir well and cook for another 5 minutes until completely heated through. Serve piping hot.

SAG ALOO

SERVES 4-6

900 g (2 lb) fresh spinach or 450 g (1 lb) frozen leaf spinach, thawed and drained	5 ml (1 tsp) black mustard seeds
60 ml (4 tbsp) ghee or oil	2.5 ml (½ tsp) turmeric
1 onion, thinly sliced	1.25 ml (¼ tsp) chilli powder
2 garlic cloves, crushed	1.25 ml (¼ tsp) ground ginger
10 ml (2 tsp) ground coriander	salt
	450 g (1 lb) old potatoes, peeled and thickly sliced

1 If using fresh spinach, wash well and put in a large saucepan with only the water that clings to the leaves after washing. Cook over very gentle heat for about 15 minutes. Drain well and leave to cool.
2 With your hands, squeeze out all the remaining moisture from the spinach. Place on a board and chop finely.
3 If using frozen spinach, cook over very gentle heat for about 5 minutes to drive off as much liquid as possible.
4 Melt the ghee in a heavy-based saucepan or flame-proof casserole. Add the onion, garlic, spices and salt to taste. Fry gently for about 5 minutes, stirring frequently, until the onion begins to brown.
5 Add the potatoes and stir gently to mix with the onion and spices. Pour in 150 ml (¼ pint) water and bring to the boil, then lower the heat and simmer, uncovered, for 10 minutes. Stir occasionally and add a few more spoonfuls of water if necessary.
6 Fold the spinach gently into the potato mixture. Simmer for a further 5-10 minutes until the potatoes are just tender. Turn into a warmed serving dish to serve.

ROSTI

SERVES 2-4

700 g (1½ lb) old potatoes, scrubbed	75 g (3 oz) butter or margarine
salt and pepper	1 small onion, finely chopped

1 Quarter any large potatoes, then put the potatoes in a saucepan of salted water. Bring to the boil and cook for 7 minutes. Drain well, leave to cool for about 10 minutes until cool enough to handle, then remove the skins. Using a hand grater, grate the potatoes into a bowl. Melt 25 g (1 oz) of the butter in a frying pan, add the onion and fry gently for about 5 minutes until soft but not coloured.
2 Add the remaining butter to the onion and heat until melted. Add the grated potato and sprinkle with salt and pepper to taste. Fry the potatoes, turning them constantly, until they have absorbed all the fat.
3 Using a palette knife, form the potato into a neat, flat cake and flatten the top. Sprinkle with 15 ml (1 tbsp) water, cover the pan and cook gently for 15-20 minutes, until the underside is golden brown. Shake the pan occasionally to prevent the potato from sticking to the bottom of the pan.
4 When cooked, place a large warmed serving plate on top of the frying pan. Invert both so that the golden side is uppermost on the plate. Serve immediately, cut into wedges. Alternatively, serve straight from the pan.

CRISPY POTATO GALETTE

SERVES 8

1 kg (2 lb) old potatoes, peeled	15 ml (1 tbsp) olive oil
	salt and pepper
50 g (2 oz) butter	parsley sprigs, to garnish

1 Cut the potatoes into very thin rings and dry thoroughly on a clean tea towel.
2 Melt the butter with the oil in a 20 cm (8 inch) non-stick frying pan or skillet with a lid. Heat until foaming, then remove the pan from the heat and add the potato rings, overlapping them in a circular pattern. Season well with salt and pepper, then press the potatoes down firmly with a metal spatula.
3 Cover the potatoes with a sheet of buttered greaseproof paper, then with the pan lid. Cook over moderate heat for 10-15 minutes until the potatoes are golden brown on the underside.
4 Transfer the covered pan to the oven. Bake in the oven at 200°C (400°F) mark 6 for 30 minutes, or until the potatoes feel tender when pierced with a skewer. Remove from the oven and leave to rest, covered, for 10 minutes.
5 Uncover the potatoes and place a warmed flat serving plate on top. Invert the potato galette on to the plate and garnish with parsley. Serve hot, cut into wedges.

COOK'S TIP

You will need a frying pan or skillet with an ovenproof handle and lid to make this galette - the French cast iron type is ideal. If your pan handle and lid knob are not ovenproof, cover them with several thicknesses of foil for protection, or bake the galette in a sandwich tin. Any leftover galette can be reheated in the oven at 200°C (400°F) mark 6 for about 15 minutes. Wrap in foil and brush with a little extra butter; unwrap for the last 5 minutes.

NEW POTATOES WITH TARRAGON CREAM

SERVES 4

700 g (1½ lb) new potatoes	4 spring onions, chopped
salt and pepper	150 ml (¼ pint) soured cream
15 g (½ oz) butter or margarine	3 tarragon sprigs

1 Cook the new potatoes in boiling salted water for 15 minutes or until just tender; drain and keep warm.

2 Melt the butter in a saucepan, add the spring onions and cook for 5 minutes until soft. Stir in the soured cream, salt and pepper to taste, and two tarragon sprigs. Heat without boiling.

3 Add the cooked potatoes to the creamy onion and tarragon mixture in the pan. Reheat gently, but do not boil.

4 Turn the potatoes and sauce into a warmed serving dish and serve garnished with the remaining tarragon.

GREEK-STYLE NEW POTATOES

SERVES 4

1 kg (2 lb) small new potatoes, preferably Cyprus	60 ml (4 tbsp) chopped coriander, mint or parsley
250 ml (8 fl oz) oil	salt and pepper
125 ml (4 fl oz) white or red wine	

1 Scrub the potatoes clean, leaving them whole. Pat the potatoes thoroughly dry with a clean tea towel.

2 With a meat mallet, hit each potato once or twice so that the flesh breaks slightly. Heat the oil in a heavy-based deep frying pan, skillet or saucepan until a stale bread cube turns golden in 2-3 seconds.

3 Add the potatoes to the hot oil and fry over moderate heat, turning them frequently, until golden brown on all sides.

4 Pour off the oil, then pour the wine over the potatoes. Add half of the chopped coriander and a liberal sprinkling of salt and pepper. Shake the pan to combine the ingredients, then cover and simmer for about 15 minutes, until the potatoes are tender.

5 Turn the potatoes into a warmed serving dish and sprinkle with the remaining coriander. Serve immediately.

COOK'S TIP

For an authentic flavour to these potatoes, cook them in Greek retsina wine. Most retsina is white, but you can use either white or red, depending on which is easier to obtain.

SWISS CHALET POTATOES

SERVES 4-6

1.4 kg (3 lb) even-sized small potatoes, peeled	good pinch of freshly grated nutmeg
salt and pepper	75 g (3 oz) Gruyère or Emmental cheese, grated
300 ml (½ pint) double cream	75 g (3 oz) Parmesan cheese, freshly grated
1-2 garlic cloves, crushed	

1 Parboil the potatoes in a large saucepan of salted water for 10 minutes. Drain well.
2 Stand the potatoes upright in a buttered baking dish. Mix the cream with the garlic, nutmeg and salt and pepper to taste, then pour over the potatoes.
3 Mix the two cheeses together and sprinkle over the potatoes to cover them completely. Bake, uncovered, in the oven at 190°C (375°F) mark 5 for 1 hour, or until the potatoes feel tender when pierced with a skewer. Serve hot, straight from the dish.

COOK'S TIP

The Swiss cheeses Gruyère and Emmental are expensive, but their uniquely sweet and nutty flavour makes them well worth the extra cost for a potato dish such as this one and you only need a small amount to appreciate their flavour.

BULGAR WHEAT PILAF

SERVES 6

75-125 g (3-4 oz) butter or margarine	600 ml (1 pint) vegetable stock or water
2 large Spanish onions, roughly chopped	salt and pepper
2 garlic cloves, crushed	75 g (3 oz) raisins
350 g (12 oz) bulgar wheat	125 g (4 oz) dried apricots, roughly chopped
225 g (8 oz) ripe tomatoes, skinned and finely chopped	50 g (2 oz) pine nuts
	5 ml (1 tsp) ground cinnamon

1 Melt 75 g (3 oz) butter in a large, heavy-based saucepan or flameproof casserole. Add the onions and garlic and fry gently for about 15 minutes until softened.
2 Add the bulgar wheat and toss to mix with the onions and butter. Add the tomatoes and mix again, then pour in the stock or water and bring to the boil. Add salt and pepper to taste, then cover and cook very gently for 25 minutes.
3 Remove the pan from the heat and fold in the fruit, nuts and cinnamon, with some extra butter, if liked.
4 Cover the pan with a clean tea-towel folded double, then with the lid. Leave to stand for 10 minutes.
5 To serve, taste and adjust the seasoning, then spoon in a pyramid shape on a warmed serving plate or flat dish. Serve immediately.

SERVING SUGGESTION

Cracked wheat pilaf makes the most delicious alternative to rice as a vegetable accompaniment. This version is quite rich and substantial, and would also make an unusual lunch dish served with thick and creamy Greek natural yogurt.

BROWN RICE RISOTTO

SERVES 4

2 onions	pinch of saffron or 5 ml (1 tsp) turmeric
1 green pepper, seeded	600 ml (1 pint) vegetable stock
45 ml (3 tbsp) oil	salt and pepper
1 garlic clove, crushed	chopped parsley, to garnish
275 g (10 oz) long-grain brown rice	freshly grated Parmesan cheese, to serve

1 Slice the onions and green pepper finely. Heat the oil in a medium flameproof casserole, add the onions, pepper and garlic and fry gently for about 5 minutes until soft.
2 Put the rice in a sieve and wash it thoroughly under cold running water until the water runs clear. Drain well.
3 Add the rice with the saffron or turmeric to the pan. Fry gently, stirring, for 1-2 minutes until the rice is coated in oil.
4 Stir in the stock, then add salt and pepper to taste. Bring to the boil, then cover the casserole tightly with its lid.
5 Cook in the oven at 170°C (325°F) mark 3 for about 1 hour or until the rice is tender and the stock absorbed. Taste and adjust seasoning and garnish with plenty of parsley. Serve hot, with the grated Parmesan cheese.

COOK'S TIP

Saffron threads are the dried stigmas of the saffron crocus, and saffron is said to be the most expensive spice in the world. The threads will give this dish a subtle colour and delicate flavour. Take care if substituting turmeric; it is more pungent so use it sparingly.

CHINESE FRIED RICE

SERVES 4

350 g (12 oz) long-grain rice	125 g (4 oz) canned bamboo shoot, drained and cut into 2.5 cm (1 inch) strips
3 Chinese dried mushrooms, or 125 g (4 oz) button mushrooms, sliced	125 g (4 oz) frozen peas
4 spring onions	30 ml (2 tbsp) soy sauce
30 ml (2 tbsp) oil	3 eggs, beaten
125 g (4 oz) beansprouts	

1 Put the rice in a sieve and wash thoroughly under cold running water until the water runs clear. Transfer the rice to a bowl, cover with cold water and leave to soak for 30 minutes.
2 Drain the rice and put in a medium saucepan. Cover with enough cold water to come 2.5 cm (1 inch) above the rice. Bring to the boil, cover tightly and simmer the rice very gently for 20 minutes. Do not stir.
3 Remove the pan from the heat, leave to cool for 20 minutes, then cover and chill in the refrigerator for 2-3 hours or overnight.
4 When ready to fry the rice, put the dried mushrooms in a bowl, cover with boiling water and leave to soak for about 20 minutes or until soft.
5 Squeeze out any excess moisture from the mushrooms, then cut into thin slivers. Cut the spring onions diagonally into 2.5 cm (1 inch) lengths.
6 Heat the oil in a wok or deep, heavy-based frying pan over high heat. Add all the vegetables and stir-fry for 2-3 minutes. Add the soy sauce and cook, briefly, stirring.
7 Fork up the rice, add to the pan and stir-fry for 2 minutes. Pour in the beaten eggs and continue to stir-fry for 2-3 minutes, or until the egg has scrambled and the rice is heated through. Serve immediately.

MICROWAVE DISHES

A variety of vegetarian recipes – designed specifically for cooking by microwave – are featured in this chapter. Choose from soups, tasty dips and terrines, quick main meals and easy vegetable accompaniments.

SPICED CRANBERRY SOUP

SERVES 4

350 g (12 oz) cranberries	45 ml (3 tbsp) clear honey
4 whole cloves	15 ml (1 tbsp) crème de cassis
1 cinnamon stick	few cranberries and mint leaves, to garnish

1 Put the cranberries, cloves, cinnamon and honey into a large bowl with 600 ml (1 pint) water. Cover and cook on HIGH for 10-12 minutes or until the cranberries are tender.
2 Cool slightly, then pass the soup through a sieve. Stir in the crème de cassis, cover and chill in the refrigerator for at least 4 hours before serving.
3 To serve, spoon the soup into individual bowls and garnish each with a few cranberries and mint leaves.

SERVING SUGGESTION

An unusual chilled soup to serve as a starter during the cranberry season.

CHILLED PEA AND MINT SOUP

SERVES 4-6

50 g (2 oz) butter or margarine	2 large mint sprigs
1 onion, roughly chopped	pinch of caster sugar
450 g (1 lb) peas	salt and pepper
600 ml (1 pint) milk	150 ml (¼ pint) natural yogurt
600 ml (1 pint) vegetable stock	mint sprigs, to garnish

1 Put the butter into a large bowl and cook on HIGH for 45 seconds or until melted. Add the onion, cover and cook on HIGH for 5-7 minutes or until softened.
2 Add the peas, milk, stock, mint sprigs and the sugar. Re-cover and cook on HIGH for about 8 minutes or until boiling. Reduce the setting and continue cooking on LOW for 15 minutes, or until the peas are really tender. Season well with salt and pepper and allow to cool slightly.
3 Using a slotted spoon, remove 45 ml (3 tbsp) peas from the soup and set aside for the garnish. Purée the soup in a blender or food processor until quite smooth.
4 Pour into a large serving bowl. Adjust the seasoning and leave to cool. Stir in the yogurt, cover and chill for 2-3 hours before serving, garnished with peas and mint.

CREAMY CARROT, TOFU AND CARAWAY DIP

SERVES 6

15 ml (1 tbsp) caraway seeds	1 small onion, finely chopped
5 ml (1 tsp) dried dill weed	275 g (10 oz) silken tofu
15 ml (1 tbsp) oil	salt and pepper
450 g (1 lb) carrots, thinly sliced	grated carrot, to garnish

1 Lightly crush the caraway seeds and put into a large bowl with the dill and oil. Cook on HIGH for 2 minutes, stirring once.
2 Add the carrots, onion and 30 ml (2 tbsp) water. Cover and cook on HIGH for 10-12 minutes or until the vegetables are tender, stirring once.
3 When the vegetables are cool, put into a blender or food processor and purée until smooth. Add the tofu and mix thoroughly together. Season to taste with salt and pepper. Garnish with grated carrot.

COOK'S TIP

Tofu is bland in flavour but high in protein. 1t has a smooth, creamy texture when whizzed in a blender, making it the perfect vehicle for dips and sauces. Carrots and caraway make an unusual dip, perfect for serving with chunks of wholemeal or granary bread. This dip may also be thinned to a pouring consistency with a little natural yogurt or vegetable stock to serve as a sauce with cooked vegetables.

AUBERGINE AND POMEGRANATE DIP

SERVES 4-6

1 large aubergine, weighing about 450 g (1 lb)	1 large ripe pomegranate
1 garlic clove, crushed	150 ml (¼ pint) natural yogurt
30 ml (2 tbsp) olive oil	salt and pepper

1 Prick the aubergine all over with a fork, then place in the oven and cook on HIGH for 6-10 minutes, or until the aubergine feels soft when squeezed gently, turning over once during cooking.
2 Leave to cool slightly, then cut off the stalk and discard it. Put the aubergine, garlic and the oil in a blender or food processor and purée until smooth. Leave to cool.
3 Meanwhile, cut the pomegranate in half and scoop the seeds out into a sieve. Hold the sieve over the bowl of the blender or food processor and push on the seeds to extract the juice. Reserve the seeds to garnish.
4 When the aubergine is cool, add the yogurt and season to taste with salt and pepper. Purée until well mixed. Leave until cold.
5 Serve cold, decorated with the reserved pomegranate seeds, with warm pitta bread or a selection of vegetable and fruit crudités.

COOK'S TIP

Aubergines are so easy to cook whole in the microwave, and they retain all of their flavour and vitamins. Once you have discovered this method of cooking them, you will never return to the arduous conventional methods of baking or grilling. Cooking in the microwave also means that the dark aubergine skin is soft enough to be included in purées, adding colour, texture and flavour.

TRICOLOUR PATE TRIO

SERVES 6

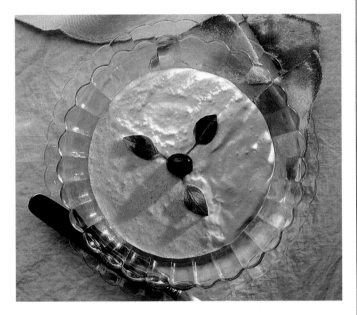

1 large red pepper	salt and pepper
175 g (6 oz) cauliflower florets	1 ripe avocado
300 ml (½ pint) natural yogurt	15 ml (1 tbsp) lemon juice
300 ml (½ pint) single cream	herbs and black olives, to garnish

1 Cut the pepper in half lengthways and remove the seeds. Place, cut side down, on a double sheet of absorbent kitchen paper and cook on HIGH for 5-6 minutes or until the pepper is soft.
2 Meanwhile, cut the cauliflower into very small florets and put into a large bowl with 15 ml (1 tbsp) water.
3 When the pepper is cooked, cook the cauliflower on HIGH for 6-7 minutes or until very tender, stirring occasionally.
4 Meanwhile, carefully peel the skin from the pepper and discard. Put the pepper, a third of the yogurt and a third of the cream in a blender or food processor and purée until smooth. Season to taste with salt and pepper.
5 Drain the cauliflower and put into the rinsed-out bowl of the blender or food processor with half of the remaining yogurt and half of the remaining cream, and purée until smooth. Season to taste with salt and pepper.
6 Halve the avocado and discard the skin and the stone. Put into the rinsed-out bowl of the blender or food processor with the remaining yogurt, cream and the lemon juice. Purée until smooth. Season to taste with salt and pepper. Leave all the pâtés to cool before serving.
7 To serve, put a large spoonful of each pâté side by side into six individual serving bowls. Shake each bowl gently from side to side allowing the pâtés to merge into one another but leaving three distinctive sections of colour. Garnish with herbs and black olives. Serve immediately, with melba toast.

STRIPED VEGETABLE TERRINE WITH SEAWEED

SERVES 4-6

	FOR THE WATERCRESS VINAIGRETTE
450 g (1 lb) carrots	
450 g (1 lb) parsnips	½ bunch of watercress
2 eggs	150 ml (¼ pint) sunflower oil
300 ml (½ pint) double cream or Greek strained yogurt	30 ml (2 tbsp) white wine vinegar
salt and pepper	5 ml (1 tsp) thin honey
3 sheets of nori seaweed, about 20 cm (8 inches) square	watercress, to garnish

1 Roughly chop the carrots and put into a roasting bag with 15 ml (1 tbsp) water. Chop the parsnips and put in a roasting bag with 15 ml (1 tbsp) water. Loosely seal the bags and cook them both at once on HIGH for 12 minutes or until the vegetables are tender.
2 Put the carrots, half the cream or yogurt and 1 egg in a blender or food processor and purée until smooth. Turn into a bowl and season with salt and pepper.
3 Purée the parsnips with the remaining cream or yogurt and egg; season.
4 Grease a 1.4-litre (2½ pint) loaf dish and line the base with greaseproof paper. Spoon in half of the carrot purée and level the surface. Fold one of the sheets of nori in half lengthways and lay on top of the purée.
5 Spoon half of the parsnip purée on top of the nori and level the surface. Fold a second sheet of nori in half lengthways and lay on top. Repeat the layers twice more, ending with a layer of parsnip.
6 Stand on a roasting rack, cover with kitchen paper and cook on MEDIUM for 12-15 minutes until just firm to the touch. Cool in the dish then turn out on to a serving plate.
7 To make the vinaigrette, process the watercress in a blender or food processor with the oil, vinegar and honey until finely chopped. Season to taste.
8 Serve the terrine hot or cold arranged on individual plates in a pool of vinaigrette, garnished with watercress.

TINY CHEESE TRIANGLES

SERVES 4

75 g (3 oz) cream cheese	75 g (3 oz) butter or margarine, in small pieces
15 ml (1 tbsp) lemon or lime juice	4 sheets of filo pastry
1 spring onion, finely chopped	75 ml (5 tbsp) natural yogurt
25 g (1 oz) chopped dried apricots or dates	15 ml (1 tbsp) lemon juice
salt and pepper	¼ cucumber, grated
	mint sprigs, to garnish

1 To make the filling, mix the cream cheese and lemon juice with the spring onion and chopped fruit; season.
2 Put the butter in a small bowl and cook on HIGH for 2 minutes or until melted.
3 Lay one sheet of pastry on top of a second sheet and cut widthways into six double layer 7.5 cm (3 inch) strips. Repeat with the remaining two sheets of pastry.
4 Brush the strips of pastry with the melted butter. Place a generous teaspoonful of filling at one end of each strip. Fold the pastry diagonally across the filling to form a triangle. Continue folding, keeping the triangle shape, until you reach the end of the strip of pastry. Repeat with the remaining strips of pastry to make 12 triangles.
5 Heat a browning dish on HIGH for 5-8 minutes or according to the manufacturer's instructions.
6 Meanwhile, brush both sides of each triangle with the melted butter. Using tongs, quickly add six triangles to the dish and cook on HIGH for 1-2 minutes until the underside of each triangle is golden brown and the top looks puffy. Turn over and cook on HIGH for 1-2 minutes until the second side is golden brown. Reheat browning dish on HIGH for 2-3 minutes. Repeat with the remaining triangles.
7 To make the sauce, mix the yogurt with the lemon juice and cucumber in a bowl. Season to taste.
8 Serve the filo triangles warm or cold, garnished with mint, with the sauce handed separately.

BRIE AND WATERCRESS TARTS

MAKES 4

125 g (4 oz) plain wholemeal flour	2 bunches of watercress
salt	275 g (10 oz) ripe Brie
75 g (3 oz) butter or margarine	45 ml (3 tbsp) double cream
	freshly grated nutmeg
	salt and pepper

1 To make the pastry, put the flour and salt to taste in a bowl. Add 50 g (2 oz) of the butter and rub in until the mixture resembles fine breadcrumbs. Add 30-60 ml (2-4 tbsp) water and mix together using a round-bladed knife. Knead lightly to give a firm, smooth dough.
2 Roll out the dough thinly on a lightly floured surface and use to line four 10 cm (4 inch) shallow glass flan dishes, covering the bases and sides with the dough. Cover and chill while making the filling.
3 Put the remaining butter in a medium bowl and cook on HIGH for 1 minute or until melted. Trim and discard the tough stalks from the watercress. Reserve a few sprigs to garnish and stir the remainder into the butter. Cook on HIGH for 1-2 minutes until just wilted.
4 Remove the rind from the cheese and cut into small pieces. Stir into the watercress with the cream. Cook on HIGH for 1-2 minutes until melted. Season to taste with nutmeg, salt and pepper.
5 To cook the tarts, uncover and prick all over with a fork. Arrange pastry side uppermost in a circle in the microwave and cook on HIGH for 2-3 minutes or until firm to the touch.
6 Leave to stand for 5 minutes, then carefully loosen around the edge and invert on to a large serving plate. Fill with the filling and cook on HIGH for 2-3 minutes or until warmed through. Garnish with watercress to serve.

HERBY AUBERGINE CHEESE TERRINE

SERVES 6

2 large aubergines, each about 450 g (1 lb), finely chopped	125 g (4 oz) curd cheese
	60 ml (4 tbsp) chopped mixed herbs
450 ml (¾ pint) boiling vegetable stock	salt and pepper
2 eggs	coarsely chopped herbs, to garnish
125 g (4 oz) breadcrumbs	

1 Put the aubergines and the stock in a large bowl, cover and cook on HIGH for 20-25 minutes or until the aubergine is very soft.
2 Beat thoroughly to make a purée then stir in the eggs, breadcrumbs, curd cheese and herbs. Season with salt and pepper.
3 Grease a deep 20 cm (8 inch) round dish and line the base with greaseproof paper. Spoon the mixture into the dish and level the surface. Cook on MEDIUM for 20-25 minutes or until just firm to the touch.
4 Turn out on to a serving plate and press coarsely chopped herbs on to the sides and top. Serve hot or cold with salad and warm bread rolls.

OYSTER MUSHROOM SALAD

SERVES 6

25 g (1 oz) butter or margarine	15 ml (1 tbsp) white wine vinegar
30 ml (2 tbsp) oil	salt and pepper
15 ml (1 tbsp) lemon juice	1 small red onion, finely chopped
450 g (1 lb) oyster mushrooms	45 ml (3 tbsp) chopped mixed herbs
mixed salad leaves, eg curly endive, radicchio, lamb's lettuce	

1 Put the butter, oil and lemon juice into a large shallow dish and cook on HIGH for 45 seconds or until the butter is melted. Add the mushrooms, cover and cook on HIGH for 2-3 minutes or until the mushrooms are tender.
2 Meanwhile, arrange the salad leaves on six plates.
3 When the mushrooms are cooked, remove them with a slotted spoon and arrange on top of the salad.
4 Quickly add the vinegar to the liquid remaining in the dish and cook on HIGH for 1 minute. Season to taste with salt and pepper. Pour over the mushrooms and sprinkle with the onion and the herbs. Serve immediately.

NOODLES WITH ORIENTAL VEGETABLES

SERVES 4

	FOR THE SAUCE
225 g (8 oz) thin wheat noodles	30 ml (2 tbsp) oil
small bunch of chives or Chinese chives	2.5 cm (1 inch) piece fresh root ginger, peeled and grated
15 ml (1 tbsp) oil	60 ml (4 tbsp) plum sauce
540 g (19 oz) can sliced lotus root	15 ml (1 tbsp) mushroom ketchup
125 g (4 oz) yard-long beans, or French beans	30 ml (2 tbsp) dry sherry
225 g (8 oz) baby corn	
12 large radishes	

1 Break the noodles in half, then divide into 4 bundles. Tie each bundle with chives. Put into a large bowl with the oil and pour over enough boiling water to cover by about 2.5 cm (1 inch). Cover and cook on HIGH for 12-15 minutes or until almost tender. Leave to stand for 5 minutes.

2 Meanwhile drain the lotus roots. Cut the yard-long beans into short lengths and twist into interesting shapes. If using French beans top and tail them. Trim the radishes. Arrange the corn and beans around the edge of a large shallow dish and put the lotus roots and radishes in the centre. Pour over 45 ml (3 tbsp) water and cover.

3 While the noodles are standing, cook the vegetables on HIGH for 5-6 minutes or until tender.

4 Drain the noodles, rinse with boiling water to remove the excess starch and arrange on 4 serving plates. Using a slotted spoon remove the vegetables from the dish and arrange on the plates with the noodles. Quickly add the sauce ingredients and 75 ml (3 fl oz) water to the liquid remaining in the dish and cook on HIGH for 1-2 minutes or until hot.

5 Pour a little sauce over the noodles and vegetables and serve the remainder separately. Serve immediately.

TOFU AND BEAN BURGERS

MAKES 6

275 g (10 oz) silken tofu	2 courgettes, grated
400 g (14 oz) can red kidney beans, drained and rinsed	25 g (1 oz) wholemeal breadcrumbs
2.5 ml (½ tsp) vegetable yeast extract	few drops of chilli sauce
5 ml (1 tsp) dried mixed herbs	1 egg, beaten
1 onion, grated	15 ml (1 tbsp) lemon juice
	grated rind of 1 small lemon
	pepper

1 Put the tofu and drained kidney beans into a bowl and mash together using a potato masher or a fork. Dissolve the yeast extract in 30 ml (2 tbsp) hot water and stir in to the tofu mixture with the remaining ingredients. Beat well together.

2 Shape the mixture into six burgers, about 2 cm (¾ inch) thick.

3 Arrange the burgers in a circle around the edge of a large flat plate. Cook on HIGH for 8 minutes. Carefully turn the burgers over and cook on HIGH for a further 8 minutes. Serve hot, with a salad or in wholemeal rolls.

LENTIL, AUBERGINE AND POTATO PIE

SERVES 4

3 medium potatoes, each about 225 g (8 oz), scrubbed	450 ml (¾ pint) boiling vegetable stock
125 g (4 oz) split red lentils	125 g (4 oz) French beans, trimmed and cut into 2.5 cm (1 inch) lengths
1 onion, finely chopped	
1 bay leaf	60 ml (4 tbsp) milk
5 ml (1 tsp) dried thyme	salt and pepper
15 ml (1 tbsp) tomato purée	25 g (1 oz) Parmesan cheese, freshly grated
1 small aubergine, roughly chopped	

1 Prick the potatoes all over with a fork and arrange in a circle on a sheet of absorbent kitchen paper. Cook on HIGH for 10-15 minutes or until soft, turning over halfway through cooking. Set aside to cool slightly.
2 Meanwhile put the lentils, onion, bay leaf, thyme, tomato purée, aubergine and vegetable stock into a large bowl and mix well together. Cover and cook on HIGH for 20-25 minutes or until the lentils and aubergine are tender and most of the liquid is absorbed. Add the beans and cook on HIGH for 2 minutes.
3 Meanwhile, cut the potatoes in half and scoop out the flesh into a bowl. Mash with the milk and season to taste with salt and pepper.
4 Spoon the lentil and aubergine mixture into a flameproof serving dish. Spoon over the mashed potato and sprinkle with the cheese. Cook on HIGH for 1-2 minutes or until heated through, then brown under a hot grill, if liked.

VEGETABLE MOUSSAKA

SERVES 4-6

2 large aubergines, cut into 5 mm (¼ inch) slices	10 ml (2 tsp) chopped basil or 5 ml (1 tsp) dried
salt and pepper	450 g (1 lb) courgettes, coarsely chopped
15 ml (1 tbsp) oil	
1 large onion, chopped	150 ml (¼ pint) natural yogurt
2 garlic cloves, crushed	5 ml (1 tsp) cornflour
400 g (14 oz) can tomatoes	125 g (4 oz) Cheddar cheese, grated
15 ml (1 tbsp) tomato purée	
5 ml (1 tsp) sugar	

1 Put the aubergines into a colander, sprinkle with salt and leave for about 30 minutes to extract any bitter juices. Rinse in cold running water and dry thoroughly with absorbent kitchen paper.
2 Put the oil, onion, garlic, tomatoes and their juice, tomato purée, sugar, basil and courgettes into a large bowl and cook on HIGH for 12-15 minutes or until the courgettes are softened and the liquid has slightly reduced. Season well with salt and pepper.
3 Spread half the tomato mixture in the bottom of a shallow flameproof dish.
4 Arrange half the aubergine slices in a single layer on top of the tomato mixture. Repeat the layers, ending with a layer of aubergines. Cook on HIGH for 10 minutes or until the aubergine is tender.
5 Meanwhile, blend the yogurt into the cornflour, then stir in the cheese and season well with salt and pepper.
6 Spread the yogurt mixture in an even layer on top of the moussaka and cook on HIGH for a further 1-2 minutes or until hot. Brown under a hot grill, if desired. Leave to stand for 5 minutes before serving.

BEAN GOULASH

SERVES 4-6

125 g (4 oz) black-eye beans, soaked overnight in cold water	10 ml (2 tsp) caraway seeds, lightly crushed
125 g (4 oz) aduki beans, soaked overnight in cold water	15 ml (1 tbsp) paprika
15 ml (1 tbsp) sunflower oil	400 g (14 oz) can chopped tomatoes
1 garlic clove, crushed	175 g (6 oz) mushrooms, thickly sliced
1 yellow pepper, seeded and roughly chopped	60 ml (4 tbsp) natural yogurt
	salt and pepper
	chopped parsley, to garnish

1 Drain the beans and put into a large bowl. Pour over enough boiling water to cover and come about 2.5 cm (1 inch) above the beans. Cover, leaving a gap to let steam escape, and microwave on HIGH for 25-30 minutes until tender. Leave to stand, covered. Do not drain.

2 Meanwhile, put the oil, garlic, yellow pepper, caraway seeds and paprika in a large ovenproof serving bowl. Cover, leaving a gap to let steam escape, and microwave on HIGH for 2 minutes, stirring once.

3 Drain the beans, rinse with boiling water and add to the pepper with the tomatoes and mushrooms. Re-cover and microwave on HIGH for 8-10 minutes, stirring once. Stir in 30 ml (2 tbsp) of the yogurt and season with salt and pepper to taste. Drizzle the remaining yogurt on top and sprinkle with the parsley. Serve hot with brown rice.

COOK'S TIP

To save time, you can substitute both kinds of beans with canned varieties. Use three 400 g (14 oz) cans of the beans of your choice and proceed from step 2.

VEGETABLE AND CHICK PEA CASSEROLE

SERVES 6

4 courgettes, cut into 1 cm (½ inch) lengths	2 garlic cloves, crushed
1 red pepper, seeded and chopped	425 g (15 oz) can chick peas, drained
1 green pepper, seeded and chopped	25 g (1 oz) almonds, blanched
2 onions, roughly chopped	5 ml (1 tsp) turmeric
2 carrots, thinly sliced	10 ml (2 tsp) paprika
225 g (8 oz) turnips, thinly sliced	2.5 ml (½ tsp) ground coriander
1 small cauliflower, cut into florets	salt and pepper
4 large tomatoes, skinned, seeded and chopped	600 ml (1 pint) boiling vegetable stock
125 g (4 oz) no-soak dried apricots, cut into quarters	chopped coriander or parsley, to garnish

1 Place all the prepared vegetables, the tomatoes, apricots, garlic, chick peas and almonds in a large bowl and stir in the spices, salt, pepper and stock. Cover and cook on HIGH for 8-10 minutes or until the vegetables come to the boil.

2 Continue cooking on HIGH for a further 30-40 minutes or until the vegetables are well cooked, stirring two or three times during cooking. Serve garnished with chopped coriander or parsley.

MUSHROOM, COURGETTE AND BEAN STEW

SERVES 4

25 g (1 oz) butter or margarine	two 425 g (15 oz) cans flageolet, borlotti or black-eye beans, drained and rinsed
1 onion, chopped	
25 g (1 oz) wholemeal flour	
450 ml (¾ pint) vegetable stock	225 g (8 oz) mushrooms, halved if large
15 ml (1 tbsp) mild wholegrain mustard	450 g (1 lb) courgettes
	45 ml (3 tbsp) chopped mixed herbs
	salt and pepper

1 Put the butter and the onion into a large bowl. Cover and cook on HIGH for 2-3 minutes or until slightly softened. Stir in the flour and cook on HIGH for 1 minute, then gradually stir in the stock.
2 Cook on HIGH for 4-5 minutes or until boiling and thickened, stirring frequently.
3 Add the mustard, beans and the mushrooms and cook on HIGH for 2-3 minutes.
4 Meanwhile, cut the courgettes into 1 cm (½ inch) slices. Stir the courgettes and half the herbs into the stew. Cover and cook on HIGH for 5-6 minutes or until the courgettes are just cooked. Season to taste with salt and pepper and stir in the remaining herbs. Serve with hot herb bread.

SMOKY STUFFED PAWPAW

SERVES 4

2 green pawpaws	125 g (4 oz) smoked cheese
1 yellow pepper	salt and pepper
125 g (4 oz) firm tofu	chives, to garnish
30 ml (2 tbsp) mayonnaise	

1 Prick the pawpaws all over with the point of a sharp knife or a skewer. Cut the pepper in half lengthways and remove and discard the seeds.
2 Put the pepper cut side down on a double sheet of absorbent kitchen paper and put into the cooker with the pawpaws. Cook on HIGH for 8 minutes or until the pepper is tender. Continue to cook the pawpaws on HIGH for 2-3 minutes or until just tender.
3 While the pawpaws are finishing cooking, put the pepper, half the tofu and the mayonnaise into a blender or food processor and purée until smooth. Pour into a bowl. Cut the remaining tofu into cubes and mix carefully into the sauce.
4 Cut the pawpaws in half lengthways and remove and discard the seeds. Scoop out the flesh with a teaspoon and roughly chop. Reserve the skins.
5 Add the chopped pawpaw to the pepper sauce and cook on HIGH for 2 minutes or until hot. Cut the cheese into cubes and stir into the sauce. Season to taste with salt and pepper.
6 Arrange the pawpaw shells on a large plate and spoon in the filling. Cook on HIGH for 1 minute or until just hot; do not overcook or the cheese will melt. Cut the chives into 7.5 cm (3 inch) lengths and scatter generously over the pawpaws. Serve immediately, with a rice pilaff.

SPICED WHEAT PEPPERS

SERVES 4

175 g (6 oz) bulgar wheat	1 large carrot, coarsely grated
4 large green peppers	1 large parsnip, coarsely grated
15 ml (1 tbsp) oil	60 ml (4 tbsp) mayonnaise
2 garlic cloves, crushed	chilli powder, to taste
175 g (6 oz) Cheddar cheese, coarsely grated	salt and pepper

1   Put the bulgar wheat in a bowl and pour over 300 ml (½ pint) boiling water. Leave to soak for 10-15 minutes or until all the water is absorbed.
2   Cut the tops off the peppers and reserve. Scoop out the seeds and discard. Brush the peppers with the oil and stand upright in a dish just large enough to hold them.
3   Mix the remaining ingredients into the bulgar wheat, seasoning to taste with chilli powder and salt and pepper. Use to stuff the peppers. Replace the reserved tops. Pour 30 ml (2 tbsp) water into the dish. Cover and cook on HIGH for 10-15 minutes or until the peppers are really tender. Serve hot or cold.

COOK'S TIP

Although this recipe is for stuffed peppers, the filling could be used to stuff other vegetables such as baked potatoes or aubergines.

SPINACH STUFFED PASTA SHELLS

SERVE 4

20 large pasta shells	freshly grated nutmeg, ground mixed spice or ground mace
salt and pepper	
900 g (2 lb) fresh spinach, washed, trimmed and chopped, or a 226 g (8 oz) packet frozen chopped spinach	150 ml (¼ pint) olive oil
	30 ml (2 tbsp) lemon juice
	10 ml (2 tsp) tomato purée
	salt and pepper
450 g (1 lb) ricotta cheese	herbs, to garnish

1   Put the pasta shells into a large bowl with salt to taste and pour over enough boiling water to cover by about 2.5 cm (1 inch). Stir once, then cover and cook on HIGH for 18-20 minutes or until almost tender, stirring once during cooking. Do not drain, but leave to stand, covered, for 5 minutes.
2   Drain the pasta and rinse in cold water, then leave to drain again.
3   If using fresh spinach, put it into a large bowl, cover and cook on HIGH for 3-4 minutes or until just cooked. If using frozen spinach, cook on HIGH for 8-9 minutes or until thawed. Drain and return to the bowl.
4   Stir in the ricotta cheese and mix thoroughly together. Season to taste with nutmeg, mixed spice or mace and salt and pepper.
5   Use the spinach and cheese mixture to stuff the pasta shells and arrange upright on a serving dish.
6   To make the tomato vinaigrette, whisk the oil, lemon juice and tomato purée together and season to taste with salt and pepper. Drizzle over the pasta shells and serve immediately, garnished with herbs.

GREEN BEANS WITH COCONUT

SERVES 4

50 g (2 oz) butter or margarine	30 ml (2 tbsp) chopped parsley
1 large onion, finely chopped	salt and pepper
50 g (2 oz) desiccated coconut	450 g (1 lb) green beans

1 Place the butter, onion and coconut in a shallow dish. Microwave on HIGH for 5-6 minutes or until the coconut turns a light golden colour. Stir once during the cooking time to coat the coconut with the fat. Stir in the parsley and seasoning and set aside.
2 Cut the beans into 5 cm (2 inch) lengths and place them in a medium bowl. Add 75 ml (5 tbsp) water. Three-quarters cover with cling film and microwave on HIGH for 12-14 minutes or until tender, stirring once. Drain the beans and place in a warmed serving dish.
3 Reheat the coconut mixture on HIGH for 2 minutes, then sprinkle over the cooked beans to serve.

COOK'S TIP

The crunchy coconut mixture can be used with other vegetables such as broccoli and cauliflower florets.

MINTED CARROTS AND BRUSSELS SPROUTS

SERVES 4

450 g (1 lb) Brussels sprouts	30 ml (2 tbsp) chopped mint
225 g (8 oz) carrots, sliced	salt and pepper
50 g (2 oz) butter or margarine	

1 Put the sprouts and carrots in a large casserole. Add 45 ml (3 tbsp) water and three-quarters cover with cling film. Microwave on HIGH for 9-12 minutes or until tender. Shake the casserole once during the cooking time.
2 Drain the vegetables and return to the casserole.
3 Place the butter and mint in a small measuring jug and microwave on HIGH for 1 minute or until melted and foaming. Pour the butter over the vegetables and toss until well coated.
4 Microwave on HIGH for 1 minute to reheat if necessary. Season to taste with salt and pepper and serve.

CUCUMBER WITH ONION AND TARRAGON

SERVES 4

1 cucumber	30 ml (2 tbsp) chopped tarragon
salt and pepper	1 bunch of spring onions, sliced
15 g (½ oz) butter or margarine	tarragon sprigs, to garnish

1 Using a sharp knife or a canelle knife, remove thin strips of skin evenly from all round the cucumber, to make a striped pattern. Quarter the cucumber lengthways and cut into 5 cm (2 inch) chunks. Place in a colander and sprinkle liberally with salt. Leave for 20 minutes, then drain and pat dry with absorbent kitchen paper.

2 Put the cucumber, butter and tarragon into a large bowl and three-quarters cover with cling film. Microwave on HIGH for 1 minute, then add the spring onions and microwave on HIGH for 2 minutes or until the vegetables are tender. Garnish with tarragon to serve.

GLAZED VEGETABLES PROVENCAL

SERVES 4

25 g (1 oz) butter or margarine	1 courgette, thinly sliced
1 garlic clove, crushed	50 g (2 oz) mangetouts, trimmed
½ red pepper, seeded and cut into strips	1 large tomato, skinned, seeded and cut into strips
½ yellow pepper, seeded and cut into strips	60 ml (4 tbsp) dry white wine
½ green pepper, seeded and cut into strips	salt and pepper
	basil sprigs, to garnish

1 Preheat a browning dish according to the manufacturer's instructions. Add the butter and garlic for the last 30 seconds of heating.

2 Add the vegetables and stir. Microwave on HIGH for 2-3 minutes or until the vegetables are slightly softened.

3 Stir in the white wine and season to taste with salt and pepper. Microwave on HIGH for 1 minute. Garnish with basil and serve.

COOK'S TIP

This dish can be prepared without a browning dish; place the butter and garlic in a large shallow dish and microwave for 1 minute, then add the vegetables and continue as above.

DESSERTS

From warming crumbles and baked puddings, through delectable
creamy desserts, to refreshing fruit salads, sorbets and ices you will find ideas to
suit all tastes and occasions in this chapter.

STUFFED FIGS

SERVES 8

225 g (8 oz) ricotta cheese, at room temperature	few drops of almond extract or rose water
150 ml (¼ pint) double or whipping cream	16 ripe fresh figs
	fig or vine leaves and rose petals, to serve (optional)

1 Beat the ricotta cheese in a bowl until softened. Whip the cream in another bowl until just standing in soft peaks, then fold into the ricotta, with almond extract or rose water according to taste.
2 With a sharp knife, cut a cross in each fig at the top (stem end). Continue cutting down almost to the base of the fig, but keeping the fruit whole. With your fingers, gently prise the four 'petals' of each fig apart, to allow room for the filling.
3 Spoon the ricotta mixture into a piping bag fitted with a large rosette nozzle and pipe into the centre of each fig. Chill in the refrigerator until serving time.
4 To serve, place the figs on individual serving plates. Alternatively arrange fig or vine leaves decoratively over a flat serving platter, place the stuffed figs on top and scatter rose petals around. Serve chilled.

INDIAN FRUIT SALAD

SERVES 6-8

3 ripe peaches	5 ml (1 tsp) cumin seeds, dry fried
2 ripe guavas	30 ml (2 tbsp) lemon or lime juice
2 ripe bananas	pinch of cayenne
45 ml (3 tbsp) caster sugar	mint sprigs, to decorate

1 To skin the peaches, plunge them into a bowl of boiling water, leave for 30 seconds, then remove the skins.
2 Cut the skinned peaches in half and remove the stones. Slice the peach flesh thinly and place in a serving bowl.
3 Cut the guavas in half, scoop out the seeds and discard them. Peel the halved guavas, then slice them neatly and add to the peaches in the bowl.
4 Peel the bananas, cut into chunks, then mix carefully with the peaches, guavas and remaining ingredients. Serve immediately, decorated with sprigs of mint.

SPICED DRIED FRUIT COMPOTE

SERVES 4

15 ml (1 tbsp) jasmine tea	125 g (4 oz) dried apple rings
2.5 ml (½ tsp) ground cinnamon	150 ml (¼ pint) dry white wine
1.25 ml (¼ tsp) ground cloves	50 g (2 oz) sugar
125 g (4 oz) dried apricots, soaked overnight, drained	toasted flaked almonds, to decorate
125 g (4 oz) dried prunes, soaked overnight, drained and stoned	

1   Put the tea, cinnamon and cloves in a bowl; pour in 300 ml (½ pint) boiling water. Leave for 20 minutes.
2   Put the dried fruit in a saucepan, then strain in the tea and spice liquid. Add the wine and sugar; heat gently until the sugar has dissolved.
3   Simmer for 20 minutes until tender, then cover and leave for 1-2 hours until cold.
4   Turn the compote into a serving bowl and chill for at least 2 hours. Sprinkle with almonds just before serving.

PINEAPPLE AND BANANA FLAMBE

SERVES 6-8

1 medium pineapple	100 g (4 oz) demerara sugar
900 g (2 lb) firm bananas	45 ml (3 tbsp) lemon juice
125 g (4 oz) dried figs	2.5 ml (½ tsp) ground mixed spice
50 g (2 oz) butter or margarine	60 ml (4 tbsp) dark rum

1   Slice the pineapple into 1 cm (½ inch) pieces. Snip off the skin and cut the flesh into chunks, discarding the core.
2   Peel and thickly slice the bananas into the bottom of a shallow ovenproof dish; spoon the pineapple on top.
3   Cut the figs into coarse shreds and scatter over the fruit. Then put the butter, sugar, strained lemon juice and spice together in a saucepan and heat until well blended; pour over the prepared fruit.
4   Cover tightly and bake in the oven at 200°C (400°F) mark 6 for 25 minutes until the fruit is tender.
5   Heat the rum gently in a small saucepan, remove from the heat and ignite with a match. Pour immediately over the fruit and bring the dish to the table while still flaming.

SERVING SUGGESTION

For a special occasion, you can serve this dessert in the pineapple shells. Any mixture which will not fit into the pineapple shells can be served separately in a fruit bowl.
To make two pineapple shells from one pineapple: with a large sharp knife, slice the pineapple in half lengthways, cutting right through the crown and base. Insert the blade of a long, serrated knife into the flesh of one pineapple half, about 5 mm (¼ inch) in from the edge of the shell, and cut all around the inside. Cut through the flesh in parallel lines, first lengthways and then crossways to produce squares of flesh (take care not to cut through the skin at the base). Scoop out the flesh with a sharp-edged teaspoon. Repeat with the second pineapple half, then turn both shells upside-down and leave to drain before filling.

SPICED FRUIT WAFERS

SERVES 8

CARAMELISED CLEMENTINES

SERVES 6-8

FOR THE WAFERS	1 cinnamon stick
75 g (3 oz) butter, softened	pared rind and juice of 1 orange
75 g (3 oz) caster sugar	6 fresh peaches, stoned and sliced
few drops of vanilla flavouring	225 g (8 oz) redcurrants
pinch of freshly grated nutmeg	225 g (8 oz) strawberries
2 egg whites	300 ml (½ pint) double cream, whipped
75 g (3 oz) plain flour	150 ml (¼ pint) Greek-style yogurt
FOR THE FILLING	icing sugar, for dusting
175 g (6 oz) caster sugar	

1 To make the wafers, cream together the butter and sugar until very soft and light. Add the vanilla flavouring and nutmeg. Gradually beat in the lightly whisked egg whites. Fold in the flour.

2 Drop heaped teaspoons of the mixture onto greased baking sheets allowing space to spread. Bake at 200°C (400°F) mark 6 for 6-7 minutes or until set and pale golden around the edges. Remove from the baking sheet and cool on a wire rack.

3 To make the filling, place the caster sugar, cinnamon and orange rind in a saucepan with 300 ml (½ pint) water over a low heat until the sugar has dissolved. Bring to the boil, bubble for 2 minutes then add the peaches and redcurrants. Simmer for 2-3 minutes or until just tender. With a slotted spoon, transfer the fruit to a bowl and add the strawberries.

4 Return the liquid to the heat, bring to the boil and bubble for 4-5 minutes or until reduced and syrupy. Add the strained orange juice and cool.

5 Mix the cream with the yogurt. Layer up the wafers with the cream and spiced fruits. Dust the top with icing sugar to serve.

275 g (10 oz) granulated sugar	oil, for brushing
18 small clementines	50-75 g (2-3 oz) caster sugar

1 First prepare the caramel sauce. Put the granulated sugar in a medium heavy-based saucepan with 125 ml (4 fl oz) water. Heat gently until all the sugar dissolves, then bring the mixture to a rapid boil. Have ready 125 ml (4 fl oz) warm water. Bubble down the sugar mixture, gently shaking the pan occasionally, until it turns a rich dark caramel. Immediately take off the heat. Cover your hand – the mixture may splutter – and pour in the warm water in one fast stream. Stir until evenly mixed, returning to a low heat if necessary, until the mixture is smooth. Pour into a heatproof jug and leave to cool.

2 Peel the clementines, removing all pith but keeping them whole. Place in a bowl. Pour the syrup over the fruit and gently stir. Cover and chill until required.

3 Line a small baking sheet with foil and brush generously with oil. Sprinkle the caster sugar evenly over the foil. Cook under a hot grill until melted and golden. Don't take your eyes off it for a second as it can suddenly catch and burn! The sugar will have run into uneven pools of caramel. Remove from the grill immediately and allow to cool slightly before peeling off the foil and breaking into pieces. Store in an airtight container.

4 To serve the fruit, transfer to a glass serving dish and scatter with the caramel pieces. Serve immediately.

CREPES SUZETTE

SERVES 4

FOR THE CREPES	FOR THE SAUCE
125 g (4 oz) plain flour	50 g (2 oz) butter or margarine
pinch of salt	25 g (1 oz) caster sugar
1 egg	finely pared rind and juice of 1 large orange
300 ml (½ pint) milk	30 ml (2 tbsp) Grand Marnier or other orange-flavoured liqueur
oil, for frying	45 ml (3 tbsp) brandy or rum

1 To make the crêpes, sift the flour and salt into a bowl and make a well in the centre. Break in the egg and beat well with a wooden spoon. Gradually beat in the milk, drawing in the flour from the sides to make a smooth batter.

2 Heat a little oil in an 18 cm (7 inch) heavy-based frying pan, running it around the base and sides of the pan, until hot. Pour off any surplus.

3 Pour in just enough batter to thinly coat the base of the pan. Cook for 1-2 minutes until golden brown. Turn or toss and cook the second side until golden.

4 Transfer the crêpe to a plate and keep hot. Repeat with the remaining batter to make eight crêpes. Pile the cooked crêpes on top of each other with greaseproof paper in between each one and keep warm in the oven while cooking the remainder.

5 For the filling, melt the butter in a large frying pan. Remove from the heat and add the sugar, shredded orange rind and juice, and the liqueur. Heat gently to dissolve the sugar.

6 Fold each crêpe in half and then in half again to form a fan shape. Place the crêpes in the frying pan in overlapping lines.

7 Warm the brandy, pour it over the crêpes and set alight. Shake gently, then serve at once with cream.

APPLE AND BANANA FRITTERS

SERVES 4-6

125 g (4 oz) plain flour	1 large cooking apple
pinch of salt	2 bananas
90 ml (6 tbsp) lukewarm water	juice of ½ lemon
20 ml (4 tsp) oil	oil, for deep-frying
2 egg whites	caster sugar, to serve

1 Place the flour and salt into a bowl. Make a well in the centre. Add the water and oil and beat to form a smooth batter.

2 Beat the egg whites in a clean dry bowl until they are stiff; then set aside.

3 Peel, quarter and core the apple. Peel the bananas. Slice the fruit thickly and sprinkle at once with the lemon juice to prevent discolouration.

4 Fold the beaten egg whites into the batter, then immediately dip in the slices of fruit.

5 Deep-fry the fritters a few at a time in hot oil until puffed and light golden. Remove with a slotted spoon and pile on to a serving dish lined with absorbent kitchen paper. Serve immediately, sprinkled with caster sugar.

SUMMER PUDDING

SERVES 4-6

700 g (1½ lb) mixed summer fruit, such as redcurrants, blackcurrants, raspberries, prepared	8-10 thin slices of day-old bread, crusts removed
about 25 g (1 oz) light soft brown sugar	fruit and mint sprigs, to decorate

1 Stew the fruit gently with 60-90 ml (4-6 tbsp) water and the sugar until soft but still retaining their shape. The exact amounts of water and sugar depend on the ripeness and sweetness of the fruit.

2 Meanwhile, cut a round from one slice of bread to neatly fit the bottom of a 1.1 litre (2 pint) pudding basin and cut 6-8 slices of the bread into fingers about 5 cm (2 inches) wide. Put the round at the bottom of the basin and arrange the fingers around the sides, overlapping them so there are no spaces.

3 When the fruit is cooked, and still hot, pour it gently into the basin, being careful not to disturb the bread framework. Reserve about 45 ml (3 tbsp) of the juice. When the basin is full, cut the remaining bread and use to cover the fruit so a lid is formed.

4 Cover with a plate or saucer which fits just inside the bowl and put a weight on top. Leave the pudding until cold, then put into the refrigerator and chill overnight.

5 To serve, run a knife carefully round the edge to loosen, then invert the pudding on to a serving dish. Pour the reserved juice over the top. Decorate with fruit and mint sprigs. Serve cold with cream.

VARIATION

Autumn Pudding
Replace the summer fruits with a selection of autumn fruits, such as apples or pears, blackberries and plums.

DANISH PEASANT GIRL IN-A-VEIL

SERVES 4

50 g (2 oz) butter or margarine	juice of ½ lemon
175 g (6 oz) fresh rye or brown breadcrumbs	sugar, to taste
75 g (3 oz) light soft brown sugar	150 ml (¼ pint) double or whipping cream
700 g (1½ lb) cooking apples	50 g (2 oz) grated chocolate, to decorate

1 Melt the butter in a frying pan. Mix the breadcrumbs and sugar together. Add to the pan and fry until crisp, stirring frequently with a wooden spoon to prevent the crumbs from catching and burning.

2 Peel, core and slice the apples. Put them in a saucepan with 30 ml (2 tbsp) water, the lemon juice and sugar to taste. Cover and cook gently for 10-15 minutes until they form a purée. (Alternatively, put the apples, lemon juice and sugar in a bowl. Cover and microwave on HIGH for 7-10 minutes until they form a pulp, stirring frequently.) Leave to cool, then taste for sweetness and add more sugar if required.

3 Put alternate layers of the fried crumb mixture and apple purée into a glass serving dish, finishing with a layer of crumbs. Chill for 2-3 hours.

4 Whip the cream until stiff. Pipe around the top of the crumb mixture and decorate with grated chocolate. Serve chilled.

COOK'S TIP

This simple but delicious pudding of stewed apples layered with fried breadcrumbs and sugar is very similar to an apple charlotte. In Denmark, where it is called *bondepige med slør*, it takes its name from the fact that the apple and crumbs are 'veiled' or covered with cream.

RASPBERRY ALMOND FLAN

SERVES 8

225 g (8 oz) plain flour	125 g (4 oz) self-raising flour
225 g (8 oz) butter or margarine	75 g (3 oz) ground almonds
125 g (4 oz) light soft brown sugar	60 ml (4 tbsp) milk
2 eggs, separated	225 g (8 oz) raspberries
	150 ml (¼ pint) whipping cream, to serve

1 Sift the plain flour into a bowl. Rub in half the fat until the mixture resembles fine breadcrumbs. Bind to a firm dough with 60 ml (4 tbsp) water.
2 Knead the dough lightly on a floured surface, then roll out and use to line a 25 cm (10 inch) loose-based fluted flan tin. Line with greaseproof paper and baking beans.
3 Bake blind in the oven at 200°C (400°F) mark 6 for 15-20 minutes until set but not browned. Remove the paper and beans.
4 Meanwhile beat the remaining fat with the sugar until light and fluffy. Gradually beat in the egg yolks. Gently stir in the self-raising flour, ground almonds and milk. Whisk the egg whites until stiff, then fold into the mixture.
5 Spoon the cake mixture into the baked flan case and level the surface. Sprinkle over the raspberries, reserving a few for decoration.
6 Bake in the oven at 180°C (350°F) mark 4 for 40-45 minutes or until the flan is golden brown and firm to the touch. Cool.
7 Whip the cream until thick, then use to decorate the flan, with the reserved raspberries. Cut the flan into large wedges to serve.

TARTE TATIN

SERVES 8

150 g (5 oz) butter or block margarine	1 egg yolk
175 g (6 oz) plain flour	15 ml (1 tbsp) water
65 g (2½ oz) caster sugar	450 g (1 lb) crisp eating apples

1 Rub 125 g (4 oz) fat into the flour until the mixture resembles fine breadcrumbs. Add 15 g (½ oz) caster sugar. Blend the egg yolk with the water and stir into the mixture. Knead the dough lightly, then refrigerate while making the filling.
2 In a saucepan, melt the remaining fat and add the remaining caster sugar. Heat until caramelised and golden brown. Remove from the heat and pour into a 20 cm (8 inch) round sandwich tin.
3 Peel, core and halve the apples and slice them into 1 cm (½ inch) pieces. Pack them tightly to fill the bottom of the tin, leaving no gaps.
4 Roll out the pastry on a floured work surface to a round slightly larger than the tin. Place on top of the apples and tuck in around the edges of the tin. Refrigerate for 30 minutes.
5 Place the tin on a baking sheet and bake in the oven at 200°C (400°F) mark 6 for 30-35 minutes until the pastry is golden. Turn out, apple side uppermost, on to a serving dish. Serve hot, with cream.

COOK'S NOTE

Correctly called Tarte des Demoiselles Tatin in French, this famous upside-down apple tart is named after the sisters Tatin, hoteliers in the nineteenth century who originated the recipe. There are now numerous versions of the original recipe, which has become something of a classic in French cookery. Most recipes use shortcrust pastry as here, although some use puff. In all versions the pastry is baked on the top so that the apples are completely sealed in with their juices, then the tart turned out upside down for serving.

SPICED PEAR STRUDEL

SERVES 8

75 g (3 oz) fresh white breadcrumbs	450 g (1 lb) pears, peeled, cored and sliced
150 g (5 oz) unsalted butter	4 large sheets of filo pastry
50 g (2 oz) light soft brown sugar	50 g (2 oz) blanched almonds, toasted and chopped
50 g (2 oz) sultanas	15 ml (1 tbsp) redcurrant jelly (optional)
2.5 ml (½ tsp) ground mixed spice	icing sugar, for dusting
2.5 ml (½ tsp) ground cinnamon	

1 Fry the breadcrumbs in 50 g (2 oz) of the butter, stirring frequently until crisp and golden. Mix together the brown sugar, sultanas, mixed spice, cinnamon and pear slices.

2 Melt remaining butter. Brush one sheet of filo pastry with a little of the melted butter. Cover with a second sheet of pastry and brush with a little more melted butter.

3 Cover the pastry with half of the fried crumbs, leaving a 5 cm (2 inch) border on all sides. Arrange half the pear mixture over the crumbs and sprinkle with half of the almonds. Dot with half of the redcurrant jelly, if using.

4 Fold the edges over the filling and brush with a little melted butter. Roll up, like a Swiss roll, starting from a long side. Place the strudel on a lightly greased baking sheet (with raised edges) and brush with melted butter.

5 Make a second strudel in the same way using the remaining ingredients.

6 Bake at 190°C (375°F) mark 5 for 35 minutes until crisp and golden, covering with foil during cooking if necessary, to prevent over-browning. Brush halfway through cooking, with butter from the baking sheet.

7 Allow the strudels to cool slightly, then sprinkle liberally with sifted icing sugar. Serve warm or cold, cut into chunky slices, with yogurt or cream.

APRICOT PASTRIES

MAKES 6

425 g (15 oz) can apricot halves in syrup	225 g (8 oz) packet white almond paste or marzipan
3 ready-rolled puff pastry sheets, each measuring about 20 cm (8 inches) square	beaten egg, to glaze (optional)
	few flaked almonds

1 Empty the can of apricots into a sieve placed over a small saucepan. Let them drain for a couple of minutes to catch all the syrup. Remove the apricots from the pan and set aside. Bring the syrup to the boil and boil for 2-3 minutes until it is reduced and thickened slightly. Remove from the heat and cool.

2 Trim the edges of the pastry squares and cut each one in half lengthways to make a total of six rectangles. Cut the almond paste lengthways into six equal slices. Using your fingers or a rolling pin, slightly flatten each slice so that it is slightly smaller than a piece of pastry. Place each piece of marzipan on a piece of pastry.

3 Arrange the pastries on a baking sheet. Brush with egg glaze, if using, then top each with two apricot halves, cut side down. Sprinkle with a few flaked almonds. Bake in the oven at 220°C (425°F) mark 7 for 15-20 minutes or until golden brown. As soon as they come out of the oven, brush with the syrup to glaze.

COOK'S TIP

These more-ish pastries look remarkably professional yet they're really quick and easy to make using ready rolled squares of puff pastry. You'll find them in the freezer cabinet in most supermarkets.

CLEMENTINE BISCUITS WITH APRICOT SAUCE

SERVES 6

75 g (3 oz) plain flour	drop of vanilla essence
pinch of salt	10 ml (2 tsp) brandy
2 egg whites, lightly whisked	30 ml (2 tbsp) ground almonds
75 g (3 oz) icing sugar, sifted	150 ml (¼ pint) double cream, whipped
57g (2¼ oz) unsalted butter, melted	6-9 clementines peeled, seeded and segmented
icing sugar, for dusting	
FOR THE FILLING	FOR THE APRICOT SAUCE
65 ml (2½ fl oz) milk	50 g (2 oz) sugar
2.5 ml (½ tsp) cornflour	225 g (8 oz) dried apricots, soaked overnight
1 egg yolk	
20-25 g (¾-1 oz) caster sugar	squeeze of lemon juice

1 To make the biscuits, mix flour, salt, egg whites and icing sugar together in a bowl. Stir in the melted butter.
2 Spoon the mixture in 12 equal rounds, spaced a little way apart, on lined and greased baking sheets.
3 Bake in the oven at 180°C (350°F) mark 4 for about 10 minutes until light golden. Leave to cool on a wire rack.
4 To make the filling, heat milk to boiling point in a pan. Blend the cornflour with the egg yolk, then stir in the hot milk. Pour into a pan and cook over a low heat, stirring, until the sauce thickens. Remove from the heat and stir in the sugar, vanilla, brandy and ground almonds.
5 Cover and leave to cool. When cold, fold in the cream.
6 To make the sauce, dissolve the sugar in about 60 ml (4 tbsp) water in a pan. Add the drained apricots and lemon juice, then simmer until soft. Purée in a blender or food processor, then leave to cool. Chill.
7 To assemble the dessert, place 6 biscuits on 6 plates. Cover with the filling, then top with clementine segments. Place the remaining biscuits on top and dust with icing sugar. Score with a hot skewer and surround with the apricot sauce to serve.

APPLE AND HAZELNUT LAYER

SERVES 8

75 g (3 oz) hazelnuts, shelled	15 ml (1 tbsp) apricot jam or marmalade
75 g (3 oz) butter	grated rind of 1 lemon
45 ml (3 tbsp) caster sugar	15 ml (1 tbsp) candied peel, chopped
115 g (4½ oz) plain flour	30 ml (2 tbsp) currants
pinch of salt	30 ml (2 tbsp) sultanas
450 g (1 lb) Cox's apples, peeled, cored and sliced	icing sugar, whipped cream and hazelnuts, to decorate

1 Cut out two 20 cm (8 inch) circles of greaseproof paper. Reserve 8 nuts and finely chop the remainder.
2 Cream the butter and sugar until pale and fluffy. Stir in the flour, salt and chopped nuts, then form into a ball and chill for 30 minutes.
3 Put the apples in a saucepan with the jam and lemon rind and cook over a low heat for 5 minutes, until soft. Add the candied peel and dried fruit and simmer for 5 minutes.
4 Divide the shortbread in half, place on the sheets of greaseproof paper and roll out into two circles. Transfer to greased baking sheets.
5 Bake at 190°C (375°F) mark 5 for 7-10 minutes, until light brown. Cut one circle into 8 triangles while warm. Leave to cool.
6 Just before serving, place the complete circle on a serving plate and cover with the apple mixture. Arrange the triangles on top. Dust with icing sugar, pipe cream on top and decorate with hazelnuts.

LEMON MERINGUE PIE

SERVES 4-6

Shortcrust Pastry made with 175 g (6 oz) flour (see page 80)	125 g (4 oz) granulated sugar
	75 ml (5 tbsp) cornflour
finely grated rind and juice of 2 lemons	2 eggs, separated
	75 g (3 oz) caster sugar

1 Roll out the pastry on a floured surface and use to line a 20 cm (8 inch) loose-based flan tin or fluted flan dish. Chill in the refrigerator for 30 minutes.

2 Line the flan case with greaseproof paper and beans. Bake blind in the oven at 200°C (400°F) mark 6 for 10-15 minutes, then remove the paper and beans and bake for a further 5 minutes until the base is firm.

3 Put the lemon rind and juice, granulated sugar and 300 ml (½ pint) water in a saucepan. Heat gently until the sugar dissolves.

4 Mix the cornflour to a smooth paste with 90 ml (6 tbsp) water and stir into the saucepan until well blended. Bring to the boil, stirring and cook for 1 minute, until thickened.

5 Cool slightly, then beat in the egg yolks, one at a time.

6 Pour the warm lemon filling into the pastry case, levelling the surface.

7 Whisk the egg whites until stiff. Whisk in half the caster sugar a little at a time, then carefully fold in the remainder.

8 Spoon the meringue on to the filling and swirl with a palette knife. The filling must be completely covered, but the meringue should not overlap the edge of the flan tin. Bake in the oven at 150°C (300°F) mark 2 for about 35 minutes. Allow to cool before serving.

RHUBARB AND ORANGE CRUMBLE

SERVES 8

175 g (6 oz) butter or margarine	two 540 g (1¼ lb) cans rhubarb, well drained
125 g (4 oz) caster sugar	125 g (4 oz) plain flour
125 g (4 oz) self-raising flour	30 ml (2 tbsp) granulated sugar
2 eggs, beaten	2.5 ml (½ tsp) ground cinnamon
finely grated rind of 1 orange	icing sugar, for dredging

1 Grease a 23 cm (9 inch) spring-release cake tin and line the base with greaseproof paper. To make the cake, beat 125 g (4 oz) of the fat, the caster sugar, self-raising flour, eggs and orange rind together until smooth and well mixed. Spoon into the tin.

2 Spoon the rhubarb over the cake mixture. To make the crumble mixture, rub the remaining fat into the flour, then stir in the granulated sugar and the cinnamon. Sprinkle the mixture over the rhubarb. Bake in the oven at 200°C (400°F) mark 6 for 45 minutes-1 hour or until firm to the touch and golden brown. Serve warm, dredged with icing sugar.

VARIATION

A light orange-flavoured sponge, topped with rhubarb and a crunchy crumble topping. Add a few chopped nuts, sunflower seeds or desiccated coconut to the topping or use other poached or canned fruit, as the fancy takes you.

SPICED APPLE
AND PLUM CRUMBLE

SERVES 6

450 g (1 lb) plums	7.5 ml (1½ tsp) ground mixed spice
700 g (1½ lb) cooking apples	175 g (6 oz) plain wholemeal flour
125 g (4 oz) butter or margarine	50 g (2 oz) blanched hazelnuts, toasted and chopped
125 g (4 oz) sugar	

1 Using a sharp knife, cut the plums in half, then carefully remove the stones.

2 Peel, quarter, core and slice the apples. Place the apples in a medium saucepan with 25 g (1 oz) of the butter, 50 g (2 oz) of the sugar and about 5 ml (1 tsp) of the mixed spice. Cover and cook gently for 15 minutes until the apples begin to soften.

3 Stir in the plums. Transfer the fruit mixture to a 1.1 litre (2 pint) shallow ovenproof dish. Leave to cool for about 30 minutes.

4 Stir the flour and remaining mixed spice well together. Rub in the remaining butter until the mixture resembles fine breadcrumbs. Stir in the rest of the sugar with the hazelnuts. Spoon the crumble over the fruit.

5 Bake in the oven at 180°C (350°F) mark 4 for about 40 minutes or until the top is golden, crisp and crumbly.

COOK'S TIP

All plums can be cooked, but dessert varieties tend to be more expensive, so it makes good sense to look for cooking plums. Whether you cook with red or yellow plums is entirely a matter of personal choice but cooking plums worth looking for are Czars, small red cherry plums, Pershore Yellow Egg, Purple Pershore and Belle de Loutain. Greengages and damsons come from the plum family and can be used in any recipe for plums, although extra sugar may be required.

BLACKBERRY
AND PEAR COBBLER

SERVES 4

FOR THE FILLING	FOR THE TOPPING
450 g (1 lb) blackberries	225 g (8 oz) self-raising flour
450 g (1 lb) ripe cooking pears, such as Conference	pinch of salt
finely grated rind and juice of 1 lemon	50 g (2 oz) butter or margarine
2.5 ml (½ tsp) ground cinnamon	25 g (1 oz) caster sugar
	about 150 ml (¼ pint) milk, plus extra to glaze

1 To make the filling, pick over the blackberries and wash them. Peel and core the pears, slice thickly.

2 Put the blackberries and pears into a saucepan with the lemon rind and juice and the cinnamon. Poach for 15-20 minutes until the fruit is tender. Cool.

3 To make the topping, place the flour and salt in a bowl. Rub in the butter until the mixture resembles fine breadcrumbs, then stir in the sugar. Gradually add the milk to mix to a fairly soft dough.

4 Roll out the dough on a floured work surface until 1 cm (½ inch) thick. Cut out rounds using a fluted 5 cm (2 inch) pastry cutter.

5 Put the fruit in a pie dish and top with overlapping pastry rounds, leaving a gap in the centre.

6 Brush the top of the pastry rounds with milk. Bake in the oven at 220°C (425°F) mark 7 for 10-15 minutes until the pastry is golden brown. Serve hot.

COOK'S TIP

Recipes with the strange-sounding title of 'cobbler' are invariably American in origin, although very little is known for certain about the meaning behind the word in culinary terms. Cobblers always have a scone dough topping which is stamped into small rounds.

EVE'S PUDDING

SERVES 4

450 g (1 lb) cooking apples, peeled and cored	75 g (3 oz) caster sugar
75 g (3 oz) demerara sugar	1 egg, beaten
grated rind of 1 lemon	150 g (5 oz) self-raising flour
75 g (3 oz) butter or block margarine	a little milk, to mix

1 Grease a 900 ml (1½ pint) ovenproof dish. Slice the apples and place in the dish. Sprinkle over the demerara sugar and lemon rind.
2 Cream the fat and caster sugar together until pale and fluffy. Add the egg, a little at a time, beating well after each addition.
3 Fold in the flour with enough milk to give a smooth dropping consistency and spread the mixture over the apples.
4 Bake in the oven at 180°C (350°F) mark 4 for 40-45 minutes, until the apples are tender and the sponge mixture is golden brown.

VARIATION

Add 25 g (1 oz) ground almonds with the flour and sprinkle 25 g (1 oz) flaked almonds over the top of the pudding.

MAGIC CHOCOLATE PUDDING

SERVES 4-6

50 g (2 oz) butter or margarine	350 ml (12 fl oz) milk
75 g (3 oz) caster sugar	40 g (1½ oz) self-raising flour
2 eggs, separated	25 ml (5 tsp) cocoa powder

1 Grease a 1 litre (1¾ pint) ovenproof dish.
2 Cream the butter and sugar together in a bowl until light and fluffy. Beat in the egg yolks and stir in the milk.
3 Sift the flour and cocoa powder together over the creamed mixture, then fold in until evenly mixed. Whisk the egg whites until stiff and fold into the mixture. Pour into the prepared dish.
4 Bake in the oven at 180°C (350°F) mark 4 for 35-45 minutes until the top is set and spongy to the touch. Serve immediately.

COOK'S TIP

This delicious chocolate pudding, which is a great hit with children, is called 'magic' because it separates magically during baking into a rich chocolate sauce at the bottom and a sponge cake on top.

CREME CARAMEL

SERVES 4

125 g (4 oz) sugar plus 15 ml (1 tbsp)	600 ml (1 pint) milk
4 eggs	1.25 ml (¼ tsp) vanilla flavouring

1 Place the 125 g (4 oz) sugar in a small saucepan and carefully pour in 150 ml (¼ pint) water. Heat gently until all the sugar has dissolved, stirring occasionally.
2 Bring the syrup to a fast boil and cook rapidly until the caramel is a golden brown. Remove from the heat and leave for a few seconds to darken. Pour into a 15 cm (6 inch) soufflé dish and cool.
3 Whisk the eggs and remaining sugar in a bowl. Warm the milk and pour on to the egg mixture. Whisk in the vanilla, then strain the custard on to the cool caramel.
4 Stand the dish in a roasting tin containing enough hot water to come halfway up the sides of the dish. Bake in the oven at 170°C (325°F) mark 3 for about 1 hour. The custard should be just set and firm to the touch.
5 When cold, cover the dish and leave in the refrigerator for several hours, preferably overnight. Take out of the refrigerator 30 minutes before serving. Carefully invert on to plates, allowing the caramel to run down the sides.

BAKED SAFFRON YOGURT

SERVES 8

300 ml (½ pint) milk	383 g (13.5 oz) can condensed milk
pinch of saffron threads	
6 green cardamoms, split	300 ml (½ pint) natural yogurt
2 eggs	1 large ripe mango, to decorate
2 egg yolks	

1 Pour the milk into a heavy-based saucepan, add the saffron and cardamoms and bring slowly to the boil. Remove from the heat, cover and infuse for 10-15 minutes.
2 Put the eggs, egg yolks, condensed milk and yogurt in a bowl and beat together.
3 Strain in the milk, stirring gently to mix. Divide between 8 ramekin dishes.
4 Place the ramekins in a roasting tin. Add hot water to come halfway up the sides. Bake in the oven at 180°C (350°F) mark 4 until firm to the touch.
5 Cool the baked yogurt desserts completely, then chill for at least 2 hours before serving.
6 To serve, run a blunt-edged knife around the edge of each yogurt, then turn out on to individual dishes.
7 Peel the mango and slice thinly on either side of the central stone. Serve with the saffron yogurts.

SERVING SUGGESTION

These individual, golden-tinted yogurts make an attractive finale to an Indian meal. They are also excellent for children at tea-time, served with fresh fruit.

COCONUT CUSTARDS WITH TROPICAL FRUITS

SERVES 8

225 g (8 oz) granulated sugar	60 ml (4 tbsp) shredded or desiccated coconut
3 eggs	2 mangoes, peeled
2 egg yolks	1 large pawpaw, peeled
30 ml (2 tbsp) caster sugar	juice of 1-2 limes
600 ml (1 pint) thin coconut milk	2 passion fruit
300 ml (½ pint) evaporated milk	

1   Have ready eight warmed 150 ml (¼ pint) ramekins. Put the granulated sugar in a heavy saucepan, pour in 150 ml (¼ pint) cold water and heat gently, until dissolved. Increase the heat and boil, without stirring, until dark caramel in colour. Immediately pour into the ramekins, swirling the caramel around the sides quickly.

2   Put the eggs, egg yolks and caster sugar in a bowl and beat to mix. Pour the coconut and evaporated milks into a saucepan and heat to scalding point. Pour over the egg mixture, stirring all the time.

3   Strain the custard into the ramekins. Place the ramekins in a roasting pan and pour in enough hot water to come halfway up the sides. Cover with lightly oiled foil, then bake in the oven at 170°C (325°F) mark 3 for 50 minutes or until set, but still wobbly around the edges. Remove from the oven and leave to cool in the pan of hot water. Chill in the refrigerator overnight.

4   Meanwhile, dry fry the coconut in a wok or heavy frying pan over low heat for 5-6 minutes, stirring, until golden. Slice the mangoes and pawpaw lengthways.

5   To serve, run a knife around the edge of each custard, then carefully invert onto dessert plates, allowing the caramel to run down the sides. Arrange a few slices of mango and pawpaw to the side of each custard, then sprinkle with lime juice and squeeze the passion fruit pulp over the top. Sprinkle toasted coconut on top.

PETITS POTS AU CHOCOLATE

SERVES 6

15 ml (1 tbsp) coffee beans	75 g (3 oz) plain chocolate
3 egg yolks	TO DECORATE
1 egg	150 ml (¼ pint) whipping cream
75 g (3 oz) caster sugar	chocolate shapes or coffee dragees
750 ml (1¼ pints) milk and single cream mixed	

1   Toast the coffee beans under a moderate grill for a few minutes, then set aside.

2   Beat the egg yolks, egg and sugar together in a bowl until very pale.

3   Place the milk, cream and coffee beans in a saucepan and bring to the boil. Strain the hot milk on to the egg mixture, stirring all the time. Discard the coffee beans. Return the mixture to the saucepan.

4   Break up the chocolate and add to the pan. Stir over gentle heat (do not boil) for about 5 minutes until the chocolate has almost melted and the mixture is slightly thickened. Whisk lightly until the mixture is evenly blended.

5   Stand six individual 150 ml (¼ pint) ramekin dishes or custard pots in a roasting tin, then pour in enough hot water to come halfway up the sides of the dishes. Pour the custard mixture slowly into the dishes, dividing it equally between them. Cover.

6   Bake in the oven at 150°C (300°F) mark 2 for 1-1¼ hours or until lightly set. Leave to cool completely.

7   To serve, whip the cream and spoon into a piping bag fitted with a large star nozzle. Pipe a whirl on top of each dessert. Decorate with chocolate shapes or coffee dragees.

COOK'S TIP

These little chocolate pots rely heavily on the flavour of the chocolate used. So it is essential to use a good quality variety.

FROZEN BRANDY CREAMS

SERVES 4

4 egg yolks	150 ml (¼ pint) double cream
150 g (5 oz) caster sugar	coffee dragees, to decorate
90 ml (6 tbsp) brandy	

1 Mix the egg yolks, sugar and brandy together in a medium bowl, stirring well.
2 Place the bowl over a pan of simmering water. Stir the mixture all the time for about 15 minutes until it thickens slightly and will just coat the back of the spoon. Do not overheat or the eggs may curdle. Remove from the heat and leave to cool for 30 minutes.
3 Lightly whip the cream and stir half into the cold brandy mixture. Pour into four small freezerproof soufflé or ramekin dishes. Cover and freeze for at least 5 hours until firm.
4 To serve, decorate each ramekin with a whirl of the remaining whipped cream, then top with a coffee dragee. Serve immediately.

VARIATIONS

Replace the brandy with Tia Maria for a coffee flavour, or Amaretto di Saronno for almond flavoured creams.

PISTACHIO AND ALMOND ICE CREAM

SERVES 6

1.4 litres (2½ pints) milk	50 g (2 oz) ground almonds
15 ml (1 tbsp) rice flour	few drops of rose water
175 g (6 oz) granulated sugar	150 ml (¼ pint) double cream
25 g (1 oz) pistachio nuts	shredded pistachio nuts, to decorate

1 Pour the milk into a large, heavy-based saucepan. Bring to the boil, then simmer gently for about 45 minutes or until the milk reduces by half. Cool slightly.
2 Mix the rice flour with a little of the cooled milk until smooth. Return to the pan and bring to the boil, stirring. Cook for 15 minutes, stirring frequently until the consistency of thin batter. Strain, add the sugar and stir until dissolved. Leave to cool.
3 Soak the pistachio nuts in boiling water for 1-2 minutes, then drain. Ease off the skins, then shred finely.
4 Stir the pistachios, ground almonds and rose water into the milk mixture. Whip the cream lightly, then fold in.
5 Freeze by hand or in an ice cream machine (see below).
6 Leave at cool room temperature for 20-30 minutes to soften before serving. Serve, decorated with pistachios.

COOK'S TIP

Using an Ice Cream Machine

An ice cream machine will freeze an ice cream or sorbet mixture and churn it at the same time, thus eliminating the need to whisk by hand periodically during freezing (see right). The results will be smooth and even textured.
There are several types of ice cream machine available; always follow the manufacturer's instructions.
Generally speaking, the cooled mixture should be poured into the machine when the paddles are moving, otherwise it tends to freeze on to the base and sides of the bowl, stopping the paddles working. When making ice cream this way, if the recipe calls for whipped cream, it should be ignored. The cream can simply be added from the carton with the custard.

RASPBERRY REDCURRANT FREEZE

SERVES 4-6

350 g (12 oz) fresh or frozen raspberries	225 g (8 oz) jar redcurrant jelly
	300 ml (½ pint) soured cream

1 Put the raspberries and redcurrant jelly in a saucepan and heat gently, stirring frequently, until the fruit is soft.
2 Purée in a blender or food processor, then sieve to remove the seeds. Chill for about 1 hour until cold.
3 Whisk in the soured cream. Freeze by hand or in an ice cream machine (see left).
4 Leave at cool room temperature for 20-30 minutes to soften before serving.

COOK'S TIP

To Freeze Ice Cream by Hand
Suggested freezing times are based on 900 ml (1½ pint) ice cream. If making a larger quantity, increase them.
1 Set the freezer to maximum or fast freeze about 1 hour before you intend to freeze the mixture.
2 Make the ice cream as directed in the recipe.
3 Pour the mixture into a shallow non-metal, freezer container. Cover and freeze for about 3 hours or until just frozen all over. It will have a mushy consistency.
4 Spoon into a bowl and mash with a fork or flat whisk to break down the ice crystals. Work quickly so that the ice cream does not melt completely.
5 Return the mixture to the shallow container and freeze again for about 2 hours or until mushy.
6 Mash again as step 4. If any other ingredients are to be added, such as nuts, then fold in at this stage.
7 Return to the freezer and freeze for about 3 hours or until firm.

MANGO ICE CREAM

SERVES 4-6

450 ml (¾ pint) milk	2 ripe mangoes, skinned, sliced and stoned, or two 425 g (15 oz) cans mango slices, drained
1 vanilla pod	
4 egg yolks	
75 g (3 oz) sugar	juice of 1 lime
	300 ml (½ pint) double cream
	lime twists, to decorate (optional)

1 Pour the milk into a large, heavy-based saucepan. Add the vanilla pod and bring almost to the boil. Remove from the heat, cover and leave to infuse for at least 15 minutes. Remove the vanilla pod.
2 Put the egg yolks and sugar in a large bowl and beat together. Stir in the milk, then strain back into the pan.
3 Cook the custard gently, stirring until it coats the back of a wooden spoon. Do not boil. Cool completely for at least 1 hour.
4 Purée the mangoes in a blender or food processor until smooth. Stir the mango purée and lime juice into the cool custard. Whip the cream lightly, then fold into the mixture. Pour into a shallow freezer container.
5 Freeze the mixture for about 2 hours until mushy in texture. Turn into a large, chilled bowl and mash with a fork. Freeze for 3-4 hours until firm.
6 Soften in the refrigerator for about 1 hour before serving, decorated with lime twists, if liked.

COOK'S TIP

Refer to instructions on page 168 for freezing in an ice cream machine.

COFFEE AND HAZELNUT ICE CREAM

SERVES 4-6

100 g (4 oz) shelled hazelnuts	300 ml (½ pint) double cream
50 ml (2 tbsp plus 4 tsp) Tia Maria	300 ml (½ pint) single cream
15 ml (1 tbsp) coffee and chicory essence	75 g (3 oz) icing sugar, sifted

1   Toast the hazelnuts under the grill for a few minutes, shaking the grill pan constantly so that the nuts brown evenly.

2   Tip the nuts into a clean tea-towel and rub to remove the skins. Chop finely.

3   Mix 30 ml (2 tbsp) Tia Maria and the coffee essence together in a bowl. Stir in the chopped nuts, reserving a few for decoration.

4   In a separate bowl, whip the creams and icing sugar together until thick. Fold in the nut mixture, then turn into a shallow freezerproof container. Freeze for 2 hours until ice crystals form around the edge of the ice cream.

5   Turn the ice cream into a bowl and beat thoroughly for a few minutes to break up the ice crystals. Return to the freezer container, cover and freeze for at least 4 hours, preferably overnight (to allow enough time for the flavours to develop).

6   To serve, transfer the ice cream to the refrigerator for 30 minutes to soften slightly, then scoop into individual glasses. Spoon 5 ml (1 tsp) coffee liqueur over each serving and sprinkle with the remaining nuts. Serve immediately.

COOK'S TIP

Refer to instructions on page 168 for freezing in an ice cream machine.

KIWI FRUIT SORBET

SERVES 6

50 g (2 oz) sugar	kiwi fruit slices, to decorate
6 kiwi fruit	orange-flavoured liqueur and wafers, to serve
2 egg whites	

1   Place the sugar in a saucepan with 150 ml (¼ pint) water. Heat gently until the sugar dissolves, then simmer for 2 minutes. Cool for 30 minutes.

2   Halve the kiwi fruit and peel thinly, using a potato peeler.

3   Place the fruit in a blender or food processor with the cool syrup. Work to a smooth purée, then pass through a nylon sieve to remove the pips. Pour into a chilled shallow freezer container. Freeze for 2 hours until mushy.

4   Beat the mixture with a fork to break down any ice crystals.

5   Whisk the egg whites until stiff, then fold through the fruit mixture until evenly blended. Return to the freezer for 4 hours.

6   Scoop into individual glass dishes, decorate with kiwi fruit and spoon over some liqueur. Serve with wafers.

BASIC SAUCES & DRESSINGS

Use this collection of savoury sauces and salad dressings to enhance the recipes in this book, or your own favourite vegetarian recipes. Remember that the secret of a good dressing lies in the quality of the oil and vinegar used.

TOMATO SAUCE

MAKES ABOUT 600 ML (1 PINT)

30 ml (2 tbsp) olive oil

1 small onion, finely chopped

30 ml (2 tbsp) tomato purée

5 ml (1 tsp) mild paprika

two 400 g (14 oz) cans chopped tomatoes

large pinch of dried oregano

300 ml (½ pint) dry red wine or vegetable stock

large pinch of sugar

salt and pepper

1 Heat the oil in a heavy-based saucepan, add the onion and fry for 5-10 minutes or until very soft. Add the tomato purée and paprika and fry for 2-3 minutes. Add the tomatoes, oregano, red wine or stock and sugar.
2 Season the sauce with salt and pepper, then bring to the boil and simmer for about 20 minutes or until the sauce is slightly reduced.

VARIATION

This makes a deliciously rich, well flavoured sauce for serving with pasta, vegetable bakes or roasts. To make a spicy sauce, add 1-2 chopped fresh chillies and a little chopped fresh coriander. Add other flavourings, such as garlic, bay leaves, thyme or rosemary, to make a sauce to complement whatever it's being served with.

CURRY SAUCE

MAKES ABOUT 600 ML (1 PINT)

30 ml (2 tbsp) oil

1 large onion, chopped

1 garlic clove, crushed

10 ml (2 tsp) ground coriander

10 ml (2 tsp) turmeric

5 ml (1 tsp) fenugreek seeds

5 ml (1 tsp) ground cumin

50 g (2 oz) split red lentils

450 ml (¾ pint) vegetable stock

salt and pepper

150 ml (¼ pint) Greek yogurt

1 Heat the oil in a heavy-based saucepan. Add the onion and garlic and fry for 5 minutes or until softened. Add the spices and fry for 2 minutes, stirring.
2 Add the lentils and stock, bring to the boil, then reduce the heat, cover and simmer for 30 minutes or until the lentils are very soft. Season with salt and pepper. Stir in the yogurt and reheat gently before serving.

HARISSA SAUCE

MAKES ABOUT 300 ML (½ PINT)

15 ml (1 tbsp) oil

1 large red pepper, seeded and finely chopped

2 red chillies, seeded and chopped

2 garlic cloves, crushed

15 ml (1 tbp) ground coriander

5 ml (1 tsp) ground caraway

30 ml (2 tbsp) tomato purée

salt and pepper

1 Heat the oil in a heavy-based saucepan. Add all the ingredients, except the salt and pepper, and cook over a medium heat for about 5 minutes or until the pepper has softened.
2 Add 300 ml (½ pint) water and bring to the boil. Reduce the heat, cover and simmer gently for 10 minutes or until the pepper is really soft. Season to taste with salt and pepper. Serve hot or cold.

BECHAMEL SAUCE

MAKES ABOUT 300 ML (½ PINT)

300 ml (½ pint) milk

1 slice of onion

1 bay leaf

6 peppercorns

1 blade of mace

15 g (½ oz) butter or margarine

scant 15 g (½ oz) plain flour

salt and pepper

1 Pour the milk into a saucepan. Add the onion, bay leaf, peppercorns and mace and bring to scalding point. Remove from the heat, cover and leave to infuse for 10-30 minutes. Strain.

2 Melt the butter in a saucepan. Remove from the heat and stir in the flour until evenly blended. Gradually pour on the warm milk, stirring well. Season lightly with salt and pepper.

3 Bring to the boil, stirring constantly, and simmer for 2-3 minutes.

VARIATIONS

Add the following to the hot sauce with the seasoning:

Cheese Sauce

Add 50 g (2 oz) grated mature Cheddar cheese and a large pinch of mustard powder.

Parsley or Herb Sauce

Add about 30 ml (2 tbsp) chopped parsley or herbs of your choice.

Blue Cheese Sauce

Add 50 g (2 oz) crumbled Stilton, or other hard blue cheese, and 10 ml (2 tsp) lemon juice.

Mushroom Sauce

Add 75 g (3 oz) lightly cooked sliced mushrooms.

Onion Sauce

Add 1 medium onion, chopped and cooked.

HOLLANDAISE SAUCE

MAKES ABOUT 150 ML (¼ PINT)

45 ml (3 tbsp) white wine vinegar

6 peppercorns

1 small bay leaf

1 blade of mace

75-125 g (3-4 oz) butter, at room temperature

2 egg yolks

salt

1 Place the vinegar, peppercorns, bay leaf and mace in a small saucepan. Bring to the boil and boil rapidly until reduced to only 10 ml (2 tsp). Set aside.

2 Soften the butter slightly. In a small heatproof bowl, cream the egg yolks with a small piece of butter and a pinch of salt. Strain the herb and vinegar mixture into the bowl.

3 Place the bowl over a saucepan of hot water on a gentle heat until the mixture becomes thick, stirring constantly.

4 Gradually add the remainder of the butter in small pieces, stirring constantly. When 75 g (3 oz) of the butter has been added, season the sauce lightly with salt. If still too sharp, add a little more butter. The sauce should be lightly piquant. Serve lukewarm.

COOK'S TIP

Hollandaise should always be served warm. It makes an ideal accompaniment to most vegetables. It curdles easily, so take care. If the mixture appears to be curdling, add an ice cube and whisk well; the sauce should come back together again.

PESTO

MAKES 300 ML (½ PINT)

50 g (2 oz) basil leaves (weighed without stalks)

2 garlic cloves, skinned

30 ml (2 tbsp) pine nuts

salt and pepper

125 ml (4 fl oz) olive oil

50 g (2 oz) freshly grated Parmesan cheese

1 Put the basil, garlic, pine nuts, salt, pepper and olive oil in a blender or food processor and blend at high speed until very creamy. Transfer the mixture to a bowl, fold in the cheese and mix thoroughly. Store for up to 2 weeks in a screw-topped jar in the refrigerator.

MAYONNAISE

MAKES ABOUT 150 ML (¼ PINT)

1 egg yolk

2.5 ml (½ tsp) mustard powder

2.5 ml (½ tsp) salt

1.25 ml (¼ tsp) pepper

2.5 ml (½ tsp) sugar

15 ml (1 tbsp) white wine vinegar or lemon juice

about 150 ml (¼ pint) oil

Put the egg yolk into a bowl with the mustard, salt, pepper, sugar and 5 ml (1 tsp) of the vinegar or lemon juice. Mix thoroughly, then add the oil, drop by drop, whisking constantly, until the sauce is thick and smooth. If it becomes too thick, add a little more of the vinegar or lemon juice. When all the oil has been added, add the remaining vinegar or lemon juice gradually; mix well.

USING A BLENDER OR FOOD PROCESSOR

Most blenders and food processors need at least a two-egg quantity in order to ensure that the blades are covered. Put the yolks, salt and pepper and half the vinegar or lemon juice into the blender goblet or food processor bowl and blend well. If your machine has a variable speed control, run it at a slow speed. Add the oil gradually, while the machine is running. Add the remaining vinegar and season.

COOK'S TIP

The ingredients for Mayonnaise should be at room temperature. Never use eggs straight from the refrigerator or cold larder as this may result in curdling. If the Mayonnaise separates, save it by beating the curdled mixture into a fresh base. This base can be 5 ml (1 tsp) hot water; 5 ml (1 tsp) vinegar or lemon juice; 5 ml (1 tsp) Dijon mustard or 2.5 ml (½ tsp) mustard powder; or an egg yolk. Add the curdled mixture to the base, beating hard. When the mixture is smooth, continue adding the oil as above. (If you use an extra egg yolk you may find that you need to add a little extra oil.)

VARIATIONS

Add one of the following flavourings to 150 ml (¼ pint) home-made or shop-bought mayonnaise.

Watercress and Lemon

Beat 60 ml (4 tbsp) finely chopped watercress and the finely grated rind of 2 lemons into the mayonnaise. Taste and adjust the seasoning, if necessary.

Thousand Island

Stir in 30 ml (2 tbsp) finely chopped green olives, 10 ml (2 tsp) each finely chopped parsley and onion, 10 ml (2 tsp) tomato purée, 30 ml (2 tbsp) finely chopped green pepper and 1 chopped hard-boiled egg. Taste and adjust the seasoning, if necessary.

Blue Cheese and Toasted Walnut

Beat 125 g (4 oz) crumbled Danish Blue cheese, 150 ml (¼ pint) soured cream, ½ quantity Vinaigrette Dressing (see right), 1 crushed garlic clove, 25 g (1 oz) toasted chopped walnuts and 15 ml (1 tbsp) chopped parsley into the mayonnaise. Taste and adjust the seasoning, if necessary.

VINAIGRETTE DRESSING

MAKES 200-250 ML (7-9 FL OZ)

175-225 ml (6-8 fl oz) olive oil

45 ml (3 tbsp) wine, garlic or herb vinegar

2.5 ml (½ tsp) caster sugar or honey

10 ml (2 tsp) Dijon mustard

salt and pepper

1 Whisk together all the ingredients until thoroughly combined. Season with salt and pepper.

VARIATIONS

Herb
Whisk into the dressing 30 ml (2 tbsp) finely chopped mixed herbs, such as parsley, thyme, marjoram, chives, sage, etc.

Mustard and Parsley
Stir in 15 ml (1 tbsp) wholegrain mustard and 30 ml (2 tbsp) finely chopped parsley

Sweet and Spiced
Add 5 ml (1 tsp) mango chutney, 5 ml (1 tsp) mild curry paste and 2.5 ml (½ tsp) turmeric.

Roquefort
Place the dressing in a blender or food processor. Add 25 g (1 oz) Roquefort cheese and 30 ml (2 tbsp) single cream. Blend until smooth.

Garlic
Crush 1-2 garlic cloves and stir into the dressing.

YOGURT AND TAHINI CREAM

MAKES ABOUT 200 ML (7 FL OZ)

90 ml (6 tbsp) natural yogurt

15-20 ml (3-4 tsp) white wine vinegar

90 ml (6 tbsp) olive oil

60 ml (4 tbsp) thin tahini paste

salt and pepper

1 Whisk together the yogurt and vinegar. Slowly stir in the olive oil until thoroughly combined.
2 Beat in the tahini, then season with salt and pepper.

INDEX